the Taste of Conquest

the Taste of Conquest

·

THE RISE AND FALL
OF THE THREE GREAT
CITIES OF SPICE

·

MICHAEL KRONDL

Ballantine Books

New York

Published in the United States by Ballantine Books,
an imprint of The Random House Publishing Group,
a division of Random House, Inc., New York.

BALLANTINE and colophon are registered trademarks of
Random House, Inc.

LIBRARY OF CONGRESS CATALOGING-IN-PUBLICATION DATA

Krondl, Michael.
The taste of conquest : the rise and fall of the three
great cities of spice / Michael Krondl.
p.   cm.
Includes index.
ISBN 978-0-345-48083-5   (hardcover : alk. paper)
1. Spices—Europe.   2. Spice trade—Europe—History.
3. Cookery—Europe—History.   4. Food habits—
Europe—History.   I.   Title
TX406.K85   2007
641.3'383094—dc22   2007026737

Printed in the United States of America on acid-free paper

www.ballantinebooks.com

2 4 6 8 9 7 5 3 1

FIRST EDITION

Book design by Donna Sinisgalli

Preface

꧁꧂

Writing this book has been a great adventure! I've gotten to eat in the homes of Indian pepper growers and Venetian blue bloods. I've met Dutch entrepreneurs and Portuguese sailors. I now know the difference between a triangular sail and a square one, and I can explain how ginger is harvested and cleaned because I've seen it done. What could be more fun than studying food?

Maybe that's why the study of the history of eating has been beneath the dignity of serious scholars for so long and why they never bothered to check their facts when they claimed that the medieval gentry ate food drowning in tsunamis of spice. Grudgingly, academia now accepts the study of culinary history into its ranks. But the subject is still new, and enormous work has yet to be done. Nevertheless, data are slowly accumulating that will eventually give us a more complete picture of what people used to eat. And then maybe we'll really understand why spices, for example, were as much an integral part of the European diet in the Renaissance as they are today in Morocco or India. And then maybe we can truly understand Europeans' taste for conquest.

I am not a specialist, which, because of the nature of this book, may have been an advantage. It has meant, however, that I have had to substitute breadth for depth. In certain cases, I have had to make deductions where the evidence is just too scanty for solid proof and to depend on the work of others. On the occasions when I have found that research to be self-evidently too shaky to stand, I've had to dig under the foundations. Given how often the construction proved faulty, I wonder how many authors I have taken on faith are just plain wrong. Which is not to say that I can blame others for my mistakes. I have surely made plenty of errors on my own. I hope and trust that others will come to correct them.

As with any project of this size, numerous people have given me assistance and offered invaluable suggestions. Many have extended their hospitality on little more than good faith. Others have held me back as I was about to place my foot firmly in my mouth—though probably not often enough.

I'd like to begin by thanking my editors, Susanna Porter and Dana Isaacson, for all their valuable suggestions. In addition, I am indebted to Elisabeth Dyssegaard, who originally championed the book at Random House and without whom it might never have taken flight. My agents, Jane Dystel and Miriam Goderich, have been fantastic throughout, going way beyond their job description at every stage of the project.

Then there are the dozens of people who helped along the way. In Venice, there is Luca Colferai, who keeps amazing me by his boundless generosity. But he was not alone. I am also grateful to Jurubeba Zancopè, Sergio Fragiacomo, Dr. Marcello Brusegan, and Antonio Barzaghi.

The Portuguese, however, were not to be outdone. I don't know what I would have done without Mónica Bello, whose journalistic skills and friendship were a godsend. I also want to thank Alexandra Baltazar, Bruno Gonçalves Neves, Hernâni Amaral Xavier, Isabel Cruz Almeida, José Eduardo Mendes Ferrão, José Marques da Cruz, and Rui Lis. Though he is not in Lisbon, my visit to Portugal would have been a pathetic failure without Filipe Castro, the naval archaeologist who opened up his personal Rolodex and thereby many doors in Portugal's capital.

When it comes to Holland, Peter Rose acted as my academic fairy godmother, fulfilling every obscure inquiry and keeping me on the straight and narrow. In the Netherlands itself, Cees Bakker, Christianne Muusers, and Anneke van Otterloo were all generous with their time and expertise. I greatly appreciate the time Frank Lavooij took out of his busy schedule, to say nothing of our lunch together.

In India, too, people's generosity was unbounded. In Cochin, C. J. Jose and his staff at the Spices Board were terrifically helpful, as were Heman K. Kuruwa, Jacob Mathew, K. J. Samson, Nimmy and Paul Variamparambil, and Ramkumar Menon. Thomas Thumpassery was especially kind to open up his home to me and show me the ways of the pepper grower. I am also grateful to V. A. Parthasarathy and his eminent staff at the Indian Institute of Spices Research for allowing me a glimpse of their inner sanctum. In Baltimore, James Lynn did me a similar favor at McCormick headquarters.

A partial list of others who helped by word or deed would have to include Amanda J. Hirschhorn, Ammini Ramachandran, David Leite, Gopalan Balagopal, Kenneth Albala, and Paul W. Bosland.

Finally, I would like to thank my wife and daughter for putting up with my extended absences and weeks of monomania.

Contents

꒰ಌ꒱

the
Taste
of Conquest

First Taste

•

S T .   A L B A N S

THE SULTAN AND THE ORGY

In my mind, flavor, smell, and memory are intertwined. To really understand a distant time and place, you should be able to sample its antique
flavors, sniff the ancient air, and take part in its archaic obsessions. But
how can you taste the food of a feudal lord? Where do you meet a medieval ghost?

I came across a likely spot on a cobbled lane in the old English pilgrimage town of St. Albans. The Sultan restaurant is located here in the lee
of a great Norman cathedral in a house that seems to stagger more than
stand on the little medieval street. I had made my pilgrimage to St. Albans
to track down the remains of a famous medieval travel writer—more on
him later—but before searching for phantoms, I was in desperate need of
lunch. To get to the Sultan's dining room, you have to climb a set of steep
and wobbly stairs to the second story, where the sagging, timbered attic has
been fitted with tables, each separated from the next by perilously low
rafters. The space cries out for blond, buxom wenches bearing flagons of
ale and vast platters overflowing with great haunches of wild beasts showered with cinnamon, ginger, pepper, and cloves. And indeed, the kitchen
door exudes sweet and fiery spice. But the waiter is skinny, male, and decidedly not of Norman stock, and if that weren't enough of a clue, the Indian hip hop on the sound system and Mogul prints on the walls will
quickly disabuse you of any illusions of stepping into Merrie Olde England.

The Sultan specializes in Balti cooking, a type of South Asian cuisine
that swept Britain by storm some years back. The style originates in

Baltistan, a place once identified with Shangri-La but now more likely to make headlines for its sectarian bloodshed. The mountainous territory stands astride a tributary of the Silk Road once used to bring spices from South India to China, Persia, and the Mediterranean. Accordingly, as is only appropriate for such a mythical land, Balti food is profoundly spicy. But is it as spicy as the food of Europe's Middle Ages, I wonder?

I order *gosht chilli masala,* a lamb stew pungent with hot Kashmiri pepper. The stainless steel tray of meat looks quite innocent, and the first taste is gentle enough. It begins with sweet notes of coriander, cardamom, and cinnamon. Then the red peppers roar in. Chilies, both fresh and dry, are blended to such incendiary effect that the occasional black peppercorn comes along as a mild respite. I gulp down my wine and pile more stew onto the flatbread.

Take away the chilies (unknown in Europe until Columbus returned from his misdirected search for the pepper isles), and I bet this is food that any self-respecting knight in armor would recognize.

While most historians agree that the Middle Ages loved its food spicy, they differ on just how spicy. The problem is that the recipes of the time are frustratingly imprecise. Typical instructions call for sprinkling with "fine spices," or as one early Flemish cookbook instructs in a recipe for rabbit sauce, "Take grains of paradise, ginger [and] cinnamon ground together and sugar with saffron mixed . . . and add thereto a little cumin." It is assumed the cook already knows what he is doing. Nevertheless, other sources do give more specific quantities and scattered descriptions of feasts where seemingly enormous amounts of spices were supposedly consumed in a single meal. The great French historian Fernand Braudel wrote of what, to his Gallic sensibility, was a "spice orgy." Some have recoiled in horror at medieval recipes that include handfuls of cloves, nutmeg, and pepper. (Today's writers warn that an ounce of cloves suffices for the preparation of an efficient anesthetic and that too much nutmeg can be poisonous.) Others just can't imagine that anyone could eat such highly seasoned cuisine. According to the Italian culinary historian Massimo Montanari, "These levels of consumption are hard to conceive of, and belong instead to the realm of desire and imagination."

I'd love to invite these academics to the Sultan restaurant. Perhaps then they would understand how perfectly credible is the medieval account that records the use of a seemingly spectacular two pounds of spices at a single bash. The figure comes from a manuscript called the *Ménagier de Paris* penned by an affluent, bourgeois functionary for his young wife in the late thirteen hundreds and includes all sorts of advice, including just what you needed to buy to throw a party. As an example, the writer describes an all-day wedding feast consisting of dinner and supper for forty and twenty guests, respectively, as well as some half dozen servants. The shopping list does indeed include a pound of ginger and a half pound of cinnamon as well as smaller quantities of long pepper, galingale, mace, cloves, melegueta, and saffron. But it also calls for twenty capons, twenty ducklings, fifty chickens, and fifty rabbits as well as venison, beef, mutton, veal, pork, and goat—more than six hundred pounds of meat in all! What's extraordinary about this meal is not the quantity of spice—at most, about a half teaspoon of mostly sweet spices for each pound of meat—but the extravagance of the entire event. If this is an orgy of food, the spices would hardly qualify as more than a flirtation.

Still, even that half teaspoon of spice would be unusual in contemporary French or Italian cooking, though it would scarcely merit mentioning at an Indian restaurant. To make the Balti *gosht,* you use way more seasoning, about a half ounce of spices (or roughly two level tablespoons) for every pound of meat. So it may well be that my medieval knight would have found my *gosht* hard going even for his developed palate. I can only imagine what the academics would say.

THE NEED FOR SPICE

A great deal of nonsense has been written by highly knowledgeable people about Europeans' desire for spices. Economic historians of the spice trade who have long mastered the relative value of pepper quintals and ginger kintars (both units of weight) and effortlessly parse the price differential of cloves between Mecca and Malacca will typically begin their weighty tomes by mentioning, almost in passing, the self-evident fact that Europeans needed spices as a preservative or to cover up the taste of rancid food. This is supposed to explain the demand that sent the Europeans off to conquer the world. Of course, the experts then quickly move on to devote the rest of their study to an intricate analysis of the supply side of the equation. But did wealthy Europeans sprinkle their swan and peacock pies with cinnamon and pepper because their meat was rank? The idea is an affront to common sense, to say nothing of the fact that it completely contradicts what's written in the old cookbooks.

Throughout human history, until the advent of refrigeration, food has been successfully preserved by one of three ways: drying, salting, and preserving in acid. Think prunes, prosciutto, and pickles. The technology of preserving food wasn't so different in the days of Charlemagne, the Medici, or even during the truncated lifetime of Marie Antoinette, even though the cooking was entirely different in each era. The rough-and-ready Franks were largely ignorant of all but pepper. In Renaissance Italy, ginger, cinnamon, nutmeg, saffron, and cloves adorned not merely the tables of merchants and potentates but also found their way into medical prescriptions and alchemical concoctions. Spices were even used as mouthwash. And then French trendsetters of the waning seventeenth century, after their own six-hundred-year dalliance with the aromas of the Orient, turned away from most spices to invent a cuisine that we might recognize today. So if spices were used for their preservative qualities, why did they stop using them? The French had not discovered some new way of preserving food. There was a shift in taste, certainly, but it was the same kind of change that happened when salsa replaced ketchup as America's favorite condiment. There were many underlying reasons for it. Technology wasn't one of them.

Old cookbooks make it clear that spices weren't used as a preservative. They typically suggest adding spices toward the end of the cooking process, where they could have no preservative effect whatsoever. The *Ménagier*, for one, instructs his spouse to "put in the spices as late as may be, for the sooner they be put in, the more they lose their savor." In at least one Italian cookbook that saw many editions after its first printing in 1549, Cristoforo Messisbugo suggests that pepper might even hasten spoilage.

Perversely, even though spices weren't used in this way in Europe, they could have been. Recent research has identified several spices that have powerful antimicrobial properties. Allspice and oregano are particularly effective in combating salmonella, listeria, and their kind. Cinnamon, cumin, cloves, and mustard can also boast some bacteria-slaying prowess. Pepper, however, which made up the overwhelming majority of all European spice imports, is a wimp in this regard. But compared to any of these, salt is still the champion. So the question remains, why would Europeans use more expensive and less effective imports to preserve food when the ingredients at hand worked so much better?

But what if the meat were rancid? Would not a shower of pepper and cloves make rotten meat palatable? Well, perhaps to a starved peasant who could leave no scrap unused, but not to society's elite. If you could afford fancy, exotic seasonings, you could certainly afford fresh meat, and the manuals are replete with instructions on cooking meat soon after the animal is slaughtered. If the meat was hung up to age, it was for no more than a day or two, but even this depended on the season. Bartolomeo Scappi, another popular writer of the Italian Renaissance, notes that in autumn, pheasants can be hung for four days, though in the cold months of winter, as long as eight. (When I was growing up in Prague, my father used to hang game birds just like this on the balcony of our apartment, and I doubt that our house contained any spice other than paprika.) What's more, medieval regulations specified that cattle had to be slaughtered and sold the same day.

Not that bad meat did not exist. From the specific punishments that were prescribed for unscrupulous traders, it is clear that rotten meat did make it into the kitchens of the rich and famous, but then it also does today. The advice given by cookbook author Bartolomeo Sacchi in 1480 was the same as you would give now: throw it out. The rich could afford to eat fresh meat and spices. The poor could afford neither.

Wine may have been another matter. For while people of even middling means could butcher their chicken an hour or two before dinner, everyone, including the king, was drinking wine that had been stored for many months in barrels of often indifferent quality. Once a barrel was tapped, the wine inside quickly oxidized. Especially in northern Europe, where local wine was thin and acidic while the imported stuff cost an arm and a leg, adding spices, sugar, and honey must have quite efficiently improved (or masked) the off-flavors.

Rather than trying to discover some practical reason that explains the fashion for spices, it's probably more productive to look at their more ephemeral attributes. One credible rationale for a free hand with cinnamon and cloves is their very expense.

Spices were a luxury even if they were not worth their weight in gold, as you will occasionally read. In Venice, in the early fifteenth century, when pepper hit an all-time high, you could still buy more than three hundred pounds of it for a pound of gold. And while it's true that a pound of ginger could have bought you a sheep in medieval St. Albans, that may tell you more about the price of sheep than the value of spice. Sheep in those days were small, scrawny, plentiful, and, accordingly, cheap. You will also read that pepper was used to pay soldiers' wages and even to pay rent. But once again, this requires a little context. Medieval Europe was desperately short of precious metals to use as currency, and if you needed to pay a relatively small amount (soldiers didn't get paid so well in those days), there often weren't enough small coins to go around. Thus, pepper might be used in lieu of small change. But sacks of common salt were used even more routinely as a kind of currency in the marketplace.

All this is to say that spices weren't the truffles or caviar of their time but were more on the order of today's expensive extra-virgin olive oil. But like the bottle of Tuscan olive oil displayed on the granite counter of today's trophy kitchens, spices were part and parcel of the lifestyle of the moneyed classes, as much a marker of wealth as the majolica platters that decorated the walls of medieval mansions and the silks, furs, and satins that swaddled affluent abdomens.

In those days, a person of importance could not invite you to a nice, quiet supper of roast chicken and country wine any more than a corporate law firm would invite a prospective client to T.G.I. Friday's. As the *Ménagier*'s wedding party makes clear, there was nothing subtle about entertaining medieval-style. Our own society has mostly moved on to other forms of conspicuous consumption—though you can still detect an echo of that earlier era in some high-society weddings that cost several times a plumber's yearly wage. But much more so than today, the food used to be selected in order to impress your guests. The more of it and the more exotic, the more it said of your place in the pecking order. When Charles the Bold, the powerful Duke of Burgundy, married Margareth of York in 1468, the banquets just kept coming. At one of them, the main table displayed six ships, each with a giant platter of meat emblazoned with the name of one of the duke's subject territories. Orbiting these were smaller vessels, each of which, in turn, was surrounded by four little boats filled with spices and candied fruit. Spices, of course, literally reeked of the mysterious Orient, and their conspicuous consumption was surely a sign of wealth. When the duke's great-grandson, the Holy Roman Emperor Charles V, visited Naples some years later, he was served peacocks and pheasants stuffed with spices. As the birds were carved, the guests were enveloped by the Edenic scent. The idea was nothing new; one of Charles's predecessors, Emperor Henry VI, in Rome for his coronation in 1191, was paraded down streets that had been fumigated by nutmegs and other aromatics when he arrived.

In the late Middle Ages, when the increasingly prosperous bourgeoisie began to be able to afford a little ostentatious display of their own, the feasts of the aristocrats had to become even more fabulous, the spicing more refined, the dishes more exquisite and artfully designed. And just to make sure the entire populace would know how fantastic was the prince's inner realm, the entire dinner might be put on display for the hoi polloi. "Before being served, [the dishes] were paraded with great ceremony around the piazza of the castle . . . to show them to the people that they might admire such magnificence," recounts Cherubino Ghirardacci, who witnessed a wedding party hosted by the ruler of Bologna in 1487. Our reporter does not mention the smell, but surely the abundance of expensive meat with a last-minute sprinkling of spice gave forth an aroma that broadcast the ruler's power even more effectively than the grand dishes glimpsed from across the road.

It was a medieval commonplace that people of different status and position not only deserved but required different foods. A peasant might fall gravely ill from eating white bread and spiced wine rather than the appropriate gruel and ale. A monk would certainly suffer painful indigestion from eating peppered venison, a food more properly reserved for knights. These rules were accepted as being part of divine providence. Inasmuch as there was a natural order among the beasts, each of which was assigned its appropriate food by the Creator, so each human being was assigned his position in the divine plan. Something of the kind still exists today in food attitudes among observant Hindus, with each particular caste having its own rules regarding what may or may not pass their lips. For an upper-caste Brahmin to eat food that is forbidden or inappropriately prepared is to disrupt the order of the universe. A similar connection existed between food and religion in Christendom before Martin

The Italian word for apothecaries was
speziali *(from* spezie, *"spices"), for the*
obvious reason that they were the ones
selling spices.

Luther upset the cart. When Saint Benedict set up his monastic communities in the early sixth century, he specified just what his monks could eat and when. (It wasn't much and it wasn't too often.) Every Catholic had to conform to the religious calendar, but within that generalized scheme, each social stratum had different rules. The Italian preacher Savonarola, best known for castigating Renaissance Florentines for their ungodly ways, also had opinions on the appropriate dining habits of various castes. "Hare is not a meat for Lords," he writes. "Fava beans are a food for peasants." Beef was apparently okay for artisans with robust stomachs but could be consumed by lords and ladies only if corrected with appropriate condiments.

Spices were supposed to be especially effective when it came to "correcting" the nutritional defects of other foods. In much the way we analyze food according to three categories (protein, fat, and carbohydrate), medieval nutritionists divided up foods according to the four humors (phlegm, bile, blood, and black bile). The diet manuals of the time were as obsessed with breaking down foods into their constituent parts as the most avid follower of the South Beach Diet. However, since the nutrients in food were seldom in balance, the cook was expected to fine-tune every dish. It was a job for an alchemist as much as a chef. Outside of the kitchen, physicians also made use of the humoral system by recommending specific foods for particular personalities and maladies, and since spices were deemed especially concentrated compounds for adjusting humoral imbalance, they were prescribed for everything from plague to impotence.

That spices were integral to an opulent lifestyle, even a "necessity" required by one group to set itself apart from another, is incontrovertible. That they were widely used as nutraceuticals is also broadly documented.

All the same, if health concerns were the main determinant of what the moneyed classes eat, customers for foie gras and forty-five-dollar-a-pound chocolates would be in short supply.

In many ways, the medieval and Renaissance elite's desire for spicy food may not be so different from today's popularity of Thai food in America and Balti food in Britain: it was exotic, it was hip, but people also assuredly liked the taste. That spices were pricey and had almost magical curative powers only added to their allure.

SIR JOHN AND THE SEARCH FOR PARADISE

Hard facts and solid reality go only so far in explaining any cultural phenomenon, and this was certainly the case for medieval Christendom. I figured if the academics didn't have the answers, maybe a ghost could give me some clues. This is why I found myself in St. Albans. The phantom in question was Sir John Mandeville, a fourteenth-century knight supposedly buried in the city's great cathedral. Sir John was the acclaimed author of the most popular travel book of his time, in which he described a trip that took him from Norman England to Venice, Constantinople, the Holy Land—and all the way to paradise. *The Voiage and Travayle of Syr John Maundeville Knight* (as it was known in one English translation) was a huge international bestseller.

Like so many travel books of its time, Sir John's story is a pilgrimage tale. The narrator, a Norman English knight, takes leave of St. Albans on Michaelmas Day, 1322. He voyages across the bejeweled Orient to famous shrines cluttered with miraculous relics. He treks through the sun-baked places where Jesus once trod. He hobnobs with the sultan of Egypt. But then comes the good part. After his grand tour of holy sites in the Levant, Sir John heads east—to mythical Christian kingdoms; to India, with its pepper groves; to the Spice Islands of Indonesia; indeed, all the way to Eden's gate. The stories get increasingly fabulous as he travels toward the rising sun. But his medieval readers were not about to split hairs between the merely astonishing and the truly unreal. Some of Asia's actual wonders were so unbelievable that many gave more credence to Sir John's mythical rulers and mouthless dwarfs than they did to the equally amazing description of Kublai Khan in Marco Polo's much more factual account. Not all of Mandeville's stories of the wondrous Orient are made up. The report of the ginger, cloves, cinnamon, nutmeg, and mace of Java and the surrounding isles is more or less on the mark, as is the description of a forest where pepper vines cling to trees bearing fruit like raisins, even if the descriptions of rivers of gems and lands of one-eyed giants might strain our own credulity. It would be hard to say if Mandeville's audience believed his stories or whether they just found him more entertaining, but the Englishman's book consistently outsold Marco Polo's narrative for a good two centuries.

Yet the book wasn't popular merely for its stories of miraculous relics and kinky hermaphrodites. At least some travelers and mapmakers took Mandeville's information altogether seriously. The German cartographer Martin Behaim used Mandeville as a source when he made the first globe of the world in the fateful year of 1492. Several of Columbus's contemporaries aver that he had a copy of the book on him as he peddled his improbable ideas from court to court. The obstinate Genoan could point to Sir John's *Travels* as proof that you could get to the fabled East Indian Spice Islands by sailing west.

But then the rigid lines between empirical data and received wisdom, between experience and revelation, between science and religion, were not as clearly delineated as they are today. When you went on a pilgrimage, as Sir John did, it was not merely a physical journey, it was a spiritual quest in search of paradise. And though the goal of the trip may have been metaphysical, the road signs pointing to every shrine and pilgrimage site were all too real. Even paradise was right there on the maps for anyone to see. When you traveled east, toward Jerusalem, you were on your way toward the earthly Eden. Then, beyond the Holy Land—as Mandeville describes in gripping detail—you needed to cross the infidel realms before reaching the great Christian kingdom of Prester John. Just beyond that, to the east of Asia, all the experts agreed, you would reach Adam and Eve's original garden. Here was a country of joy and plenty, evergreen trees would whisper in the gentle wind, and verdant meadows were irrigated by fountains of youth. (The tourist boards of every Caribbean island are thoroughly versed in the same concept.)

Eden didn't just have a location and an address, it had a taste and an aroma. Paradise smelled like spices, for it was there these precious com-

modities grew. The connection was made explicit when melegueta pepper
was called "grains of paradise," despite its African origin. The thirteenth-
century travel writer Sire de Joinville describes the fishermen in the Nile
dragging up nets "filled with the goods which this [distant] world produces, with ginger, rhubarb, sandalwood and cinnamon; and it is said that
these come from the earthly paradise." Purportedly, the spices that grew
in Eden's groves were shaken loose by that gentle elysian breeze and fell
into the headwaters of the Nile. Saints and their remains supposedly
smelled of spices, since they were already halfway to heaven. Moreover,
this idea of an unearthly scent was not unique to Christendom. Persian
and Arabic sources also describe a sweet afterlife filled with perfumed
plants and food. Even the Chinese thought cinnamon was the bark of the
tree of life. So it's hardly surprising that when later European adventurers traveled halfway across the world in their quest for the precious seasonings, they were ever on the lookout for Shangri-La. Many, just like
Christopher Columbus, brought along Mandeville as a guide. On the
third voyage to his "Indies," the Genoan adventurer wrote to his patrons,
"There are great indications of this being the terrestrial paradise, for its
site coincides with the opinion of the holy and wise theologians . . . all of
whom agree that the earthly paradise is in the East." You will recall that
he still thought he was just east of Asia.

All this is not to say that the main reason for Columbus's epochal voyage was a quest for the Garden of Eden. Most spice seekers were more interested in getting rich quick than in the rewards of the afterlife. But all
the same, you can't entirely discount the religious drive. Let's not forget
that Columbus was in the pay of Queen Isabella, the *conquistadora* of
Granada, the last Muslim refuge in western Europe. The "Most Christian" monarch and her shock troops, the mounted conquistadors, saw
themselves as heirs to the Crusaders, and, like those earlier warriors, their
ultimate goal was to liberate Jerusalem. (Admittedly, they did get a little
sidetracked.) The story of Columbus's great rival Vasco da Gama is even
more clear-cut. He was specifically charged with searching for the legendary Christian ruler Prester John when he headed for India's spice
coast. There, too, greed outshone more metaphysical aspirations, yet that
does not mean that the people of the time did not take their religious mo-

tivations seriously. Indeed, the early Iberian expansion can only be understood when seen as a tale of armed pilgrimage in which the quest for spices is just one chapter.

The idea that you might reach paradise by traveling east has a certain logic to it, given the times. We are so accustomed to thinking of European civilization as the vanguard of the world that we forget that for much of human history, the European peninsula was at the receiving end of the miracles of the East. Over the millennia, innovations such as Mesopotamian agriculture, the Phoenician alphabet, Greek philosophy, and Arab bookkeeping all flowed from east to west. Both Christianity and Islam followed the same route. So did wheat, olives, sugar, and spices. The historian Norman Pounds has depicted this flow of technological and cultural innovation from the Middle East as a "cultural gradient" that was tilted down toward Europe throughout the greater part of human history. It is certainly true that when Sir John traveled from England to Italy, Byzantium, and finally the Middle East, he would have been encountering progressively more advanced technologies, economic structures, and cultures, to say nothing of more sophisticated cuisines.

This gradient, however, was set to shift decisively in Europe's favor some hundred years later, when Mandeville's book was set in movable type. It is worth noting that while the slope of civilization went downhill from east to west, spices were desired, but just when that demand peaked, the slope reversed, and the mythical Oriental aromatics began to lose their allure in Europe. By the time of the Italian Renaissance, innovation, culture, and conquest began to flow in the opposite direction. The first tentative voyages in search of paradise and pepper gave way to the aggressive expansion of European power across the globe.

Unfortunately for Mandeville's reputation, once actual travelers had seen the fabled Spice Islands, they found he had embroidered the truth. Pearls were common enough, and pepper was a scruffy weed that hardly merited cultivation. More recently, academics have even dismissed his very existence. My ghost may never have been more than a fiction. But whether he existed or not, the protagonist of the *Travels* had provided medieval Europe with a taste of paradise. The trouble was that once Eden had been ransacked and colonized, it lost its scent of spice. The transformation was in small part a result of Mandeville's success, but it was also to be his undoing.

BLACK GOLD

While their mythical origins in the East gave Oriental aromatics a marketing advantage over local seasonings, the money you could make buying them in one place and selling them in the next gave traders more than enough motivation to get into the spice business. The pepper grown in the hills of India's Malabar Coast could change hands a dozen times before reaching the shops run by the pepperers guild in Mandeville's England. And each time the pepper changed hands, passed a customs checkpoint, or was subject to taxes, its price shot up. According to one study of the fifteenth-century trade, the Indian grower might be paid one to two grams of silver for a kilo of pepper; when it reached Egypt's main port of Alexandria, the price had shot up to ten to fourteen grams; the traders at Venice's spice market on the Rialto were charging fourteen to eighteen; and by the time it was offered to London's gentry, the price had increased to some twenty to thirty grams of silver. Not that any individual link in this chain made a killing. It's been estimated that the Venetians, who did as well by this trade as anyone, made a comfortable but not extortionate net profit of 40 percent. Still, that was twice the return on investment that Florentine bankers were getting at the time. It's worth noting that today's profit margins can be almost as plush: pepper was recently trading at about $1.60 per kilo wholesale in India, while an upscale grocer in New York was charging $5.49 for a 1.62-ounce jar (that's $120.00 per kilo!) for McCormick "Gourmet" Black Pepper. But the big difference between then and now is that there were few other commodities with this kind of moneymaking potential. And once the Portuguese, and later the Dutch, entered the Asiatic trade, their profits could be even more spectacular. In the sixteenth century, the Portuguese could earn *net* profits of 150 percent or more from the pepper they bought in South India and sold in Lisbon. Nutmeg could fetch a hundred times in Europe what it cost in Malabar. The margin was even greater when it was purchased at its source in the Spice Islands of today's Indonesia.

AN ANCIENT TRADE

The fantastic profits to be made from the spice trade had attracted businessmen for millennia and not only, or even primarily, in Europe. A thriving spice trade existed among India, China, and the islands of Southeast Asia long before the Portuguese and Dutch bullied their way in. The Chinese ruling classes of the Tang dynasty (618–907 C.E.) were as fond of Indonesian and other spices as any Burgundian lord. Marco Polo claimed that for every Italian spice galley in Alexandria, a hundred docked at the Chinese port of Zaiton (Quanzhou). By some estimates, the percentage of spices that reached the European market was never much more than about a quarter of what Asia produced.

If we can rely on the reporting of the Old Testament, Joseph was sold to a caravan carrying spices into ancient Egypt. Just what kind of spices we aren't told, but chances are they brought at least a little pepper. A pharaoh who died in 1224 B.C.E. has been found embalmed with peppercorns up his nose. In later years, when the queen of Sheba made a courtesy call on King Solomon, she reportedly brought along camels bearing spices as a house gift. Perhaps a more trustworthy source is an archaeological dig in Syria that has unearthed cloves dating back to about 1700 B.C.E.—and that in the kitchen of an ordinary household! When the Romans arrived on the scene, they, too, imported spices from Asia, though at nothing like the later European rate. Pepper seemed to have been popular, as was cinnamon and its look-alike, cassia, though some scholars have argued that these last two were actually altogether different spices from the ones we recognize by those names today. In time, the western empire collapsed, and pepper was a rare sight indeed in the former Roman provinces. Elsewhere, though, spice merchants continued to keep the tables of the rich and powerful well supplied. China, India, Persia, and the Arab states of the Middle East still used spices just like they always had, as both tonic and seasoning. Even the Eastern Roman Empire—or Byzantium, as it came to be known—kept up its culinary habits more or less as before.

In Europe, things were different. With the collapse of Rome, the orderly territories north of the Alps were ravaged. Wheat fields were bludgeoned into wastelands, and vineyards were trampled into dust. Trade was throttled. Great cities shriveled to hamlets. Ordinary folk resorted to scavenging for roots and nuts, while the warrior class tore at great haunches of roasted beasts, swilling beer all the while. Or that, at least, is our image of the Dark Ages. Undoubtedly, there were pockets of polished civilization amid the roughened landscape, especially in the monasteries, where fragments of a Roman lifestyle remained. Italy, in particular, retained active ties to both the current "Roman" empire in Byzantium as well as the memory of the old stamping grounds of the Caesars. All the same, whatever else you might say about the invasions of the Germanic and Slavic tribes that swept across the continent in those years, their arrival was hardly conducive to the culinary arts.

In the meantime, as Europe spiraled down into a recurring cycle of war, hunger, and pestilence, the Middle East flourished under a *Pax Arabica*. In Baghdad, the imperial capital, Persians, Arabs, and Greeks sat down at the same table to argue about medicine, science, the arts, and, naturally, what should be served for dinner. Arab merchants sent their agents to China, India, and Indonesia to shop for silks and jewels, but most especially for the spices that were the essential ornament to any sophisticated cuisine. Incidentally, it was those same spice traders who brought Islam to Indonesia and Malaysia. Meanwhile, in the West, Muslim armies had overwhelmed the Iberian Peninsula and penetrated deep into France. They took Sicily and all but a fragment of the Byzantine Middle East. In Jerusalem, mosques towered over Christian remains. For a time, the cries of muezzins calling the faithful to prayer could be heard from the dusty plains of Castile to Java's sultry shores.

Quite reasonably, Christian Europe felt under siege, and its response came in a series of assaults on the Middle East between 1096 and 1291 that we call the Crusades. Yet the short-lived military success of the Crusaders in the Holy Land (they held Jerusalem for just eighty-eight years) pales in comparison to the ideological, cultural, and economic aftershocks that followed those first Catholic jihads.

Cultures typically gain their identity not only from what unifies them but, more important, from what sets them apart from their neighbors and foes. Today, for example, Europeans are united as much by the way they grouse about Americans as they are by the euro. In much the same way, the early medieval idea of Christendom—given the enormous political and economic differences within Europe—could not have been possible

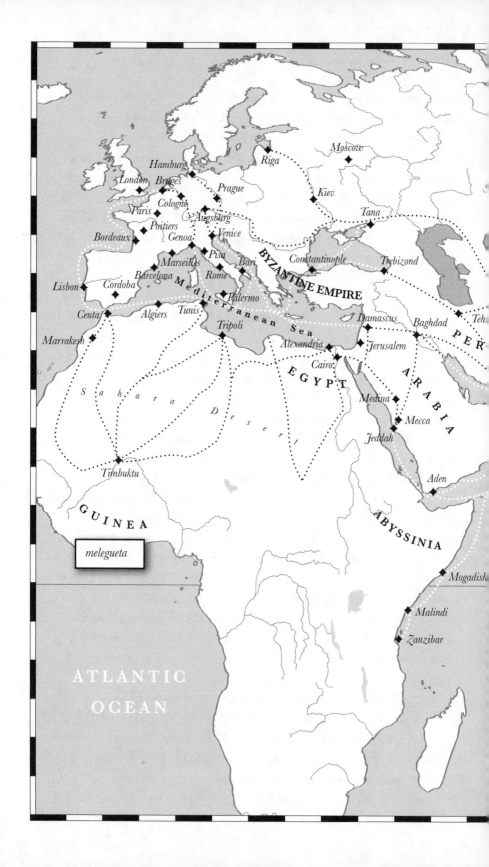

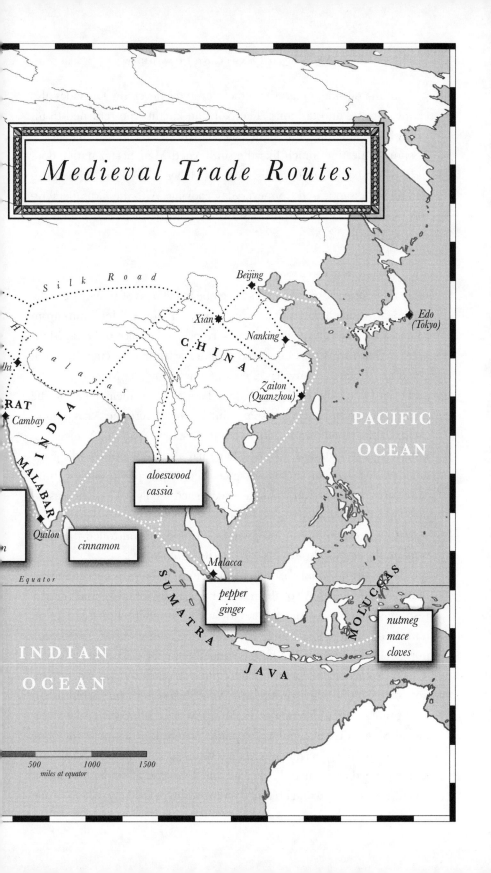

Medieval Trade Routes

Silk Road

Beijing

Xian

Nanking

CHINA

Zaiton
(Quanzhou)

Edo
(Tokyo)

PACIFIC

OCEAN

Himalayas

hi

RAT

Cambay

INDIA

MALABAR

Quilon

aloeswood
cassia

cinnamon

Equator

SUMATRA

Malacca

pepper
ginger

MOLUCCAS

nutmeg
mace
cloves

INDIAN

OCEAN

JAVA

500   1000   1500
miles at equator

without the outside threat. On a more everyday level, the Crusades also changed tastes and fashions. The Norman knight who returned to his drafty St. Albans manor brought back a craving for the food he had tasted in sunny Palestine, much like the sunburned Manchester native does today when he returns from his Turkish holiday. In the Dark Ages, spices had all but disappeared from everyday cooking. With the Crusaders' return, Europeans (of a certain class) would enjoy well-spiced food for the next six hundred years.

HARBORS OF DESIRE

Over the centuries, people across the globe made piles of money from the European desire for pepper, cinnamon, and cloves. Merchants from Malacca to Marseilles built fabulous fortunes in the spice business. Monarchs in Cairo and Calicut financed their armies from their cut of the pepper trade. London, Antwerp, Genoa, Constantinople, Mecca, Jakarta, and even Quanzhou could attribute at least some of their wealth to the passage of the spice-scented ships. But nowhere were the Asian condiments the lifeblood of prosperity as in the great entrepôts of Venice, Lisbon, and Amsterdam. Each took her turn as one of the world's great cities, ruling over an empire of spice. Venice prospered longest, until Vasco da Gama's arrival in India rechanneled the flow of Asian seasoning. Then Lisbon had her hundred years of wealth and glory. Finally, Amsterdam seized the perfumed prize and ruthlessly controlled the spice trade in the century historians call the city's golden age.

There are probably as many similarities among the three cities as there are differences. All of them ran (or at least dominated) small, under-resourced countries, and so they didn't have much choice but to go abroad to make good. Kings and emperors sitting on fat, tax-stuffed purses never had the same kind of appetite for the risky spice business. The great harbors were renowned for their sailors and shipbuilders (and, not coincidentally, their prostitutes). Nevertheless, they prospered in different times and in different ways. Venice was, in some ways, like a medieval Singapore, a merchant republic where business was the state ideology and the government's main job was to keep the wheels of commerce primed and tuned. Pepper was the lubricant of trade. Lisbon, on the other hand, lived and breathed on the whim of the king, who had one eye on the spice trade even as the other looked for heavenly salvation. In the fifteenth century, Portugal had the good fortune to have a run of enlightened, even inspired monarchs who figured out a way to cut out the Arab middlemen by sailing right around Africa. Whether this pleased God is an open question, but it certainly gratified the pocketbook. The Dutch were much more down-to-earth. In Amsterdam, they handed the spice trade over to a corporation, which turned out to be a much more efficient and ruthless way to run a business than Lisbon's feudal approach. Decisions made at the headquarters of the Dutch East India Company would transform people's lives halfway across the globe. By the time the Hollanders were done, the world was a very different place from the one Mandeville wrote about in his *Travels*.

In the meantime, the role of spices in European culture gradually shifted, from the talismans of the mysterious East carried on Venetian galleys, to exotic treasure packed in enormous carracks emblazoned with the Crusaders' cross, and finally to a profitable but rather mundane commodity poured like coal into the holds of Dutch East Indiamen. All this as Europe was transformed from a continent joined (if intermittently) in its battle against Islam, united in its religion, and with an educated class conversant in the same language to a battleground of nation-states, divided by creed and vernacular. People still used plenty of pepper and ginger in post-Reformation Europe, but that's mostly because they had become relatively cheap. The trendsetters had grown tired of spices, though, and the cuisine favored by generations of Medici, Bourbons, Hapsburgs, and Tudors was about to fundamentally change.

It was just around the time when the road to European world domination opened for business that Europeans' tastes began to come home. Crusades and pilgrimages went out of fashion. And the orgy ended. Certainly not overnight and not everywhere, but in the fashion centers of Madrid and Versailles, spices no longer made the man. The vogue that had built Venice from a ramshackle fishing village on stilts into Europe's greatest metropolis, the transient tastes of a few cognoscenti that had transformed Lisbon from a remote outcrop at the edge of Christendom into the splendid capital of a world-spanning empire, the culinary habits of a minute fragment of this small continent's population that had lifted Amsterdam out of its surrounding bog and briefly made teeny Holland one of the great powers of the world—all this was over. Fashion had moved on.

A NEW WORLD

The voyages in search of the spiceries, whether successful like da Gama's or misdirected like Columbus's, had effects both profound and mundane. We all know of the disastrous fallout for Native Americans once Europeans arrived and the subsequent horrors of the transatlantic slave trade. Perhaps less well known is the genocide perpetrated by the Dutch East India Company in the nutmeg isles of Indonesia. Or the slave trade that flourished in the Indian Ocean to provide the Portuguese with sailors for their spice ships and to supply workers for Dutch nutmeg plantations. The Afrikaner presence in South Africa, the Boer War, and even the subsequent apartheid regime would never have existed if the Dutch hadn't sent colonists to the Cape of Good Hope to supply their pepper fleets. Other consequences of the spice trade were more narrowly economic. The European appetite for Oriental luxuries meant that money kept flowing ever eastward. Armadas of silver sailed from Mexico and Peru to Europe but then, just as assuredly, kept going all the way to Asia to pay for the pepper that was sent back home. Asians wanted silver pieces of eight for their black gold. But the pepper ships weighed down with silver brought another kind of cargo on their outbound voyage. Franciscans and Jesuits came in the lee of the spice trade, and although their proselytization efforts could never keep up with the Muslim spice traders, at least Christianity was added to Asia's assortment of religions. A cargo of perhaps even greater consequence was the foods brought along with the priests and the doubloons. New World crops such as corn, papayas, beans, squashes, tomatoes, and chilies were all transported in Portuguese ships bound for Africa, India, and the Spice Islands. Not that all the aftershocks of the spice trade were of seismic proportions. Everyday fashions were influenced by contacts with the East. The Portuguese penchant for blue and white tiles, for example, came about when they tried to imitate the Ming porcelain brought back with the pepper, and in Amsterdam, Indian fabric embroidered in the Mogul style was all the rage in its day.

We have been taught that history moves on great wheels, on world wars, on Napoleonic egos, on the revolutions of the masses, on vast economic upheavals and technological change. Yet small things, seemingly trivial details of everyday existence, can lead to convulsions in the world order. In trying to find a modern commodity that has the same transformative role played by spices in the expansion of Europe, historians have tried to make the analogy with today's dependence on Middle Eastern oil. But that comparison is deeply flawed, for petroleum is absolutely critical to the day-to-day functioning of virtually every aspect of modern existence. Great oceans of petroleum are sent around the world every day. By contrast, in the early fifteen hundreds, almost all of Europe's pepper arrived in a yearly armada of a half dozen Portuguese ships. It's easy enough to understand why nations would go to war to safeguard oil, the lifeblood of their economy, but to risk life and limb for a food additive of virtually no nutritional content that only a tiny fraction of the population could even afford? Spices have about as much utility as an Hermès scarf. Yet it is precisely this inessentiality that makes them a useful lens for examining the human relationship to food. Once people no longer fear starvation, they choose to eat for a whole variety of reasons, and these were not so different at the court of the Medici than they are at the food courts of Beverly Hills. Food is much more than a fuel; it is packed with meaning and symbolism. That ground-up tree bark in your morning oatmeal once had the scent of heaven, the grated tropical nut kernel topping your eggnog set in motion a world trading network, and those shriveled little berries in your pepper grinder gave the cue for Europe's entry onto the world stage and its eventual conquest of the world. The origins of globalization can be traced directly to the spice trade.

RETROFITTING EDEN

It is often assumed that people's taste preferences are conservative, and while this may be true for a particular individual, the cuisines of societies are regularly transformed within a generation or two. The fondness that many adult Americans exhibit for that sugary mélange of Crisco and cocoa powder called Oreos was most surely not shared by their parents. Italians as a whole were not obsessive pasta eaters until after the Second World War. Today, the eating styles of entire nations are in flux. And they are converging. It could be argued that the world—at least, that part of it that doesn't fear starvation—is eating more alike than it has since the

Middle Ages. Of course, food is only a small part of this phenomenon. There is a kind of modern-day, international gothic, not only in art and architecture (as the term is typically used by art historians) but also in food, music, fashion, and language. English is the new Latin. Hip-hop emanates from clubs in Nairobi and Mumbai. McDonald's, Coca-Cola, and their imitators dot the globe.

Of all the world's great cities, it is perhaps London that has undergone the most dramatic culinary transformation over the last generation. Good food is surprisingly easy to find here, much of it imported from halfway across the world.

As I set out one evening to explore London's cosmopolitan vibe, it appeared I had not entirely left St. Albans's ghostly knight behind. How else to explain that I stumbled onto the hundred yards or so of pavement named Mandeville Lane? Up the block, the lane changes its name to Marylebone High Street. With its parade of French pastry shops, nail salons, Starbucks, and other multinational chain stores, it is typical of contemporary English main streets. Here, the upscale pubs are filled with a tanned crowd sporting that lightly disheveled look that passes for well groomed among the English in-crowd. The trendiest of the local watering holes is a spot called Providores, renowned among London foodies for its New Zealand variant on jet-set fusion cuisine. I think Sir John would have liked the place, especially the Tapa Room (it is decorated with a large Polynesian tablecloth called a tapa). It is a rambunctious space vibrating with percussive laughter, where aromas of distant tropical gardens waft from the passing dishes.

Kiwi chef Peter Gordon has actually visited the places mentioned in Mandeville's medieval travel guide. The restaurant's website credits the New Zealander's extensive travels through Southeast Asia, India, and Nepal as the source of his culinary inspiration. Gordon, like many of his generation, is a television celebrity; he's a draw at charity events across the land and a consultant on at least three continents. He epitomizes the globe-trotting style that has become the standard upper-crust cuisine from Miami to Bangkok. It, too, is spicy, if in a different style from the dishes eaten by the lords and ladies of Sir John's Europe.

Still, the exotic flavors of the Providores kitchen titillate as much as the stories Mandeville brought back from his fictional voyages through the Indies, and in much the same way. Here, too, the exotic Orient is repackaged for its Western consumer. Where the itinerant knight gave his audience stories of industrious pygmies in the employ of the Chinese emperor, the traveling chef gives us crab *laksa,* a spiced crab cake aswim in Thai curry sauce. And in place of fantasies of wife-swapping inhabitants of an unnamed isle, we can indulge in the flavors of an imaginary land where French-cooked fish are served on a bed of Indian-spiced vegetables. But the food here is as much of a fiction as Mandeville's tales. The exotic tropical flavors spirit you away from the English drizzle to a far-off isle where the sun is always shining and azure water laps gently on rosy coral shores. We, too, want our paradise. And if we can't board a plane to get there, at least we can sip a Caribbean cocktail and nibble a spicy Balinese hors d'oeuvre. It's a quest I think Sir John would endorse.

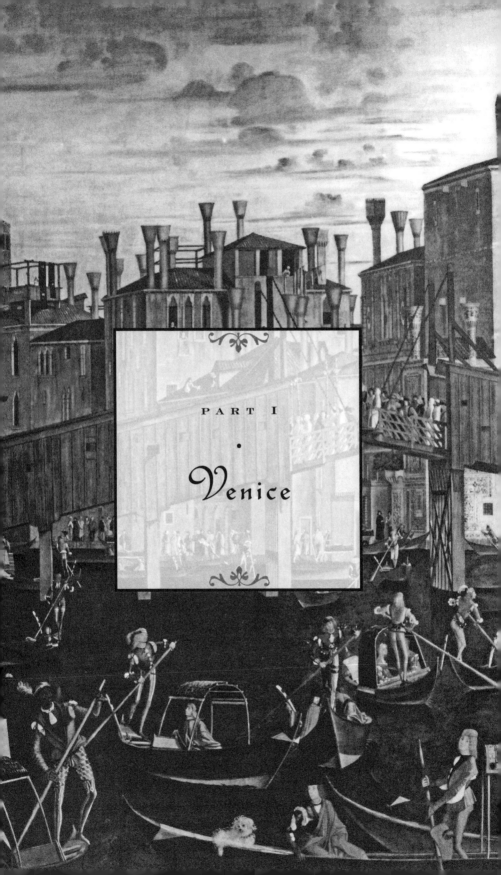

PART I

·

Venice

I ANTICHI

What I remember best from that dinner on Campo San Maurizio are the *canoce,* a tangle of milky pink sea creatures spilling across a great silver platter. And Luca, looming in the low kitchen doorway, in an outfit of leather pants, royal blue velvet blouse, and Day-Glo orange boots, a huge grin splitting his satyr's face as he paused dramatically to hold up the dish so that we might admire his succulent prize. *Canoce* are about the size of a fat man's index finger and belong to the same family of tasty exoskeletal sea life as shrimp and saltwater crayfish; however, they are distinctly more buglike in appearance, lacking the bright color and exuberant claws of other crustaceans. In flavor, though, they are far more delicate, infused with sweetness and brininess in exquisite balance. When they arrive at the table, I give up on my knife and fork so that I can methodically rip each luscious beast apart to extract its sweet belly and slurp on my fingers to secure each salty drip. I try to remember the instructions from a pamphlet on etiquette published in 1483, when everyone ate with their hands: "Eat with the three fingers, do not take morsels of excessive size and do not stuff your mouth with both hands." Success is elusive.

Like most Italian cooking today, the *canoce* recipe is simple: the crustaceans are bathed in a little olive oil and seasoned with salt and pepper. It is Venetian food at its most elemental, a dish that comes from the bounty of the lagoon that fed local fishermen long before Venice became Europe's pepper dealer and continued to do so long after the city was washed up in the spice trade. The pepper is still there, but there's not even a trace of the other seasonings—the ginger, the cinnamon, the nutmeg, the cloves—that once filled the city's great galleys and suffused her suppers with Oriental scents. It's as if the ancient town can no longer recall yesterday's spiced debauch and instead, as the old often do, has retreated to the memories of her youth, before the parvenu aristocrats began to dress her up with baubles from abroad. Luca explains that this method of cooking *canoce* is more *popolare,* of the people, the way the old ladies make them, the only ones who can still make Venetian food. The recollection of feasts gone by fades the rake's smile to melancholy.

I had come to Venice to try to pry off her mask, to uncover some of the antique flavors, to sniff out her ancient peppery smells. I figured Luca could make the introductions. After all, he has spent his forty-something years consorting with the old dowager on the lagoon. Along the way, he has reproduced Renaissance feasts complete with trained bears, sword-fights, and period trumpet serenades, where the gilded pheasants and cinnamon-scented ravioli were served from ornate platters and golden bowls. Although he is more a jack-of-all-trades than a Renaissance man, he has often dressed the part of the latter. Imagine Paul Bunyan in silk tights topped by an exquisite doublet of pink and gold. In other towns, Luca Colferai might have been a punk rocker in his youth, but here, his rebellion took the form of organizing erotic poetry festivals and resurrecting Casanova. So you can understand that when his grandiloquent dinner invitation arrived, I could hardly refuse.

One of Luca's many roles is to play a guiding spirit to I Antichi, a confraternity of like-minded families known as a *compagnia de calza* (literally, "society of the stocking"). "Our *compagnia* is made up of a small lunatic fringe who just want to have fun during *Carnevale*" is how Luca describes his companions. In fact, the society's mandate, to organize celebrations during Carnival, is fully approved and authorized by the Venetian municipal government. Given that this is Venice, the idea goes back to the sixteenth century, when groups of elite young men formed these associations to throw parties during Carnival. This was a time when the city's commercial prowess, and the spice trade in particular, was under siege. To the sons of privilege, drinking and whoring till dawn seemed much more sensible than risking their lives in the increasingly precarious pepper business.

The original I Antichi was founded by a group of Venetian nobles in 1541 with the motto *Divertire divertendosi*, which might be roughly translated as "Throw parties so you can party." The group was reinvented by a Venetian lawyer and antiquarian named Paolo Zancopè in the late 1970s and subsequently passed into Luca's hands upon the founder's death. Zancopè's residence, where our *canoce* feast was held, has become a kind of clubhouse for I Antichi, presided over by the effervescent presence of his Brazilian widow, Jurubeba.

Emptying yet another bottle of fizzy Prosecco, Luca recounts a golden past of grand regattas and mask-filled balls. The membership of I Antichi ranges from street sweepers to multimillionaires, from butchers to poets. They come together for the many official festivals that mark the Venetian calendar: for the *Festa della Salute,* which commemorates the end of the plague of 1631, when a third of Venice perished; for the *Festa di Redentore,* another party in memory of an epidemic; for the *Festa della Sensa,* when Venice recalls a time when the doge, the elected Venetian leader, would symbolically marry the sea; and, of course, for *Carnevale,* the pre-Lenten festival that overruns Venice and can seem as execrable as a plague when the narrow alleys swarm with the tourist hordes. The menu for every holiday follows age-old traditions: cured, spiced mutton for the *Salute;* artichokes for the *Sensa; bigoli* for the *Redentore.*

Jurubeba interrupts Luca's reminiscences to consult on the state of our *bigoli.* (The *canoce* were only one course among many.) He breaks off midsentence to attend to the important matter at hand. *Bigoli* are a kind of thick whole wheat spaghetti that are typically served entangled in a sauce of caramelized onions and anchovies, the saltiness of the fish and sweetness of the onion providing the perfect, if unsubtle, condiment for the rough pasta. They are very traditional, especially to the Jews of the Ghetto Nuovo, the original "ghetto." (The Jewish variant uses garlic instead of onions.) But today, it seems, all that's left of the Ghetto's ancient community are Hassidic Jews from Brooklyn—and they know about as much about *bigoli* as they do about prosciutto. These days, there is little traditional food to be found in Venice. When I invite Luca to a restaurant, he grimaces, insisting that there are no more "honest" restaurants left, that they're all for the tourists now.

All the same, Venetian food hasn't entirely disappeared (yet), and if you dig hard enough, you can still unearth hints and clues of what food might have tasted like two hundred, five hundred, even a thousand years ago. Many restaurants still serve *sarde in saor,* a dish of fried sardines mounded with onions and raisins, seasoned with vinegar, sugar, and occasionally even cinnamon. Its combination of sweet and sour is typical of the Middle Ages; there's even a fourteenth-century recipe for much the same dish. You can also taste the past in the confections called *peverini*, sold in every Venetian *pasticceria*. They are barely sweet with molasses but distinctly seasoned with pepper, the pungency a faint echo of the city's past renown as spice supplier to the Western world.

Still, most of the food that Venetians call their own, the cooking of their grandmothers, is of much more recent vintage. In Marco Polo's day, our *canoce* would have been showered with a medieval blend of spices on top of today's salt and pepper; even as late as the seventeen hundreds, Casanova sprinkled his pasta with sugar and cinnamon. Indeed, the very idea of Venetian food as a regional Italian cuisine is largely an invention of the nineteenth century, much like the Italian state itself. It was only when Venice lost her overseas empire that her cuisine became dependent on local "Italian" ingredients. The occasional spiced dishes of the Renaissance held on, but only as obscure local specialties. Pelegrino Artusi, who wrote the nineteenth-century bible of Italian bourgeois cooking, is bemused and a little horrified when he writes of the way spices were used in the past.

While there's no way to know just how the food of the past tasted (the meat, the wine, even the onions, were different from what we have today), the spiced mutton served at the festival of the *Madonna della Salute* probably comes the closest in flavor to the food eaten by Shakespeare's merchants of Venice. Preparations for the November holiday begin in the spring, when the meat is prepared by curing a castrated ram with salt, pepper, and cloves before it is smoked and then air-dried for several months. It is still exported from Dalmatia (better known today as the countries of Albania and Croatia), as it would have been when the ancient republic used the preserved meat to feed her sailors. The flavor is strong and complex—and anachronistic. It is entirely alien to Luca's four-hour feast of simply seasoned *bigoli, canoce,* roast *triglie* (red mullets), shrimp, and grilled radicchio and a world apart from the simple dessert of mascarpone and biscotti that arrived to finish our memorable evening.

I can't help but see a parallel between today's cooking, with its absence of spice, and the general amnesia you find in Venice about the importance of the spice trade. It didn't used to be like that. When Venetians found out that the Portuguese had arrived in India, at the very source of the pepper that made the city's economy hum, many panicked. The loss of the spice trade "would be like the loss of milk and nourishment to an infant," wrote the spice dealer Girolamo Priuli in his journal in July 1501. And in many ways, it was, though it wouldn't be until a hundred years later that the Dutch finally choked off the teat of prosperity.

Bemoaning the city's fate has been a favorite pastime ever since. But there may be more to it now. The city's population has shrunk by a third in the last twenty years. Foreigners do arrive to settle in the city, just as they have always done, but they are a trickle compared to the exodus. Jurubeba, in her mellifluous Brazilian accent, murmurs how, yes, Venice is shrinking but how the community is *più profondo*, "deeper." I don't ask if becoming deeper in a city that is sinking is necessarily the best thing. Luca shakes his head as he finishes his Prosecco: "The shrinking of the population is a shock to the system. All the food stores are closing so that they can sell masks, but not only masks. Lately, for some reason, everyone is opening lingerie stores. A great explosion of intimate apparel!" Luca bursts into laughter—he doesn't find this entirely displeasing.

DOGES AND FISHERMEN

Luca is right about the lingerie stores: I counted four as I made my way—a little unsteadily—to the Museo Correr the next morning. The musty civic history museum is tucked into one of the homely, neoclassical palaces that hem in the much-photographed Piazza San Marco. Like Venice itself, the Correr is all hype and illusion. Every society is a Potemkin village to some degree, built to appear as it would like to be seen, but nowhere is this more true than in the city that sprouted from the lagoon, where marble façades mask simple brick structures teetering on wooden sticks stuck in mud. When Venice's role on the world stage shrank to insignificance in the sixteenth—but most especially, the seventeenth—century, its inhabitants rewrote her history and rebuilt the backdrop to reflect the new story line. As with the cuisine, the myth of Venice was fossilized into its current form in the nineteenth century, and much to my frustration, the spices are almost as absent from the myth as they are from the cooking.

The Museo Correr is an institution devoted to this willful amnesia, its permanent exhibition a particularly bombastic staging of the nineteenth-century myth. Grand pictures of battles and displays of guns and armor tell a magnificent epic of a mighty imperial power ruled by great doges resplendent as any European prince. In the Correr's version of history, the most glorious moment came in 1571, at the Battle of Lepanto, when a Venetian-led navy cleared the Mediterranean of the infidel Turk. What you won't get from the operatic paintings of dueling triremes plunging through roiling waves is that the famous skirmish is widely seen as Venice's last gasp of power in the inland sea, that in its aftermath, the Turks systematically annexed Venice's overseas possessions. As you walk from room to room, staring up at portrait after portrait of majestic doges done up in kingly, gold-stitched robes, you never find out that, before Lepanto, just about every one of them had started out as a businessman dealing in grain, wine, cheese, salt, but above all, in spices. As you admire vitrines filled with shiny gold ducats, zecchini, and *scudi d'oro*, you may notice the plaque that explains that the coins circulated from Europe to India—though, of course, it doesn't mention why Indian museums are chockablock with old Venetian coins.

All the same, there is a certain logic to the Correr myth. By 1571, the Republic was on its way out as a commercial superpower, and so it only made sense for Venetians to reinvent themselves. The great trading entrepôt turned itself into the entertainment capital of Europe. Gambling at the casinos took the place of speculating on the spice market, and shopping for local gimcracks replaced dealing in exotic merchandise. The museum's back rooms are full of roulette wheels and card games, acrobats tumbling out of pictures, and fantastic human pyramids, eight men high. In 1523, even as the old pepper-laden fleet had shrunk to the odd, pathetic boatload of spice, the new doge, Andrea Gritti, started to invite poets, artists, and musicians to a city better known for its merchants and insurance underwriters. Stone bridges and civic monuments were scenically arranged to reflect the city's splendor in the milky waters of the canals. This is the Venice you see today; it's what draws the visitors and pays the bills. Under Gritti, *Carnevale,* long the disorderly flip side to the city's carefully constructed social order, came under central control. Where now tourists compete for the privilege of being smothered by the Piazza San Marco's famous pigeons, the doges used to sit on their reviewing stands watching official parades that were part church procession and part Fourth of July parade (bands and all). The razzle-dazzle kept the tourists coming even while overseas Venice was washed up.

So if the Correr is all sham and show, where can you find out about the city's history? The best place to start may not be a museum at all; it may be a fish market. To get there, follow the signs to the Rialto Bridge, then go down the Ruga Orefici and Ruga Speziali (the goldsmith and spice seller streets) until you see a large neo-Gothic pavilion. This is the Pescaria, the city's ancient fish market. It's a place where you can get an almost visceral sense of Venice's origins and its first real source of wealth. You can see it in the masses of sparkling seafood, in the wriggling live shrimp no bigger than a roach and the giant six-inch shrimp that belie the name, in the translucent *canoce* and bags of razor clams the color of mother-of-pearl, in the giant tuna whose eyes glisten in the morning light, and in the *scorfano* whose pink getup seems hardly appropriate to a fish with such a fearsome grimace. Here, you understand how the Queen of the Adriatic was spawned in the wriggling lagoon just like the fishy bounty beneath the canopy of the Pescaria.

Recent archaeological digs under the murky waters of the canals have revealed that the dependable riches of the local tides drew people here as early as the third century. The proudly separate Venetians like to think that their city was founded by Italians from the mainland escaping marauding barbarians in the fifth and sixth centuries. (Luca still refers to the mainlanders, those from the terra firma, as barbarians.) But more likely, those early marsh dwellers were just looking for a spot to set up camp near the fertile fishing grounds. They eventually settled on one of the few islands that remained dry during high tide. They called it *Rivo Alto*, meaning "high bank," later shortened to Rialto.

At first, the city of Venice was no more than a stretch of wetland, scattered with a handful of boggy islands. Streams meandered through the marsh, one of which would eventually become the Grand Canal. It was a highly improbable place to build a town. Those early Venetians had to drain the boggy landscape, shore up banks, transport soil from miles away, and drive wooden stakes into the sludge. The city was built first of mud and wattle; then bricks; and finally, to give the impression of solidity, sheets of marble facing were shipped in to cover the plain brick. Nevertheless, the city kept sinking, even as it does today. Archaeologists calculate that by the eleventh century, when the mosaic floors of the great churches at Torcello and San Marco were laid, the ground level had already been raised by more than six feet at the two sites. For the city to remain above water, neither the people nor the government could ever let up on their efforts to keep the houses from flooding and the canals from silting up. This kind of cooperative spirit would come in handy when Venetians started to go into business overseas.

That lagoon not only brought piscatory plenitude but also provided the first Venetians with a salable commodity in the form of salt. Needless to say, this naturally occurring chemical was critical to every human economy before the advent of refrigeration. While food might be preserved by other methods, salt was essential to keeping meat and fish from one season to the next. This is hard to appreciate when, on our tables, salted foods like ham, anchovies, and capers are no more than incidental accessories. But for most Europeans, until very recently, fresh meat was a rare luxury. Salted meats, prepared much like the holiday specialty of spiced mutton, used to be the norm.* Whereas in northern Europe, salt came from deep mines, in the Mediterranean, the supply came from evaporating seawater. Just about anyone with a suitable spot could produce salt, and trying to control production was a virtual impossibility.

Nevertheless, the Venetians gave it a try. The fishermen who had settled on the islands around the Rialto had been working local salt pans since at least the sixth century; however, they could never keep up with the region's main salt producer, which was the town of Comacchio, some fifty miles down the coast. The Venetians' solution was as simple as it was brutal. In 932, they rowed their galleys up to Comacchio, burned its citadel, massacred the inhabitants, and carried off the survivors. Once in Venice, the Comacchians were forced to swear an oath of loyalty to the doge before they were freed. While differing in the particulars, these harsh methods developed by the racketeers who ran the Venetian salt business became a template for the violent strategies of later spice

---

* Some have argued that the enormous quantities of beer consumed in northern Europe were a result of this very salty diet. One study, for example, showed that about a quarter of the cargo shipped from the German port of Lübeck to Stockholm in both 1368 and 1559 consisted of salt. Another 19 percent was in the form of hops, a critical beer ingredient.

traders—and not only Italians in the Mediterranean but also their Portuguese and Dutch successors as they rampaged through Asia.

Venice did eventually give up trying to control salt production, but trade was another matter. Through a combination of business smarts, diplomacy, and murder, the city eventually controlled all the salt that passed through the region. In much the same way as they later set up a government unit to control the spice trade, the Republic's leaders organized a department to determine how, where, and when salt could be sold.*

The men who devised these policies came from a loose cluster of prominent families. They were generally old, experienced businessmen, much like the patricians who sit on American boards of directors, and like those corporate board members, they periodically elected a chief executive officer, the doge, to run the day-to-day operations of Venice Inc. This CEO was expected to fill the role for life; though, when it seemed like the boss was pursuing vainglorious adventures that could jeopardize the bottom line, he could be reined in and, at times, even sacked. (In 1355, when Doge Marin Falier got too high and mighty, the ruling Council of Ten's idea of a golden parachute was to slice off the chief bureaucrat's head on his own palace stairs.) Even though the Republic of Saint Mark could never be confused with a democracy, it was also nothing like the usual feudal medieval state. Here, the ruling class was made of merchants intent on making a buck rather than armed knights more interested in hunting one. It was a government of businessmen by businessmen for businessmen. Which is not to say they had much use for free trade. Nevertheless, they did keep an eye on the little guy and set ground rules under which even small-time merchants could prosper. In this business-friendly environment, ambitious young men with no capital could set up partnerships with established financiers and wealthy widows. With a dose of savvy and a little luck, both sides could profit from the arrangement. But it wasn't just the entrepreneurs who benefited from a government organized to maximize commercial profits. Shipbuilders and

---

* By the 1350s, no salt could move on the Adriatic unless it was in a Venetian ship on its way to or from the city. As late as 1578, the Republic's navy destroyed the saltworks at Trieste. At this point, Venetians were making an 80 percent profit on salt sold on the Italian mainland.

sailmakers, sailors and stevedores, provisioners and prostitutes, along with the bankers and insurance underwriters, all had a direct stake in the merchant republic.

In other places, princes and caliphs skimmed as much of the surplus as they could from their own merchants, but not in Venice. Here, money bred money. As a result, the relatively puny republic could take on vastly bigger and more populous powers such as the kingdom of Hungary, which repeatedly (and unsuccessfully) tried to muscle in on Venice's backyard, and more fatefully, even populous Byzantium. The vast sums that eddied and flowed down the Grand Canal made it possible for a city of fewer than one hundred thousand souls to take on an empire of millions.

When it comes to the Byzantines, once again, *La Serenissima* suffers from selective memory. In the beginning, Venice had been a part of that Eastern realm—though, admittedly, an inconsequential little town on its western periphery. The city was officially a part of the empire until the early ninth century, when, through a series of treaties, it entered a kind of legalistic limbo, still technically a province of Byzantium but paying tribute to the German emperors. As late as 1082, the emperor would refer to the Venetians as "true and faithful servants," and at least theoretically, they remained subject to the same laws as Byzantines. In the early years, Venetians took full advantage of this intimate relationship; later, they ruthlessly exploited it and then finally slit the throat of their once-great overlord. Yet you don't hear much about this in Venice. There is an almost Oedipal reluctance to discuss the city's indebtedness to Byzantium. Still, much of the history of Venice, and especially her role as the spice merchant of Europe, makes sense only when you remember her origins in that ancient empire.

VENICE AND BYZANTIUM

Right next to the great Basilica of Saint Mark and the eponymous piazza is the long quay called the Molo. This is where everybody stands to take the stereotypical snapshot of the green lagoon with the sparkling white church of San Giorgio Maggiore in the background. If you want to buy a gondolier's hat for your nephew or a Carnival cap for your niece, a dozen kiosks here will be happy to oblige. This is where you catch the ferry to the beach on the Lido or to visit the glassworks on Murano or make the trip to the airport. Ships have unloaded passengers and cargo here for a thousand years. It was from this wharf that each doge mounted his gilt-encrusted galley for the annual ceremony in which he married the sea. This has always been Venice's front porch. Yet what is notable, though not immediately obvious, about the pier is its orientation: the Molo faces south and east. It turns its back on the European mainland, the terra firma of the barbarians, to look in the direction of Constantine's glittering metropolis.

When they originally built Saint Mark's, it was no more than the doge's modest private chapel, propped up right next door to his walled fortress. Its claim to fame was that it held the relics of Saint Mark the Apostle, stolen from a church in Alexandria in the ninth century. (Legend claims that the merchants sandwiched the remains between slices of pork to keep the caliph's customs officials at bay.) Some two hundred years on, though, the city had come of age, and like every medieval city of ambition, it needed a grand church to announce her coming out. For a model, the Venetians turned, as they usually did, to Constantinople. They decided to crib the design from the Church of the Holy Apostles, not least because it had been commissioned by Constantine the Great. The doge could now boast of a church to rival the one built by a legendary Roman emperor, with bragging rights to relics just as good as any Byzantine church.

Much of medieval Venetian culture was in fact stitched together from scraps imported from the East. Venetian law followed the Roman tradition of the Eastern Empire more than it did the legal approach of the mainland.* The design of war galleys and the idea of a state-managed arsenal were both largely derived from Byzantium. Taste in clothes, art, and food looked for inspiration to Constantinople. In Venice, Eastern styles of dress—richly brocaded and hanging loose from the shoulders—as well as Greek-inspired icons remained in favor long after the Florentines and Mantuans had turned to tight-fitting, form-revealing outfits and moved on to patronizing the likes of Botticelli and Leonardo.

---

* In Venice, almost uniquely in Europe, women retained legal control of their often considerable dowries. Moreover, it was not unusual for women to invest fairly large sums in overseas trade in spices, silks, and other commodities.

Venetians not only tried to dress like the Byzantines, they aped their eating habits, too. Not that every Eastern culinary innovation was immediately embraced. The imported fork, for example, was initially demonized as "an instrument of the devil." When the doge's son Giovanni Orseolo returned from Constantinople around 1004 with his Byzantine bride, Maria, she immediately elicited gossip not least because of the highly suspect implements in her trousseau. "She did not touch food with her hands," wrote a scandalized reporter years after the event, "but the food was cut up into small pieces by her servants and she would pick up these tidbits, tasting them using a golden fork with two tines." And as if her eating habits weren't peculiar enough, Maria had a proclivity for bathing, in perfumed water no less! Some even blamed her arrival for the plague that devastated the city at the time. (This is not as far-out as it sounds, since the plague was, in fact, as much a Byzantine export as forks and perfume.) Forks were by no means an overnight success, but by the late thirteenth century, the delicate little implements (they were about the size of today's oyster fork) were appearing in wills and inventories. You can see them in a Botticelli painting from the mid-fifteenth century in which two young women delicately hold these tiny forks, and later Venetian banquet depictions are littered with them. Though the sources don't mention it, Maria must have brought her cooks, too. Imagine a finely drilled brigade of Parisian chefs arriving in a Wild West frontier town and you might get some sense of the scandal and wonder engendered by the spiced aromas that now wafted from the kitchens of the doge's palace. Eleventh-century Venice still had a long way to go to keep up with the Byzantines.

Even as western Europe languished in the Dark Ages, Constantinople was the Mediterranean's greatest and most cosmopolitan city. At its height, in the reign of the Emperor Justinian (527–565), the imperial capital likely exceeded half a million people (some estimates go as high as a million). No city in Europe would reach that figure for more than a thousand years! As late as 1204, when the Venetians were about to ravage their increasingly decrepit former mistress, one of their company was still awed by what he saw:

Those who had never seen Constantinople before were enthralled, unable to believe that such a great city could exist in the world. They gazed at its high walls, the great towers with which it was fortified all around, its great houses, its tall churches more numerous than anyone would believe who did not see them for himself; they contemplated the length and breadth of the city that is sovereign over all others.

The city at the gates of the Bosporus had always been a magnet for people from across eastern Europe and western Asia. A Western Crusader described Constantinople's melting pot in 1096: "Greeks, Bulgarians . . . Italians, Venetians, Romanians [the contemporary term for mainland Greece], Dacians [from today's Romania], English, Amalfitans, even Turks; many heathen peoples, Jews and proselytes, Cretans, Arabs and people of all nations come together here." Not surprisingly, the local culture was inflected by all these foreign accents and the city's cuisine seasoned by flavors from across the empire.

Byzantine kitchens largely depended on the abundant local fish and produce (much as Turkish and Greek cooking does today), but the imperial capital could also count on supplies of grain from far-off Crimea, cheese and wine from the Aegean Islands, and oil from mainland Anatolia. As far as seasoning goes, *garum* (*garos* in Greek), the fermented fish sauce so essential to ancient Greek and Latin cuisines, remained in favor here long after western Europe gave it up. The old Roman influence also showed up in a love of herbs, spices, and other exotic seasonings. The taste for spices, it seems, grew more pronounced over the years. Ancient Roman cooks had mostly limited their use of Asian condiments to black and long pepper (*Piper nigrum* and *Piper longum*), despite the fact that there was a more or less direct route that delivered spices from South India to Italy. Other aromatics were mainly used medicinally, though priests and embalmers found them handy as well. Tacitus informs us, for example, that after murdering his wife, Poppaea, in 65 C.E., Nero used a year's supply of Rome's cinnamon to bury her.

In Byzantium, as the connection to ancient Rome faded, spices began to leach from the apothecary's cabinet to the stewpot. This was remarked upon by an early Christian killjoy, Asterius of Amasea, around 400 C.E. "Becoming more elaborate as every day passes," he notes with the usual religious ascetic's breast-beating, "our luxury now impels us to

plaster our food with the aromatics of India. Nowadays the spice merchant seems to be working not for the physician but for the cook!" Asterius was probably overstating the case so he could pep up his sermon.
Spices remained important in the physicians' medical kit, their therapeu-
tic value appreciated perhaps even more than before as people became
ever more familiar with the humoral system. If anything, the curative
properties of the Asian exotics only enhanced their prominence in Byzantine cooking.

A wide range of spices was used in the kitchens of Constantinople.
Apparently, at least one of the emperors, Constantine VIII, was even an
amateur cook, "a highly skilled mixer of sauces, seasoning his dishes
with colors and flavors so as to arouse the appetite of all types of eaters."
Our source, a contemporary chronicler, adds that the imperial gourmet
was addicted to food and sex and, as usual, came to a bad end. The flavors in the emperor's pantry would be only partially familiar to us. Mas-
tic, produced from the sap of trees on the island of Chios, was a great
favorite used in bread and cakes but also as a kind of chewing gum to
freshen breath. (Turks and Greeks still add it to chewing gum to similar
effect.) Storax and balsam, produced in much the same way in the southern reaches of the Middle East, perfumed soups and wines. Spikenard,
an extract of a leafy Himalayan plant, and putchuk, a plant from the
highlands of Kashmir, were just two of the many Indian seasonings the
debauched ruler mixed into his sauces and soups. He could also turn to
black pepper, long pepper, ginger, cassia, cinnamon, cloves, nutmeg,
mace, and the equally pricey sugar to arouse those jaded appetites. It's
hard to know just how much of these imported seasonings the high-
living emperor stirred into his pots, but if we can trust the few recipes
that actually give quantities, the seasoning was varied but not overly
prodigious.

It doesn't seem that the fine spices we associate with medieval and
Renaissance Europe were especially valued over other condiments in the
middle years of the Byzantine Empire. More likely they were part of a
multihued palette of local and imported seasoning. Perhaps they were not
as exotic to the Byzantines, who were in constant contact with the spice-
savvy culinary cultures of Persia and Baghdad. When the Byzantine

army marched into the Persian palace at Dastagert in 626, we find out they looted about seventy-five pounds of aloeswood (another resinous compound used in cooking), but when it came to the silk, linen, sugar, and ginger they also pilfered, it seems they were not sufficiently impressed to bother noting the quantities. Spices certainly fetched a good price in Constantinople, but they were assuredly less expensive than in Venice, and vastly less so than in France or England. Was there perhaps less snob appeal to spices because they were relatively affordable here?

All the same, in Constantinople, spice dealers made a good living off these exotic roots and berries for well over a thousand years. Some traveled as far west as Burgundy to peddle their wares, and at least one Byzantine merchant was apparently spotted at the court of Ceylon sometime around 550. Typically, though, most of the profits fell in the laps of other middlemen who controlled a network spanning more than eight thousand miles across a continually reconfigured chessboard of shifting nations and inconstant religions. For cloves and nutmeg, the long voyage began in the Moluccas, a minute archipelago of volcanic outcroppings in Southeast Asia, where Indian and Chinese traders loaded their ships for the three-thousand-mile sail to India's pepper coast. At the end of that trip, the resident merchants—Indians, Chinese, Arabs, and Jews—exchanged silver and gold for pepper and nutmeg before loading up the waiting dhows. The little ships, once filled, would flit with the autumn winds across the Indian Ocean and into the Red and Arabian seas. Once more, the spices were reloaded, this time onto thousands of camels, which marched like never-ending columns of ants across the dusty plains to deliver their scented booty to their spice-hungry sovereigns in Egyptian Alexandria and Byzantine Trebizond, on the Black Sea. Then finally came the Mediterranean galleys and Constantinople. After the seventh century, all the overland routes were under Islamic rule, but at least the last leg was run by the Byzantines. But not for long. The Venetians were waiting in the wings.

It should be noted that the Venetians weren't the only ones to muscle in on the Mediterranean spice trade. The Genoese and even the Pisans gave them a good run for their money. Still, in the end, the fishermen from the boggy lagoon prevailed.

MERCHANTS AND PIRATES

Look at a map of the Mediterranean and you'll see a body of water broken up into numerous gulfs, inlets, and estuaries. If you consider it as a whole, though, you'll notice the sea divides more or less neatly in two uneven halves: the smaller, western Mediterranean, which ends at the Italian boot, and the larger, eastern half, which lies south and east of Sicily. Constantinople, today's Istanbul, sits more or less in the middle of the northern coast of the eastern half, perched like a spider above the web of sea-lanes in the Aegean and strategically located to control all traffic with the Black Sea. On the arid southern coast, the great city of Alexandria is located at the very western end of the fertile Nile Delta, the outlet of the caravans bringing pepper and other luxury goods up from the Red Sea. Venice is positioned at the very northwest corner of the Adriatic, the largest gulf of the eastern Mediterranean and just across the Alps from the German-speaking lands. From Venice, it's more or less a direct shot down the eastern Adriatic coast, skimming mainland Greece, past the island of Crete, and then straight down to Egypt. This voyage is easily the most direct path between the spice emporia of the Orient and the silver mines in the heart of Europe.

Controlling this route became the dominant foreign policy concern of the rulers of the Republic of Saint Mark from the moment they began to send their galleys out of the Aegean. To safeguard its program, the city gradually expanded its sphere of influence, first by setting down trading colonies in ports along the route, then strong-arming them into protectorates, and finally, especially after 1204, seizing them outright as colonies. If you travel this route today, you can still see mini-Venices all down the Dalmatian coast, and plenty of Greek towns in the Aegean continue to be overshadowed by the wrecks of Venetian citadels.

The merchants who ran the Venetian state often resorted to the techniques they had learned in the salt trade. This meant that no one who interfered with the Republic's business was off-limits. The Venetian navy was sent to fight Italian city-states just as often as any other interlopers. In particular, the wars with Genoa came almost as regularly as the tides throughout most of the Middle Ages as the two cities wrestled for control of the eastern Mediterranean. But violence wasn't always the best ap-

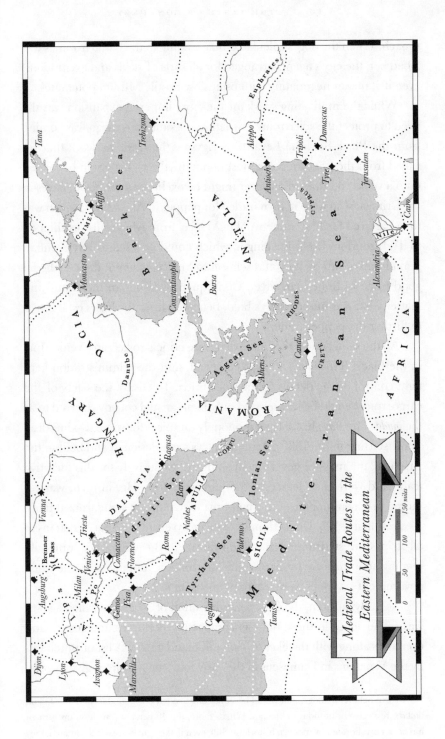

Medieval Trade Routes in the
Eastern Mediterranean

proach. When the doges calculated that sending in the battle triremes was a bad bet, the city's agents arranged for all sorts of deals and exemptions, even if it meant negotiating with ostensibly hostile Muslim potentates.

While the motivating spark for the city's imperial expansion was the need to protect the spice route—whether the odiferous cargo was coming from the Black Sea, the Levant, or Egypt—the trade network that resulted from the policy involved just about anything that could be loaded onto a vessel. So Bohemian silver might be exchanged for Slavic slaves in the Crimea, who were in turn traded for pepper in Alexandria, which was then bartered for Florentine wool in Venice, from whence it was shipped to Trebizond and sold for ginger, which could be used to buy Apulian grain in the south of Italy and sent on to Venice, where it then fetched a good price in Bohemian silver. Consequently, Venetian merchants, no matter what was in their ship's hold, benefited from the bases established to further the pepper trade.

All the same, it was the spices that were critical to keeping Venice Inc. in the black. This was widely recognized, and the administration kept tight control of the details of the spice trade. To ensure the safety of the cargo, spices could be transported only in an armed convoy referred to as the *muda*. The *muda* had a legal monopoly on spices for some two hundred years, starting in the 1330s. Armed galleys were designed and built in the Arsenale, the massive government shipyard, exclusively for this lucrative trade and were then leased to the highest bidder. He, in turn, was required to accommodate even small-time merchants at standardized rates. As a result, in 1423, Doge Tomasso Mocenigo estimated that Venetians of all stripes invested some ten million ducats in the spice trade, annually reaping an impressive profit of some four million, and this at a time when government revenues were less than one million!*

As in Byzantium, the European definition of what was called a spice was rather loose in those days, encompassing perfumes, medicines, and even dyes along with the likes of cinnamon and ginger. A list of purchases by the Venetians in Damascus in the early fourteen hundreds gives a good

---

* If we can believe the doge, that would be something like ten billion dollars and four billion dollars, respectively, in today's currency. What's more, the 40 percent return on investment has been corroborated by modern historians. Still, even if the figures are a little inflated, they give a sense of the kind of money involved.

idea of what was in demand. The Italians loaded up on what we would call "spices" of varying qualities, including black pepper and long pepper, five kinds of ginger, galingale (similar to ginger), zedoary (related to turmeric), nutmeg, mace, cloves, clove stalks, three types of "cinnamon," cubebs (a kind of pepper), cardamom, but also several varieties of incense, dyes, and a half dozen drugs and other chemicals, some thirty items in all. But this long list is a little misleading, since most of these Oriental exotics were traded in minute quantities. The only two commodities that were traded in bulk (making up some 50 to 65 percent of the Damascus spice purchases) were pepper and ginger. And pepper was king. In the fifteenth century, Venetians imported some five pounds of pepper for every two pounds of ginger. Moreover, the quantity of black pepper traded was typically more than all the other spices combined. Accordingly, when Venetian doges fretted about keeping their sea-lanes safe and their ships well provisioned, they were mostly concerned about the flow of the wrinkled black berries from Malabar.

Most traders made a perfectly good living buying and selling more mundane commodities, so why the obsession with spices? The short answer is money. On average, Venetian traders earned a *net* profit of some 40 percent from spices. The great Florentine bankers of the time were getting half that return on investment. Other merchandise might earn 15 to 20 percent if you were lucky. And although certain commodities, especially grain in times of famine, could occasionally be more lucrative, the market for spices remained nice and steady, fat years and lean. Moreover, you did not need a huge investment to enter the market. As a young man with limited resources, a twenty-something merchant could get on a boat to Egypt and return with a couple of sacks of pepper and still make it worth his while. To make a similar profit on grain, you would need to invest serious money, hire an entire ship, and fill it with literally tons of wheat.

But spices had something else going for them, a seldom-remarked quality that may explain why pepper, in particular, was the bait that drew so many Venetian galleys to trade with the infidel and later lured the Spanish and the Portuguese to distant oceans. Spices don't spoil—or at least, not quickly. We are so used to nibbling Chilean grapes and chomping on shrimp from Thailand that we may forget how difficult it used to be

Pepper, as depicted in Garcia da Orta's late-sixteenth-century herbal.

to transport all but a few specialized commodities over any great distance. There would have been no demand for Indian-grown pepper in medieval Europe if the dry little berries had not been light enough and sufficiently nonperishable that they could withstand being shipped halfway across the world. For a bale of pepper to get from Quilon to Cologne, it would likely endure months of transportation by ship, camel, and mule, interrupted by many more months of storage in every port along the route—and all this without a noticeable decline of quality. Pepper, in particular, is remarkably stable and can be stored up to a decade as long as it's kept reasonably dry. Imagine trying to ship a sack of mangoes halfway across the world or lugging a crate of china across the Alps. And while Asian spices were never really worth their weight in gold, they were a whole lot lighter for those camels to carry! The only other goods that were worth transporting over such a long distance were precious stones and silk. Marco Polo's trading family, for example, seems to have specialized in pearls and such when they trekked across Asia in the late twelve hundreds. The problem with jewels, though, was that they were relatively pricey even at the point of purchase, and thus, the potential for profit was inevitably smaller. Spices, on the other hand, were a cheap agricultural commodity that was easily obtained by low-skilled foragers in the forest. This explains why princes and businessman could get away with jacking up the price 1,000 percent between the time the dried condiments left Asia and their arrival at the Adriatic port.

Still, the long-distance trade wasn't without its risks. Overseas were alien rulers who wanted to wring ever more revenue from the trade; foreign merchants demanding a fatter slice of the pie; and rivals from Genoa, Barcelona, and Marseilles bidding up the price. Once your cargo was loaded, you had to worry about shipwrecks, pirates, and, once again, the European competitors, who could be worse than the pirates. The merchant who not only wanted to make a profit but also to survive needed to keep one hand on the hilt of his sword as the other reached for his purse. In some ways, even to characterize the traders aboard Mediterranean galleys strictly as merchants is a little misleading. Rather, imagine highly organized, well-armed gangs prowling the sea, en route from port to port, seizing any opportunity that might present itself. Throughout most of history, whether a transaction ended up as looting or trade often depended on the strength of the opponent. The Venetians were always calculating whether to haggle or fight, but in either case, it was wise to be well armed if for no other reason than that the threat of harm might result in a better price. While fellow citizens of the Republic were generally considered off-limits for piracy, other Italians were considered fair game, especially if a precious cargo of spices or pearls was suspected on board. The situation on land was not much better, and while all sorts of treaties and legal statutes were supposed to regulate trade in the spice ports, there was always the possibility one side might not like the deal and pull their daggers. Even once the goods were in hand, they had to be locked up under vigilant guard. In part, this is why local authorities sometimes permitted or acquiesced in the erection of surprisingly elaborate fortifications for each trading "nation."

The Venetian semimilitarized vessels had a distinct advantage over the lightly armed merchantmen of the Byzantines. The rulers of the Eastern Empire put what resources they had into their navy, which was a strictly military outfit and did not meddle in trade, whereas the large, heavily armed crews of the Venetian ships were not only able to ward off potential attackers, they could attack at will, buying and selling all the while. Recognizing their naval prowess, Byzantine emperors hired Venetian navies on at least two occasions to fend off Norman incursions. As a reward, Venetians would enjoy tax-free status throughout the empire.

It wasn't just shipping that was subjected to Venetian attack, though. The poorly garrisoned coastline of the southern Aegean was a tempting target for the Venetian corsairs as well. As they passed through, the armed galleys would descend on undefended fishing ports at will, demanding provisions (if you were lucky) and kidnapping children and young adults to sell into slavery (if you weren't). Technically, Christians were supposed to sell only nonbelievers into slavery, but this distinction was not always strictly observed. It isn't that Venetians were any more rapacious than the others; they were just the most capable predator in a shark-infested sea.

At first, the Venetians took over the export trade from Byzantium to the Adriatic; then, along with the Pisans and Genoans, they began to supply Constantinople itself; and finally, by the time of the First Crusade, Italians were doing most of the shipping inside the empire. The splendid old dominion of the eastern Caesars was having a tough time of it all around. Central authority had broken down to such an extent that most of the provinces were now run by regional strongmen who seldom bothered to send any tax revenue to the capital. In the East, Seljuk Turks had gradually consumed large chunks of what is now Turkey. By the late eleven hundreds, all that remained of the realm that had once controlled the entire eastern Mediterranean were the Balkans and fragments of coastal Turkey. As the once-great empire wasted away, Venetians moved in to feed off the carcass, swelling, in turn, the purses of the upstart republic. In 1204, Frankish and Venetian pilgrims, armed for the Fourth Crusade, arrived to deliver the fatal blow.

COOKS AND CRUSADERS

As you arrive in Venice today, the city that floats upon the sea presents a skyline of soaring cupolas and pointed bell towers. Every *campo*, every square, every neighborhood, is dominated by a church. Many are still graceful and limber, even though others are increasingly doddery and infirm. But still, with all those domes and steeples, you'd think the Venetians a religious lot. The truth is rather more nuanced. As far as the rest of medieval Europe was concerned, the Venetians were always on the verge of apostasy. They were particularly notorious for cutting deals with the Moor to maintain their trading privileges. The popes regularly excommunicated the entire town—though, admittedly, there was usually a political motive for this. In the Republic of Saint Mark, local clergy were strictly subordinated to the secular authorities. Here, the slogan was *Veneziani, poi Christiani!* ("Venetians [first], then Christians!"). As a result, many historians have attributed Venice's involvement in the Crusades to purely mercenary motives; the whole bloody affair as little more than a hostile-takeover bid for the pepper business. But that's just too pat. To discount religion from Venice's strategy toward the Arab world would be as simplistic as it would be to remove the ideological component from America's adventures in the Middle East. Sure, pepper (like oil today) was important, but that didn't mean the Venetians weren't dedicated Christians just like every other medieval European. Which isn't to say that—much like fervent American Christians today—the Venetians let their religion get in the way of their business practices.

By the time the Italian city-states became involved in the pepper trade during the waning years of the first millennium, the Mediterranean world was irrevocably split between the Christian North and the Islamic South. After Muhammad's death in 632, Muslim armies thundered across the Middle East and North Africa. They seized Iberia and Sicily. Their mounted horsemen surged deep into France, where they were finally checked by Christian knights at the battle of Poitiers in 732. In the aftermath, there was a more or less stable entente between the faiths for the next three hundred years. By the early years of the new millennium, however, an increasingly prosperous Europe was emerging from the slumber of the Dark Ages. One sign of this was a new imperial religiosity, a widespread desire to push back the borders of Islam. When, in 1095, Pope Urban II appealed for a crusade to liberate Jerusalem, men (and even some women) across Europe took up the cause by the thousands, donning the white tunic emblazoned with the red Crusaders' cross.

Lacking any navy to speak of, the Frankish knights of western Europe had to charter ships in order to get their men and horses to the Holy Land. Consequently, they turned to the nautically endowed Italian city-states. Genoa offered a measly 13 ships. Pisa was more generous, providing a flotilla of about 120 vessels. The Venetian authorities took close to a year to sort out the pros and cons of joining the holy war, but when they finally did, their 200 ships were to be the single largest contribution to the Crusader navy. There were certainly many Venetians who were swept up in the religious fervor of the time; nevertheless, there were also a good number who were more calculating in the matter. When the then-current doge, Vitale Michiel, exhorted his fellow citizens to join the jihad, he did not forget to add that the potential for gain was not merely of the spiritual variety. Under the terms of the deal, the Italian cities were supposed to get one-third of any territory captured in the Holy Land in payment for transport. Though the Italians never got quite as much as the contracts stipulated, they did get enough territory to set up commercial bases across the Levant.

For the Venetians, the Crusades were undoubtedly an enormous strategic as well as financial windfall, whereas, for the rest of Europe, the consequences were ultimately to be more cultural than directly economic or even political. The Latin knights who disembarked, first in Byzantium and then in the Holy Land, were in for a culture shock. Only when confronted with the plush lodgings and refined cuisine of the East would most of them have realized just how dank and dismal were their drafty donjons and how dull their diet back home.

In Constantinople, the great lords of Europe were fed spiced delicacies in the perfumed palace of the emperor, but even lesser souls were exposed to the decadent ways of Byzantium at inns and bathhouses across the great metropolis. The imperial capital was the kind of place where, on Easter Sunday, the ruler would parade to the world's largest church, the Hagia Sophia, past a fountain "filled with ten thousand jars of wine and a thousand jars of white honey . . . the whole spiced with a camel's load of [spike]nard, cloves and cinnamon," an event reported by a Muslim hostage a century earlier.

Meanwhile, in the boomtowns of Palestine, common Italian merchants lived better than Burgundian princes. Their salons were decorated with mosaics and marble and decked out with carpets of plush damask. Perfumed meats arrived on platters of silver, if not gold. Fresh water ran from taps, carried by the still-standing Roman aqueducts. Chilled wine flavored with the spices of the Orient filled delicate goblets and beakers.*

Many Crusaders would have spent as much as a year exposed to Constantinople's spice-laced cooking, though, of course, this was nothing compared to the decades some would spend in Palestine—or Outremer, as they came to call it. Western European pilgrims came to the Holy Land by the thousands. There were those who settled so that they could live a step closer to paradise. Others found God in more earthly rewards. "Those who were poor [in France]," wrote the royal chaplain, Fulcher of Chartres, "God has made rich here. He who had a few pennies possesses bezants [a gold coin] without number; he who held not even a village now by God's grace enjoys a town." But for every pilgrim made rich by con-

---

* Archaeologists have found a relative abundance of glass bottles from the period in Lebanon, especially near the Venetian-dominated town of Tyre. Glassware was apparently a Jewish specialty at the time. The technology the Venetians learned here would later become the basis of Murano's famous glass industry. By the fifteenth century, the Venetians were in a position to export glass back to the Near East. They confirmed their reputation for doing anything to make a buck by manufacturing mosque lamps, decorated with both Western floral designs and pious Koranic inscriptions, which they sold to the infidel.

quest or trade, there were many more who spent their last penny to get here, and then they were stuck. Yet as numerous as they were, the Catholic immigrants remained a tiny minority among the indigenous Syrian Christian and Muslim population. What's more, since most of the conquerors were male, they were desperate for local women to be their consorts, servants, and cooks—and they found them, whatever the means. If all else failed, the necessary help could be purchased at the slave market, though buying women slaves for sex was technically illegal. Fulcher describes the mutation he witnessed: "We who were Occidentals have now become Orientals. He who was a Roman or a Frank is here a Galilean or a Palestinian. . . . We have already forgotten the places where we were born. . . . Some have taken as his wife not a compatriot but a Syrian or an Armenian, or even a Saracen [that is, Muslim] who has received the grace of baptism."

Whether they liked it or not, the Europeans ate a largely Arab, Middle Eastern diet. No doubt, many were nauseated by the local cuisine and, much as some homesick Americans resort to McDonald's when in Rome, stuck to a western European diet of thick beer, plain meat, garlic, and beans. But less conservative palates would surely have thrilled to the new ingredients and flavor combinations. The local cuisine was closely related to what they had tasted in Byzantium—after all, the region had been a part of the Eastern Roman Empire for centuries—but it must also have echoed the kind of sophisticated food that was dished up in Baghdad and Alexandria. Baghdad, in particular, was the foodie capital of its day, where (much like today) cookbooks were written as much to be read and discussed as to be utilized for their directions. At a time when European dukes and counts were satisfied with great, gristly haunches of grilled venison, the connoisseurs of the Arab capital could dine on pasture-raised mutton and tender chicken redolent of imported Asian spices; they could pick and choose among a wide assortment of freshly baked breads and nibble on confections crafted of local fruits and imported sugar. These delicacies could even be cooled with ice that was carried from distant mountains, something that hadn't been seen in Europe since Roman times. In Baghdad, a host was judged by the diversity of ingredients and the variety of preparations rather than crude quantity. The Arabic cookbooks of the time give us recipes aromatic with spices layered over a distinctly sweet-and-sour taste. To give just one representative example, an Egyptian fish stew called *sikba* was seasoned with pepper, "perfumed spices," onion, saffron, and sesame oil as well as honey and vinegar to give it the requisite tang. Of course, the Arab cooks in Palestine could hardly have been up to the standards of a caliph's court, but they surely had some idea of what the Muslim gentry were eating.

However, the pilgrims who made it as far as Jerusalem didn't always get to taste the best local cooking. We can infer this from the name given to the central market where Westerners got their takeout. They called it the *Malquisinat,* or "Place of Bad Cookery." Presumably, the food was better in the Crusaders' quarters, where Western residents of the city would typically employ local women to do their cooking. Arab cooks were in high demand, at least according to Usmah ibn Munqidh, a Muslim warrior and courtier who seems to have been a regular visitor in the occupiers' homes. He writes that some Franks—though apparently not the majority—had become acclimated to local customs. During the course of a social call at the home of a soldier of the original Crusader generation, Usmah was offered lunch. "The knight presented an excellent table with food extraordinarily clean and delicious. Seeing me abstaining from food, he said, 'Eat: be of good cheer! I never eat Frankish dishes, but I have Egyptian women cooks and never eat except their cooking.' "

So, clearly, in spite of the antagonism between the faiths, the mounted, mailed, malodorous invaders holed up in their fortified Jerusalem residences must have had at least an inkling of how the other side lived. For they, too, hired couriers to bring snow from the mountains of Lebanon—a two- to three-day run—in order to chill their wine in the heat of summer. They, too, sprinkled their food with sugar. (This luxurious "spice" had been cultivated in well-watered enclaves of the Holy Land for generations and exported to Europe in minuscule quantities.) And apparently, the Crusaders even started to bathe! In imitation of local ways, the Frankish women are known to have gone to the baths three times a week, and it is supposed that men, who were less constricted, might have gone even more often.

Moreover, for Europeans, their culinary education wasn't limited just to the Holy Land. After all, Muslims ruled most of the Iberian Peninsula well into the twelfth century (Islamic Granada held out even longer, until it was conquered in 1492) as well as Sicily for more than two hundred years. In their day, Moorish Palermo and Córdoba were the largest cities in Europe and accordingly major outposts of Muslim culture and cuisine.* And as Usmah's memoir shows, relations between the two confessions were not always combative. Especially in Spain, Christians and Muslims (and Jews) lived together in relative harmony for centuries. The dominant culture of these western caliphates was naturally Arabic and drew inspiration for its music, literature, and food from Baghdad and points east. The introduction of oranges, lemons, eggplant, and other fruits and vegetables to the West is generally ascribed to Arab intervention. Pasta as we know it seems to have been invented in Moorish Sicily. Arabic recipes soon insinuated themselves into Italian compilations, while these were, in turn, disseminated north. Culinary ideas flowed across Europe in much the way that Gothic art and architecture spread across the continent. In the same way that the Arabic arch was incorporated into Western cathedrals and then transformed into an indigenous art form, the Middle Eastern way with spices was adapted to the European kitchen. John of Salisbury, a twelfth-century English Crusader and scholar, gives us some sense of the new culinary melting pot when he criticizes a dinner he was served at the house of a merchant in the southern Italian province of Apulia. The menu reportedly included "the finest products from Constantinople, Babylon, Alexandria, Palestine, Tripoli, Syria, and Phoenicia," but then the priggish pilgrim has to add, "as though the products of Sicily, Calabria, Apulia, and Campania were insufficient to adorn such a refined banquet."

Needless to say, the Arabic influence wasn't limited to food and architecture. The Middle East had plenty to teach the Western barbarians about mathematics, philosophy, astronomy, and medicine. Most medieval nutritional theory came straight from Arabic writers, who had, in turn, picked up the earlier Greek medical tradition. The scholars in Baghdad, however, altered the old system to suit their taste and culture, giving their dietary advice a distinctly Arab accent. It is no coincidence that medieval

---

* According to some estimates, Moorish Palermo boasted a population of 350,000 in the year 1050 and Córdoba as many as 450,000. Other estimates would cut these numbers to a third. Still, Venice numbered maybe 45,000 at the time, and it was the biggest Christian city west of Constantinople.

dietitians in Bologna and in Paris would suggest the same ingredients (expensive Eastern imports such as spices, sugar, dried fruit, citrus, almond milk, and rose water) as their Muslim sources.

There was virtually no influence flowing in the opposite direction. Usmah's admiration for the Western invaders was limited to their fighting skills, dismissing them "as animals possessing the virtues of courage and fighting, but nothing else." But even the knights' pugilistic prowess couldn't save them when confronted by the superior forces of Salāh Ad-dīn Yūsuf ibn Ayyūb, better known in the West as Saladin. After a bare eighty years in control, the Franks were expelled from Jerusalem in 1187, though Europeans managed to hold on to parcels of what is now the coast of Lebanon, Israel, Syria, and Turkey until 1291.

During these almost two hundred years of colonialism and crusade, tens of thousands of Italians, Germans, English, and French had traveled back and forth across the whole Mediterranean. The ruling classes of Europe wouldn't be this well traveled until the invention of the jet set. The ex-colonists who returned to Cologne, Bordeaux, and St. Albans brought with them a remarkably similar idea of what made up sophisticated cuisine. Like the tourist who returns after a week's stay in Tuscany toting olive oil and porcini mushrooms, those ancient travelers must have craved the complex flavors left behind. As a consequence, the European gentry would increasingly demand that their pigeon pie be flavored with imported seasonings. And, of course, it was Venice that was best placed to take advantage of this burgeoning need.

There are few hard numbers on just how much spice was imported into Europe in the years following the Franks' capture of Jerusalem. The spice trade had never entirely dried up in the Dark Ages, and elite cooks were certainly sprinkling pepper and possibly ginger, cloves, cinnamon, and galingale onto lordly joints by the time Pope Urban II called Christendom to arms, but just how much of these seasonings made it to Western ports is anybody's guess. Most historians do think, though, that there was a steady increase that came with the Crusades. In part, this was because there was just more back-and-forth traffic across the Mediterranean. Undoubtedly, the demand was also fueled by a contemporary European population explosion. In the Christian West, there were more people and more money to pay for more and more imported pepper.

It was no accident that the expansionist Crusader era happened to coincide with one of the most prosperous times Europe would see until the nineteenth century. The twelfth century was an age of broadening horizons and progress in just about every field, from agriculture to mining, from transportation to banking. As a result, feudal lords were able to skim off increasingly greater profits from the multiplying mills, fishponds, breweries, and mines under their control. And what did they do with their profits? A lot of them (sometimes more than the petty knights could afford) were spent on life's little luxuries. The ruling classes of Europe finally had the time and money to be bored, to need entertainment. You might say that the mounted heirs to the Vandals and Huns had gone soft. Instead of bloody battle, men showed their mettle through (relatively) genteel jousting, hired poets to compose weepy romances, and lingered over increasingly complex tasting menus. As usual, we find out about the improved quality of contemporary life by people's griping about it. Around the end of the thirteenth century in Milan, the curmudgeonly Galvano Flamma contrasted the honest and simple past with the current prosperity:

Life and customs were hard in Lombardy [at the beginning of the century]. Men wore cloaks of leather without any adornments, or clothes of rough wool with no lining. With a few pence, people felt rich. Men longed to have arms and horses. If one was noble and rich, one's ambition was to own high towers from which to admire the city and the mountains and the rivers. The virgins wore tunics of *pignolato* [rough cotton] and petticoats of linen, and on their heads they wore no ornaments at all. A normal dowry was about ten lire and at the utmost reached one hundred, because the clothes of the woman were ever so simple. There were no fireplaces in the houses. Expenses were cut down to a minimum because in summer people drank little wine and wine-cellars were not kept. At table, knives were not used; husband and wife ate off the same plate, and there was one cup or two at most for the whole family. Candles were not used, and at night one dined by light of glowing torches. One ate cooked turnips, and ate meat only three times a week. Clothing was frugal. Today, instead, everything is sumptuous. Dress has become precious and rich with superfluity. Men and women bedeck themselves with gold, silver, and pearls. Foreign wines and wines from distant countries are drunk, luxurious dinners are eaten, and cooks are highly valued.

Despite the fact that you could now finally get a decent meal in northern Italy, Flamma's Milan was by no means the fashion center it is today. At this point, Italians—or at least, the ones in the up-and-coming merchant republics of Florence, Genoa, and Venice—were more interested in making money than spending it. In early medieval Europe, the fashion makers were to be found at the courts of rich and powerful princes, not in places run by bankers and businessmen. It was the feudal magnates who had to secure their position by spending fortunes to impress potential rivals and awe their underlings. And mostly, these aristocrats spoke French—or at least, some variant of it. In the thirteenth century, the rulers of England, France, the Low Countries, Naples, and Sicily as well as the Crusader kings of the Holy Land were all part of the French sphere of influence. Even in the city-states of northern Italy, the Provençal dialect of French was the trendy vernacular in the twelve hundreds. The account of Marco Polo's travels (1298) was originally distributed in French, and some have suggested that Dante almost wrote the *Divine Comedy* (circa 1308–21) in Provençal rather than in the Tuscan dialect that he would eventually choose. So perhaps it should come as no surprise that the first "Italian" cookbook that we're aware of, *Liber de coquina*, came out of the royal court in Naples, ruled by members of the French house of Anjou.

In fact, the culinary fashion had much in common wherever French was spoken. This was the cuisine partially adapted from the Arabs, with a similar penchant for sweet and sour complemented by a robust addition of spice mixtures. Specific spices went in and out of vogue, but remarkably, this approach to seasoning, even while it became more artful and incorporated new ingredients, did not go out of style until the seventeenth century. Accordingly, no self-respecting nobleman could make do without a steady supply of spice. This "need" for imported luxuries (not only spices but silks, pearls, and gemstones) meant that every prince and aspiring aristocrat could be counted on as a cash cow for the Italian city-states.

The Florentines, Genoans, and Pisans were all well located to be the middlemen in the growing luxury trade precisely because they were in the middle, between Byzantium and the Arabs, and the Catholic kingdoms to the north. Typically, Genoa and Pisa supplied France and the Low Countries, while Venice provisioned central Europe. But there were other players in the spice trade, too. Both Marseilles and Barcelona gave the western Italian towns a run for their money. Venice, on the other hand, not only had no competition across the Alps, she was also the closest of the major spice-trading powers to the Oriental ports as well as the silver mines of Germany and Bohemia. As the Germans sent silver down the Brenner Pass, the merchants of Venice sent pepper-laden mules back. Though Venice wouldn't be able to monopolize the spice trade until the early fourteen hundreds, in the interim, she was clearly the leader, and she meant to keep it that way.

As the Asian aromatics became increasingly important to the city's dynamic economy, the government paid more and more attention to securing the pepper galleys. The armed convoy system of the *muda* solved the problem of piracy, but even before this was in place, the Republic was confronted with a more pressing issue. In Byzantium, the people were increasingly getting fed up with the aggressive tactics of the Adriatic upstart. As a result, Venetian residents were targeted for violence, but what was even worse, the emperor had begun to cozy up to the Genoans. Back at the doge's palace, the decision was made that Venice's "national interest"—mainly, the route to the Eastern spice emporia that ran straight through the heart of the empire—was at risk. The leadership's solution to the problem was to mount a military assault in the guise of a crusade, an action that would culminate in one of the most egregious incidents of "collateral damage" in the whole history of the spice trade.

THE CRUSADER DOGE

I am always reminded of the shrunken assemblages of New York and Paris they've built on the Vegas strip when I see the Basilica of San Marco. It, too, is a pastiche, though this one of Constantinople. There is, however, at least one significant difference between the design of the gaudy church and the garish casino hotels in the desert. Here, the fragments of the Eastern imperial capital are real, not simulated. The great, glittering chapel is encrusted with genuine Byzantine loot both inside and out: the undulating corkscrew columns planted into the façade; the famous bronze racehorses cavorting—incongruously for a city devoid of horses—above the basilica's entry; the very altar, the gorgeously bejeweled *Pala d'Oro,* many of its two thousand plus emeralds, rubies, amethysts, pearls, and 255 icons ripped out of Byzantine churches and monasteries. And these are just the most obvious. At one time, there used to be an ampoule with the blood of Christ, the arm of Saint George, and a segment of the head of Saint John the Baptist brought back to the basilica to keep Saint Mark's body parts company. The resulting edifice also sent a different sort of message than the playful desert casinos. This was dead serious. It was Venice's signal to the world that she now owned and ruled the remains of the old Eastern Empire, that the Queen of the Adriatic had donned the mantle of ancient Rome.

The motives for the Fourth Crusade and the subsequent looting of Constantinople by Franks and Venetians were an unfortunate, if all too common, collusion among religion, greed, and realpolitik. As such, it foreshadowed the later actions of Portuguese conquistadores in Africa and the Indies. These Crusaders, though, weren't going after Muslims (like the earlier Franks and later Iberians); their target was a city of fellow Christians. Of very wealthy Christians, it's worth adding. When I read contemporary descriptions of the Fourth Crusade, I keep thinking of American dollar bills with their motto "In God we trust." To the Crusaders, their faith and their greed were simply the opposite sides of the same coin. The accounts of the day point out how especially adept the Venetians were at manipulating a holy war to serve their financial goals. Which is not to say they weren't all practicing, devout Catholics, I'm sure.

The Venetians had long maintained a sizable colony in the Byzantine capital, and though they were nominally subject to imperial law, they largely acted as they pleased. A Greek eyewitness (admittedly not the most impartial judge) describes the resident merchants as morally dissolute, vulgar, and untrustworthy, "with all the gross characteristics of seafaring people." Their insolence apparently knew no bounds, so that they even abused and assaulted the local Greek nobility. It didn't help matters that they paid no taxes while the locals got squeezed. In 1172, the emperor, who was increasingly concerned by the Adriatic city's sway, decided to trade in the Venetians for the Genoese, but just to make sure the Republic didn't cause trouble, he seized ten thousand of her citizens as hostages. Eventually, most of the people were recovered, but the spice trade was in shambles, and it became all too evident that the Venetians needed a longer-term solution to the Byzantine problem. Then, conveniently, in 1198, Pope Innocent III called for yet another crusade to retake Jerusalem.

As usual, the (mostly) French knights needed transport and turned to the only city capable of mass-producing a navy, Venice, for "there they might expect to find a greater number of vessels than in any other port," to quote Geoffroi de Villehardouin, one of the French noblemen who led the expedition. The Venetian doge cut a deal with the Crusaders to provide food and transport for their men and horses in exchange for eighty-five thousand marks as well as half the booty derived from the operation.* Supposedly quite taken with the whole enterprise, the nearly blind ninety-year-old Doge Enrico Dandolo declared that he, too, would take on the cross and join the Crusaders. This was an unusual move for the Venetian executive, though how close to Jerusalem he intended to take his pilgrimage is less than clear. Dandolo came from a long line of Venetian merchants and politicians. Like most of Venice's wealthy elite, the family's business interests spread across the eastern Mediterranean, from Alexandria and its spice markets to the imperial capital on the Bosporus. While we have little information on the doge before he was elected to the leadership in 1192 (at the age of eighty!), it is a safe assumption that he spent a good portion of his youth traveling on business—this was the pattern in almost every Venetian family of note. We do know that in his later years, he served as a sort of ambassador in the Middle East. He also seems to have taken part in a disastrous rescue operation meant to free the emperor's Venetian hostages in 1172, which must have given him firsthand incentive to remove the Byzantine obstructionists once and for all.

When the flotilla was ready in 1202, only a fraction of the expected Crusaders showed up. The ships were ready, but there weren't enough

---

* To get some sense of how much money that was, a galley captain earned some 33 *lire* (a lire was worth a little more than a mark) a month, so figure just the cash part of the transaction was worth at least $8.5 million in today's currency.

men to cover the costs for the trip. At first, the Republic threatened to deny the foreign army food and drink until they paid up, but then Dandolo wrangled a new deal in which the Venetians would get their share of the Crusaders' booty before anyone else got theirs.

In the meanwhile, Constantinople was in the midst of a dynastic squabble that involved fraternal eye-gouging and other unsavory acts. The emperor was deposed, and in the aftermath, his young son Alexius showed up in Venice, hat in hand. This gave Dandolo and the Crusaders what they had been waiting for all along—a rationale for a profitable detour.

From a purely mercenary standpoint, gold-filled Constantinople was a much plumper fruit to pick than the war-ravaged cities of Palestine, and her defenders an easy target when compared to the formidable Muslim battalions in the Holy Land. Venice could regain her strategic commercial base in the Byzantine capital and secure the spice route; the knights could come home rich. To their credit, some of the pilgrims—most notably, Cistercian monks—refused to take part in this sham crusade, and the pope expressly forbade it. But even as the dissenters went home and the pope's missives went mysteriously missing, the majority of the Latin army sailed for Constantine's city, and on April 12, 1204, after a long siege, Venetian and Frankish soldiers breached the walls. The ensuing rampage was heartrending.

"How shall I begin to tell of the deeds wrought by these nefarious men!" writes a Byzantine survivor. "Alas, the images, which ought to have been adored, were trodden under foot! Alas, the relics of the holy martyrs were thrown into unclean places!" Our reporter, Nicetas Choniates, describes the altar of Hagia Sophia torn into pieces; mules and horses brought into churches, where they were laden down with booty; the doors of monasteries ripped down and the nuns raped. "In the alleys, in the streets, in the temples, complaints, weeping, lamentations, grief, the groaning of men, the shrieks of women, wounds, rape, captivity, the separation of those most closely united."

What distinguished the sack of Constantinople from the conquest of other medieval cities was hardly the brutality and greed shown by the attackers. The viciousness experienced in the sieges of Jerusalem, by Christians and Muslims alike, was, if anything, worse, and we can point to all too many equally reprehensible war crimes committed in our own time.

But what made the sack so remarkable was its sheer scale and the cold-hearted calculation that went into it. While it is unlikely that Constantinople held two-thirds of the world's riches, as one of the veterans of the attack claimed, the gold and jewels in its churches and palaces exceeded those of any other Christian city by several orders of magnitude.

For Doge Enrico Dandolo's merchant republic, the Fourth Crusade turned out to be one of the best mergers and acquisitions in history. Not only did the city earn a handsome profit in transport fees and a huge windfall in the form of gold, silver, and precious jewels, but the adventure amounted to a vast real estate coup, giving Venice three-eighths of the empire. Henceforth, each doge would be known as "Lord of One Quarter and One Half [of a quarter] of the Empire of Romania," or three-eighths of the Roman Empire. The spice route was secure.*

When young Alexius refused to cooperate with the conquerors, Doge Enrico dismissed him. "We have raised you off the dunghill, and on the dunghill will we cast you back again" was his send-off to the man who would be emperor. He was duly thrown into prison and strangled. Thereupon a French nobleman grabbed the imperial throne. And although the Greeks did eventually get the seat back after sixty years of Latin rule, the emperor's palace would be a gloomy place from now on. In 1453, its light was extinguished once and for all by Mehmed the Conqueror when his Turkish troops bombarded the city into subjection. However, the Ottoman conquest of Byzantium wasn't a loss merely for the Greeks. The inevitable result of the Muslim invasion was that Venice's entire strategic plan for the eastern Mediterranean began to crumble. Her fate had always been tied to Constantinople, whether as satrap or as conqueror, so once the Islamic crescent rose above Hagia Sophia's great dome, it was only a matter of time before Venice's star would set. Still, in the intervening 250 years, the Queen of the Adriatic would become the undisputed ruler of Europe's spice trade.

* In 2004, Pope John Paul II arrived in Istanbul bearing the remains of Saint John Chrysostom and Saint Gregory of Nazianzus, part of the relics looted in 1204. The bones came with an apology for what theologians call "sins of action and omission" by Roman Catholics against Orthodox Christians, which, in this case, includes the sack of Constantinople. As yet, Venetians have not followed suit.

PEPPER ON THE RIALTO

In Enrico Dandolo's day, the church of San Marco was by far Venice's flashiest structure, towering over a town much homelier than today's panorama of churches and palazzi glittering in the reflected sunlight. A map from about 1150 shows a watery village of modest dimensions. The great basilica looks across a canal at the stocky walls of the doge's fortress. The famous Piazza San Marco is a muddy meadow. Much as it is today, the city depicted on the map is a jigsaw puzzle of islands fitted around the double arc of the Grand Canal, but instead of the cheek-by-jowl stone façades and paved squares that surround you today, you would have seen wooden houses, vineyards, and plots of vegetables. The walk from San Marco to the Rialto commercial district took you through the most densely built-up part of town. Here, pedestrians had to dodge garbage flung out of windows, tiptoe past pig feces in the alleys, and make sure they didn't sink too deep into muck during the rainy weather or high tide. (Mud was so ubiquitous that Venetians invented platform shoes a foot or more high to keep themselves above the filth.) Pigs were encouraged in the alleys so that they would consume the accumulating garbage, while along the banks of the Grand Canal, cows grazed, as best they could. But then, just as you approached the wooden Rialto Bridge, which was freshly built in the Crusader doge's old age to let people cross over the cattle-lined canal, you would be enveloped by a perfumed haze.

For here, on the Campo San Bartolomeo, was the epicenter of Europe's spice trade. In the three hundred years that followed the Fourth Crusade, this long, rectangular piazza was where spice merchants just returned from Alexandria and London would trade their bales of pepper and precious cloves and exchange gossip—rumors as well as hard intelligence—about deals on cinnamon in Damascus and the going rate of ginger in Bruges. It was here that the whispers of the Portuguese arrival in India were greeted first with derision and then with dismay. The two decades following da Gama's trip were a dismal time for the traders on the Campo San Bartolomeo, but then business picked up. By the mid-fifteen hundreds, happy days seemed to have returned. Nonetheless, by century's end, the flow of spice was finally and definitely cut off by the sharp-eyed financiers of the Dutch East India Company. In the interim, though, the city grew up into the ravishing vision you still see today.

If you could stand at the peak of the nearby Rialto Bridge (it was a drawbridge all those years to allow for the passage of sailing ships) and watch the scene unfold for the centuries between the Latin Crusaders' sack of Constantinople and the Dutch conquest of the Spice Islands, you would see a city transformed. Grand warehouses arise, erected for both Venetians and foreigners. The Germans build their trading house, the Fondaco dei Tedeschi, and hire Titian and Giorgione, two of the most glorious painters Venice ever produced, to decorate the exterior. In later years, the Turks move into their own business center, the Fondaco dei Turchi, constructed in a typically Venetian Gothic-Byzantine style. As you look down to the water's edge, the wooden piers are torn out and replaced by broad stone wharves. Palazzi grow in place of the grass and cow dung that once framed the canal. The bell towers of splendid churches sprout amid the skyline of soaring masts. Yet the one thing that's constant is the gold and merchandise that slip from hand to hand—even as they do today.

In the galleries of the Accademia, there is a picture of this very spot from about 1500 by Carpaccio, the same painter who was later the namesake of a twentieth-century dish of raw beef and shaved cheese (supposedly because he had a thing for red and white). Though the painting is titled *The Miracle of the True Cross at Rialto,* the real subject is the beautiful people of Venice, the young aristocrats and businessmen who rub velvet-clad shoulders on the embankment by the Grand Canal. If you want to look in the face of a fifteenth-century Venetian (whether merchant or slave) and examine the fine points of his grooming and haberdashery, no artist is more useful. The voluminous cloaks and tight-fitting hose shimmer with silk, furs, and gold trim. You can see a hint of the city's international population in the Greek costumes of two men at the edge of the canvas, in the turban of a Turk conferring with a fellow countryman in the background, and in the gaudy livery of a black African gondolier poling a boat across the green waters under the wooden bridge. There is something of Norman Rockwell in Carpaccio's obsession with the everyday, and like the American illustrator, he often included his friends in the pictures. Luca Colferai is a dedicated student of Carpaccio because he can practically take one of the paintings to a tailor, the depictions of the outfits are so detailed. Even better for his purposes, many of the canvases are peopled by members of the *compagnie de calza,* recognizable by their insignia.

Yet what do we really know of these dapper merchants who stand around in paintings of miracles and wonders? There are occasional contracts, wills, and account books, but they tell us little of the risky trips from port to port or of the tricky transactions required to secure a better price on a bale of spice. Most Venetian businessmen were none too keen to set down their professional secrets, and few had the time or the writing skills to pen idle thoughts as they waited for their ships to come in. There is, however, at least one diary composed by a young Venetian nobleman who profited from the Indian summer of Venice's spice trade in the middle years of the fifteen hundreds.

Alessandro Magno sailed for Alexandria on April 4, 1561, bringing with him two thousand ducats and silk cloth to trade. The spice business had changed since the days when Venetian galleys had evacuated the last Crusaders from the Holy Land, but not as much as you might think. There weren't as many traders now. In Venice, money had become concentrated in fewer and fewer hands, and whereas spice merchants of an earlier generation might have been content to come home with a couple of bales of cloves, the entrepreneurial classes of Renaissance Venice had more cash at their disposal. The sailing conditions were better, too. In the old days, the young traders would spend the trip down to Alexandria in the back of an open galley, with no more than a canopy to keep the rain off their heads. Alessandro at least had a cramped little cabin on the Egypt-bound *Crose,* now that large, round sailing ships had replaced the narrow medieval galleys.

But, just like in the old days, Alessandro traveled as an independent agent, and his goal was the same as it had been for thousands of Venetians before him: to buy spices and, in particular, pepper. The journey of some fifteen hundred miles took about a month, and on his arrival in the Egyptian harbor, he was assigned a room in the *fondaco,* the walled Venetian compound. There must have been something of a college dorm atmosphere to these concentrations of twenty-somethings, with nothing to do but wait for the spice caravans to arrive. Given the inevitable collision of alcohol and boredom, it should come as no surprise that there were frequent complaints of brawls among the different Italian colonies in Alexandria and Constantinople. At night, at least, the young men were locked in by the Muslim authorities, but during the day, the Christian merchants were more or less free to wander at will. But there was very little for them to do.

Used as he was to the cosmopolitan vibe back in Venice, Alessandro quickly grew bored of the *fondaco*'s stultifying atmosphere and Alexandria's provincial scene. The formerly great harbor that was once second only to Caesar's Rome was now little more than a second-rate port town barely scraping by on the passing trade. Alessandro, hankering after the big-city life, exchanged part of his cash and all of his silk for pepper and hopped on the first barge headed up the Nile to Cairo. The Egyptian capital was easily a match for Venice. "I do not think that there exists another city in the world as populous, as large, as rich, and as powerful as Cairo," a European visitor had described it a few years earlier. During his weeks there, Alessandro did what anyone with time on his hands in Egypt would do: he went sightseeing. He spent a good part of the torrid Egyptian summer exploring the pyramids and other sites around Cairo. Then, just before leaving the capital, he must have witnessed the weeklong party that celebrated the annual rise of the fertile Nile. He watched people ride out on rug-bedecked boats as they spent all their savings on food, perfume, and musicians. Add in the wine drinking and sexual promiscuity that were apparently the rule, and you can imagine how homesick Alessandro must have been for his own *Carnevale*.

Due to the pattern of the monsoon in the Indian Ocean, spices typically arrived in the Red Sea ports in the fall and then made their way by caravan to Cairo and Alexandria to arrive a couple of months later. Naturally, prices fell when the camels unloaded their plentiful cargo. But unfortunately for Alessandro, the caravan did not show up on time, and the captain of the *Crose* decided not to wait. The ship was making preparations to leave even as the young merchant arrived from his summer vacation. Alessandro reports how he was caught up in a scrum of desperate dealing. "Everyone began to buy furiously," he writes. "Pepper, which before had been worth twenty ducats a *cantar* [about ninety pounds] went to twenty-two, and could not be had, and everything else similarly." Alessandro decided to cut his losses and invest in cloves and ginger. Even though she sailed in October, before the caravan had arrived, the *Crose* was still packed with more than half a million pounds of spices. According to records of the Venetian consulate—the spice trade remained a matter of the utmost importance to the Republic—pepper accounted for about 80 percent of the cargo, while various kinds of ginger made up the bulk of the remainder.

The ship would sail back the way it came, stopping in Crete to pick up provisions, perhaps adding to its cargo some of the local wine, the thick, syrupy malmsey they loved to guzzle in the transalpine courts, and definitely loading up on the hard Cretan cheese produced for the export market. We're told that each sailor was supposed to get about an ounce and a half per day as part of his ration, admittedly not much to flavor the daily pound or more of dry biscuit! If you wanted more, you could apparently buy it, much as discount airlines sell snacks today.

Typically, the armed spice convoy made it home by the late fall. You can get some sense of what the arriving Alessandro would have seen if you take the *traghetto,* the passenger ferry, from Lido Island across the lagoon. Pretend for a moment that the stench of diesel that permeates the boat is the smell emitted by half a million pounds of spice. Ignore the plastic seats and fluorescent life jackets. The ship glides from the choppy, deep blue Adriatic into the placid waters of the bay. Far to the north, you can barely make out the shimmer of snowcapped peaks. The lagoon is aswim with traffic. Oar-propelled galleys, *fuste,* and *galeotte* slice through the salt green sea. Cogs, *barze,* and *galeoni* lumber along under their partly furled sails. Look ahead to where Venice floats upon the horizon, her white edifices washed pink by the failing winter light. The city resounds with bells, welcoming you and your odorous cargo to her piers. Alessandro was back in Venice on November 18 and managed to sell his spices for almost twice what he'd paid. He figured he made about 266 ducats on the whole trip, a decent but hardly extraordinary profit margin. But certainly enough to throw a party. I can see Alessandro, seeking out his friends, perhaps the original I Antichi, in order to celebrate his return, in order to fulfill the confraternity's mission, *Divertire divertendosi.*

The annual return of the spice ships poured new life and fresh cash into the wintry alleys and squares. The trade in Asian aromatics, even though it was hardly Venice's only source of wealth, structured not just its foreign policy but also the very rhythm of the city. The collusion of money and leisure that came with the return of the pepper convoy turned the city into one nonstop party that would end only with *Carnevale*. That pattern persisted for centuries, even when the pepper on the Rialto arrived in Dutch and English ships.

MALABAR

In Carpaccio's picture, just behind the Turks, there is a dark-skinned man climbing the steps of the wooden bridge. He is dressed in only a loincloth and doubled over beneath the weight of a large white sack. I was reminded of him when I stood in Jew Town Street, some forty-five hundred miles distant, as the crow flies, from the Rialto, and saw barefoot Indian men clothed in the same basic way, loading and unloading large sacks of spice. Whereas, in Venice, the spice trade sometimes seems no more than a skeleton in the family closet, here in the city of Cochin, spices are still the mother's milk of prosperity. What's more, the pepper business has changed surprisingly little in India in the last couple of thousand years.

Cochin (Kochi on the official government maps) is the bustling commercial capital and principal port of the southern Indian state of Kerala, a region long known to Arabs and Europeans as Malabar. I arrived during the pepper harvest, in January, to see those little black berries picked and dried, to get a more intimate whiff of the aromatic cargo that drove at least some medieval Europeans to go on holy war. In the bustling spice market of the old city's "Jew Town," you get a sense of the biting aromas that must have hovered across the quays of the Rialto five hundred years back. In the winter, the warehouses are filled with enormous mounds of ginger, so, as you pass the open doors of the wholesale traders, the scent of the tangled knobs wafts out of every other doorway, flavoring the noonday heat with their sickly sweet smell. If you should step inside, the aggressive perfume invades your nostrils and quickly coats the throat with incendiary grit.

Medieval texts distinguished between some half dozen varieties and grades of ginger, and the Keralan spice was considered the best. In Europe, *micchino* ginger (named after Mecca, where it was marketed) typically costs less than pepper, whereas *colombino* (named after the Malabar

city of Quilon, or Kollam) could be as much as 50 percent more.* When
you taste it today, there is a clear difference between the local ginger,
which has a much denser, earthier quality, and the lighter, almost lemony
roots (technically, rhizomes) typically imported from Hawaii into the
United States. Keralan ginger is much better suited to the complex seasoning mixtures used in Indian cooking than the varieties grown in East
Asia. Similarly, it would have been a good fit for the spice-rich recipes of
medieval Europe.

The spice merchants of today's Kerala are as eclectic a mixture of religious and ethnic groups as the blend that goes into the Indians' beloved
masala powder. Over the years, the port of Cochin has attracted Christians, Muslims, Hindus, but especially Jews, who give the spice market its
name. Depending on the season, they deal in ginger, cardamom, cinnamon, and imported cloves, but pepper is still the black gold that pays the
bills. Up until very recently, when the winter pepper harvest arrived, they
all used to crowd into the faded pink block that houses the pepper exchange and stand on a central platform yelling out bids under the
whirring fans. That is one thing that has changed. Since 2004, the business transactions are now funneled through a small, threadbare room lit
up by a computer screen, and mouse clicks have replaced the shouts and
murmurs.

Mostly, though, the pepper business is as it's always been. Just a few
steps from the exchange, down a crumbling passageway, is the Kishor
Spices Company. Downstairs, as you enter the company complex, a squat
pyramid of hundreds of pounds of pepper is protected by a large blue
tarp and secured behind thick bars while barefoot bookkeepers sit cross-
legged and shuffle papers in a cramped alcove next door. Upstairs, on
the other hand, the owner's air-conditioned office might as well be in an
Atlanta corporate park; yet, even so, his business model would have been
familiar in Enrico Dandolo's day. Traders such as the Kuruwa, the company owners, acquire their pepper mostly from small-scale farmers who
might have as little as ten pounds to sell. These small lots are collected

---

* In addition to *colombino*, there was *beledi*, or "white" ginger, which could come from Malabar
or the interior. *Deli* and *micchino* were inferior grades, the former smaller and less white than
the other varieties, the latter often tinted red because it had been preserved by adding clay.
Ginger preserved in syrup had its customers as well.

through a network of country dealers and brought to the company's warehouses, where they are cleaned and shipped across the world. In the old days, the middlemen had to lug bales of rice and salt up the mountain paths to exchange for the pepper; rupees and SUVs make that part a lot easier now. Heman Kuruwa, the third generation in the family firm, assures me that the locals would never be enterprising enough to run this sort of import-export business. His family are Muslims from the northern Indian state of Gujarat. He reminds me that Gujaratis have dominated this trade for hundreds of years, that they were here long before the Portuguese ever nosed their way into the Indian sea.

The method of growing pepper has seen even fewer changes since that time. It would be hard to improve on the fourteenth-century description of the Italian friar Odoric of Pordenone:

> [Pepper grows in a] certain kingdom where I myself arrived, being called Minibar [Malabar], and it is not so plentiful in any other part of the world as it is there. For the wood wherein it grows is 18 days journey around. . . . In the foresaid wood, pepper is had after this manner: first it grows in leaves like unto potherbs, which they plant near great trees as we do our vines, and they bring forth pepper in clusters, as our vines do yield grapes, but being ripe, they are of a green color, and are gathered as we gather grapes, and then the grains are laid in the sun to be dried, and being dried are put into earthen vessels: and thus is pepper made and kept.

At the behest of the pope, the thirty-year-old friar had embarked from Venice in 1318 on a journey that would take him across Asia. His account was written down upon his return in 1330 and was widely read in Europe, including by the author of Mandeville's *Travels*. (Parts of Mandeville's pepper forest description are lifted almost verbatim.) The pepper groves of southwest India were noted by every traveler who passed through this part of the world. Marco Polo describes the kingdom of Coilum (Quilon), where pepper "grows in great abundance." The Arab travel writer Ibn Batūtah describes the city as one of the finest in Malabar, "with splendid markets and rich merchants."

Quilon is a slow, three-hour ride south of Cochin on India's improbable answer to a rail system. What remains of the ancient city today is a modest provincial town of middling size, depending more on rubber than pepper to fill the cash registers. The spice ships had long since moved north to Cochin and Calicut even before da Gama and his lot started meddling in Malabar.

I was met at the Quilon train station by Thomas Thumpassery, a local planter, who had consented to give me a tour of one of Friar Odoric's pepper woods. He was waiting for me on the platform, cell phone in hand, waving down the Westerner amid the parrot hues of swirling saris, circling food vendors, and Indian businessmen on the march. A moment later, I was bundled into a brand-new SUV, and we sped out of town. The drive from Quilon was a blur of magenta, lime, and tangerine, the road lined with somnolent cows standing before huge billboards of sexy, sari-enveloped models and with rice paddies little bigger than tennis courts hemmed in by ragged banana bushes. About an hour later, the flat coastal landscape gave way to thick and lovely hills.

Thomas, I soon learned, is part poet, part schemer, part dilettante. "I'm lazy," he says more than once over a glass of *chai* that we drink at a minimall just opposite the ritual pool of a Hindu temple. His latest scheme is a hamburger bar–cum–billiard parlor, and he is full of questions on the minutiae of hamburger and pizza making. He comes across as skinny and younger than his thirty-five years and clearly amused by his own wacky ventures, a penchant he seems to have inherited from his father along with the family plantation. His estate is mostly planted with rubber trees, though there are a few small plots devoted to ginger, nutmeg, bananas, and coconut palms. But he also grows about eight hundred pounds of pepper annually, as a sort of sideline, a kind of insurance. This is typical for India, where pepper plants are cultivated in the shade of other, more dependably profitable crops.

One of those soft south Kerala hills is covered by the Thumpassery plantation, the whole thing, from top to bottom, forested with rubber trees, each of which is tapped like a sugar maple to yield a milky sap, which is then dried into raw rubber. But there is also pepper in the woods. As the SUV pulls up to the ranch house that sprawls across the hill's summit, Thomas almost knocks a worker off a stool to avoid the mat spread in the middle of the driveway covered with drying peppercorns. Driveways are particularly well suited for drying pepper, especially when they are flat and exposed to the sun. For farmers without paved driveways, the Indian Spices Board (a government agency) provides subsidies to pave a section of their property in concrete.

At first, the pepper vines are hard to identify, but when you look carefully, the scruffy vines are everywhere, climbing up spindly *arepa* palms, gangly mango trees, or whatever else happens to be growing in the area. Here, there are none of the prim lines of a European farm or vineyard. Instead, there is jungle, with the unruly pepper vines looking more like rapacious weeds rather than the fountain of wealth for distant empires. The palm-sized leaves surround the supporting trees like ten-foot-high hula skirts, with the dark green pepper clusters, referred to as "spikes," hiding out among the heart-shaped foliage.

Thomas takes me deep into the pepper wood. Its air is clear and fragrant, filled with clucks and cackles that easily drown out the barely audible cadences of the Hindu prayers coming from a distant temple. He explains how the bisexual pepper flowers, the color of clotted cream, are pollinated by early morning mist, the dewdrops condensing on the flowers and dripping from tiny blossom to blossom. He tells me about the one hundred or more wild varieties that still grow in the high hills and the hundreds more that have been domesticated. He points out the wild long pepper vines that meander in the shadows.

Friar Odoric was quite correct about the harvesting of black pepper, which takes place when the berries are dark green. In Kerala, this typically occurs in January. Once picked, the berries are spread out to dry on bamboo mats for several days until they turn a rich black. Although piperine, the chemical that gives pepper its bite, is contained in the berry itself, most of the flavor components are in the skin. To make white pepper, the green berries are blanched in boiling water, and the outer peel is removed before they are dried. Indians, though, have little use for white pepper, which, while just as hot as black, lacks much complexity. Thomas's mother laughs when I ask her about white pepper. They sell all of it to Western-style hotels, she tells me, to season the food of foreigners. Green peppercorns, however, leave her puzzled, having never heard of such a thing. Thomas has read about them on the Internet, and he informs her of their use in fancy French recipes. She shakes her head as she returns to the kitchen, where dinner is cooking over a wood fire.

Ironically, Keralans use very little pepper in their cooking. For them, it is the money that grows on trees, and most would prefer to sell rather than eat it, or better yet, store it up for a rainy day. People in the business give all sorts of estimates of how much pepper is being held in reserve in India. Heman Kuruwa, the dealer in Cochin, guesses twenty thousand tons, but this is not something anyone can really know. Thomas alone has some two tons of it, a bulging pile of plastic mesh bags, shoved against the back of a shed that is also used to store smoked sheets of rubber. Some growers will keep pepper up to ten years, waiting for the price to rise or perhaps using it to pay a daughter's dowry. Thomas has three young daughters. Though, in his case, I wonder whether the pepper will still be there when he needs it or whether it will be the capital for another improbable scheme.

Though pepper originates in the Western Ghats, the mountains that rise from India's western coast, it was probably transplanted to Sumatra (and possibly other parts of today's Indonesia) as early as two thousand years ago and was certainly quite common throughout the region by the time Marco Polo passed through on his way home in the late twelve hundreds. Today, pepper is grown in Brazil and China as well, while Vietnam has overtaken India as the world's largest exporter. In Europe, though, they still like Indian pepper best.

Europeans have been importing pepper from this part of India at least since Roman times. Large numbers of Roman amphorae have been excavated at Pondicherry, in South India, dating to the first and second centuries C.E. The route remained more or less the same for the next fifteen hundred years, and at least some pepper continued to be shipped over the old caravan routes long after the Portuguese opened the route around Africa.

Nevertheless, the routes did shift over all those years, depending on the vagaries of geopolitics. The Silk Road of Marco Polo's day, which carried spices, jewels, and silks between China and the Middle East, endured only as long as Genghis Khan and his successors kept an iron grip over central Asia. But once their empire fell in the early years of the fourteenth century, the flow of Eastern luxuries had to be sluiced through a new set of channels. Now the bulk of Malabar's riches was loaded onto Arab dhows (but also some Chinese junks), which skimmed up the Red and Arabian seas, then at Aden, and later Jeddah, the spices were loaded onto enormous camel caravans. In his early days, Muhammad had the job of supervising one of these dromedary delivery services between Mecca and Syria. For later Arab merchants, one of the attractions of the port of Jeddah was its proximity to the Prophet's hometown; Muslims were just as adept at mixing business and religion as any Venetian Crusader. The processions of camels, each beast laden down with a quarter ton of spice, passed through Mecca in caravans that grew to be so huge they took two days and nights to pass through the gates on the last leg of the journey to Damascus or Alexandria.

Once in the Mediterranean, the spices passed into Christian hands. At first, the western Mediterranean market was split up among the Genoans, Provençals, and Catalans, who kept the spice flow coursing not only to western Europe but also to Arab towns in western North Africa, while Venetians sent most of their pepper across the Alps. But by the early fourteen hundreds, Venice began to monopolize the spice route straight through to the Atlantic, even sending her perfumed galleys all the way to England and the Low Countries. All over Christendom, the appetite for spice, whetted by the Crusades, would grow and grow for at least five hundred years. Generations of (well-off) Europeans would grow up with the taste of Malabar on their tongues.

A TASTE FOR SPICE

Just what the food in the Middle Ages and Renaissance tasted like is impossible to say. The old cookbooks are too imprecise, the technology is hard to replicate, and the ingredients are utterly different. Animals, fruits, and vegetables were all smaller. Even the spices were different. The spices we have today have undergone centuries of selective breeding to concentrate and standardize their flavor, whereas most of the aromatics of 1400 were still gathered in the wild from bushes and trees. Then there is the issue of freshness and storage. When you consider that cloves, nutmeg, and mace might have been in transit for an absolute minimum of a year, and all the spices were often stored for years at a time under often dubious conditions, you have to wonder just how potent they were.* Under ideal storage conditions, pepper holds up extremely well, but the others have nothing like pepper's shelf life. No doubt, many of the spices that reached such European backwaters as England and Scandinavia were about as fresh as the jar of allspice that has sat in my spice cupboard for the last six years.

But just because it's impossible to replicate the cuisine of the past hasn't stopped anyone from trying. I am particularly intrigued by the efforts of Sergio Fragiacomo in Venice to try to turn gastronomic time travel into a business model. Sergio owns a restaurant, some five minutes' walk away from Piazza San Marco, called, somewhat incongruously in French, Bistrot de Venise. Sergio comes across more like a genial professor than a restaurateur, and like so many Venetians, he is an amateur (in the old sense of the word) on the subject of Venice. He has the old lover's devotion to the city, enamored as much of her foibles as her charms. "I want to have a conversation with her past," he tells me. His obsession is to bring the old tastes alive, to introduce the tourists not merely to mortar and marble but to the very flavors of the ancient republic. But he also has to make a living, so he offers two menus, one of traditional Venetian food—grilled fish, polenta, risotto, and such—and another inspired by old Venetian sources. "The other restaurateurs think I'm crazy," he tells me as we sip a distinctly twenty-first-century cocktail of Prosecco and pomegranate juice. "There is no sense of the history of our culinary culture in today's Venice," he says. "It's so stupid!"

The mostly French and English tourists ("The Italian public think with their stomachs," he grumbles) who order from the historical menu can sample dishes that date back to the fourteenth, fifteenth, and sixteenth centuries. That the flavors can never be entirely authentic goes without saying. At best, this is culinary tourism; however, in a sense, Sergio's re-creations are no less representative of the past than the medieval palazzi that have been ripped apart and reassembled to install indoor

---

* In later years, the Dutch East India Company would periodically burn its twenty-year-old stock of spices because they were considered unsellable. Does that mean it was sometimes selling fifteen-year-old nutmeg and cloves?

plumbing and fiber-optic lines. In the same way that the sensitively modernized mansions remind us of a glorious past, the attractively arranged plates give us hints of ginger, turmeric, and pepper, sufficient to recall the spice-laden galleys but sparing us too much authenticity. I suppose I am just as pleased to do without the medieval city's stinking canals, drafty rooms, and omnipresent fleas, even if I long for a little more spice.

Dinner proceeds in small, delicate courses, beginning with a fennel soup gently scented with cinnamon. We then move on to "ravioli," more like superdelicate gnocchi in this case, with an admixture of sweet spices and herbs resting atop a yellow ocher reduction thickened with rice flour and turmeric—all this inspired by an anonymous fourteenth-century recipe compilation known as the *Anonimo Veneziano*. Next, a dish of sea bass arrives. The sweet fish is topped with an almond crust arranged atop a little ginger-infused puddle, the sauce with that slightly bitter, even chalky flavor that reminds you that ginger is dug out from the earth. The menu pointedly reassures the diner that although the ingredients are strictly traceable to the great Renaissance chef Maestro Martino, the recipe has been adapted to modern taste. Sergio insists I finish with *fritelle da imperador magnifici,* two small fritters of ricotta and pine nuts, gently crunchy on the outside, creamy inside, resting like two little pillows on a coverlet of sauce composed of *vin cotto,* honey, cinnamon, and cloves. The fritters (though not the sauce) are also cribbed from the *Anonimo Veneziano.* The original fourteenth-century recipe calls for a mixture of egg whites, fresh cheese (that is, ricotta), flour, and pine nuts. Once fried, they are sprinkled with sugar—lots of sugar to make them worthy of an emperor, the *imperador* of the name. I'll forgive Sergio the sauce, because it happens to be delicious and I can't resist his quiet enthusiasm. He's probably right—authenticity has its limits.

Sergio insists that the moderate hand with the seasonings reflects the past as much as his desire not to offend contemporary European palates. Like Luca, he believes that the scholars who speak of an "orgy of spice" are talking through their hats. If only those medieval cookbooks were just a little more precise! One of the few medieval texts that is pretty consistent in its instructions is the *Anonimo Veneziano.* Perhaps because it was intended for a Venetian audience that was predominantly bourgeois, the quantities needed to be more specific than similar compilations used by highly trained professionals in aristocratic homes. Oddly, recipes from the Venetian cookbook are often used to prove how those insensate medieval diners consumed enormous quantities of spice. Luca thinks the misunderstanding comes from a faulty assumption about portion size. It may simply be that most historians just don't know how to cook for a crowd. A quick glance, for example, at a recipe for *ambrosino*, a kind of chicken stew with dried fruit, would lead you to believe that a dozen guests will be consuming a dish seasoned with almost half a pound of spices (mostly ginger and cinnamon but also some bay leaves and a very small quantity of nutmeg, saffron, and cloves), in addition to a little more saffron and nutmeg. The problem with this analysis is that there is no way twelve people could eat this much food.* Unlike the discreet little portions that arrive at Bistrot de Venise, the medieval tables of the wealthy were enormous smorgasbords where only a small portion of the food was likely to be eaten by the guests. That all the food was not intended to be eaten at these feasts is nicely illustrated in the *Ordinaciones* of 1344, a set of rules promulgated by Peter III (the Great) of the Iberian kingdom of Aragon. The king brought an accountant's precision to the table arrangements: "Since it is appropriate that some persons are honored more than others according to their status, we desire that our plate should include food enough for eight persons." The royal princes, the archbishops, and the bishops dining with the king would receive enough for six, while lesser prelates and ordinary knights were assigned a portion for four.

Nevertheless, even the moderate quantity of spice called for by the *Anonimo Veneziano* is a great deal more than Sergio's clients are used to when they go out for Italian food. (Italians are just about at the bottom of Europe's generally measly spice consumption statistics, each contemporary Italian eating less than a quarter pound per year.) But that is probably the wrong comparison. The flavor combinations in contemporary Italian food have very little to do with medieval tastes. North Africa would be a better model. The ingredient list of the *ambrosino*—almonds, dates, raisins, prunes, ginger, cinnamon, and saffron cooked with chicken—

---

* When you read on, it turns out that the spices were meant to season six capons, which works out to some thirty pounds of meat! In other words, less than a sixth of an ounce of spice (about 1½ teaspoons) for every pound of capon. Numerous other recipes in the collection have a similar spice-to-meat ratio.

reads like a contemporary Moroccan recipe, and the spicing is only marginally more copious. Indeed, the Arabic influence on medieval food is always implicit even where it is not explicit. The slightly earlier Neapolitan cookbook *Liber de coquina*, mentioned above, has several typically Arabic recipes, including a Saracen-style soup. That collection, originally written in Latin, was one of the first widely disseminated cookbooks in Europe. It calls for spices in many of its recipes, though nowhere near as many as the Venetian compilation. It would seem to make sense that in Venice, where Oriental seasonings were considerably cheaper than elsewhere, and where the Near Eastern cultural influence was the strongest, a more liberal hand with seasoning would prevail.

All the same, the late-fourteenth-century *Ménagier de Paris,* roughly contemporary with the *Anonimo Veneziano,* seems at least as generous with the spicing—though, admittedly, this can only be deduced from the few recipes that actually give quantities. A recipe for meat in aspic has you cook a pig, four calves' feet, two chickens, and two rabbits with ten or twelve *cloches* (knobs) of ginger and five or six *cloches* of galingale (a spice similar to ginger) as well as much more modest quantities of melegueta, mace, zedoary, cubebs, spikenard, bay leaves, and nutmeg. All these spices are ground up and tied up like a big tea bag to stew along with the meat. Although it's hard to know just how big a *cloche* of ginger is, it is safe to say we're dealing with close to a pound of ginger and another ounce or two of the other spices combined. But then we're also cooking well over a hundred pounds of meat! What's more, the *Ménagier's* pound of ginger, after its long trek round the world, was certainly not as spicy as it would be today. To make *ypocras,* the spiced wine that medieval Franks loved just as much as the Byzantines, the author instructs you to add a little sugar and half an ounce of a mix of cinnamon, ginger, melegueta, nutmeg, and galingale to a *quarte* (a little over two liters) of wine—in other words, about a quarter teaspoon of spice in each wineglass. But even this was typically served in modest doses at the end of dinner as a sort of digestif. For anyone still convinced that the wealthy people of the time buried their food under avalanches of spice, it's worth parsing the shopping directions the *Ménagier* gives for throwing a wedding party. This is the famous two pounds of spices intended to season the dinner (and supper) of some forty guests that appears on the same checklist as some 650 pounds of meat! In other words, a paltry few grams, less than a half teaspoon for every pound of meat.* Of course, looking at averages won't tell us how much seasoning went into any particular dish. Some were surely spicier than others. But it does tell us something about the level of spicing in the cuisine overall.

Though cookbooks of the time from Venice, France, Catalonia, England, and Germany are all more or less generous with Oriental seasoning, the fashion for spice was not uniform across western Europe. The French, as is clear from the *Ménagier*'s recipes, seemed much more eclectic in their choice of spices than the Italians. The slightly earlier *Viandier* (circa 1375), attributed to the French royal chef Taillevent, mentions some seventeen "spices," including those Byzantine favorites zedoary and spikenard along with the more common mace and cinnamon. By comparison, the *Anonimo Veneziano*'s spice rack is limited to about a dozen. German collections are more restricted still. Yet despite certain other regional preferences (melegueta shows up regularly in France but hardly ever in Italy; pepper more often in Germany than France), the similarities among the cookbooks are more striking than the differences. In the fourteenth century, the trendy spices are the same everywhere. Ginger is by far the favorite, with saffron coming a close second.

Interestingly, pepper is less common, especially in the French collections. Was it already assumed that you added pepper (the recipes don't include salt either) to your food without having to spell it out? Or, perhaps more likely, pepper was already too commonplace to be served to the genetically stuck-up consumers of these culinary style sheets. Early account books tend to back up the latter argument. Typically, as you went up the social scale, the shopping list for spices grew longer and longer, while more common people could afford little more than pepper. Thus, the French king Jean II and his entourage, while imprisoned by the English in the 1350s (evidently under rather cushy conditions), went through some

---

* Another oft-repeated statistic is that the Duke of Buckingham went through close to half a ton of spice in a single year (1452–53), but when you look at the actual account books, it is more like 400 pounds of spices (pepper and ginger make up more than three-fourth of this) for a household that consumed some 1,500 sheep, 250 cattle, 80 pigs, and easily 5,000 fish during the same year. What's more, spices were typically sold in "light pounds" of about twelve ounces at the time, so it was likely a scant pound of mostly pepper and ginger feeding between one hundred and two hundred people a day.

dozen spices but no black pepper. A roughly contemporary French vis-count limited himself to four: pepper, ginger, cinnamon, and saffron. Pepper by itself, on the other hand, is mentioned as part of a 1258 consignment to a French poorhouse and commended as a "sauce for field laborers who mix it with broad beans and peas" by at least one medieval diet guide.

Needless to say, trying to figure out what fourteenth-century Europeans actually ate based on elite cookbooks is about as easy as extrapolating the typical American's diet from a Martha Stewart entertaining guide. Here, some numbers serve as a useful corrective, even if coming up with any sort of hard statistics for the Middle Ages is a tricky affair. Economics historians do have a rough idea of how much spice Europeans were importing, at least after the fourteenth century, when Venice ruled the spice trade.* In 1400, it's been estimated that Christendom consumed about two million pounds of pepper and perhaps another million of the other Asian spices, with ginger by far the most popular of these, followed at a distance by cinnamon, cloves, nutmeg, mace, and the others. When you consider that there may have been about three or four million people (roughly 5 percent of the population) who could afford the more expensive aromatics, you realize that average per capita consumption couldn't have been all that high. To give some sense of comparison, Americans today eat about 1½ pounds of spices per head every year. Contemporary Europeans eat about half that, and Moroccans roughly double. So was the medieval elite eating food that, on the whole, was about as spicy as what most Americans eat now? Well, perhaps the kings and queens were, but for the rest, spicy dining must have been a special-occasion treat. There just weren't enough spices to go around for everyone to eat spicy food day in and day out. What's more, many of the more expensive and obscure spices ended up in medicine, and even the likes of cinnamon, ginger, and melegueta were used to season beer and wine as often as food.

* Before 1400, the data are just too fragmentary to paint a complete picture. Prices of at least some spices do seem to go down as the centuries march on, which would imply an increased supply. So, presumably, spices were more exclusive at the time of the Crusades than two hundred years later. Scattered statistical evidence seems to indicate that this was the case at least in remote England, though trying to project English numbers onto the rest of the continent is iffy at best.

Even the embalming business swallowed up some unknown percentage of the imports. So, at best, that top 5 percent may have been eating something on the order of two or three ounces of spices (other than pepper) a year in 1400, and perhaps double that a hundred years later.

Of course, average numbers obscure the fact that not every meal was as spicy as the next or that some people just didn't go in for all that much seasoning. But that is as true today as it was in medieval France. No doubt the hyperelite consumed quite a bit more. For them, those special-occasion meals of spiced capons and hippocras were an everyday occurrence. You could compare them to today's executives on expense accounts who don't think twice about dropping several hundred dollars on a restaurant dinner that less privileged mortals eat once or twice a year. But even so, it isn't likely that King Jean II, even after his return home from English captivity in 1360, would have been eating much more than the monthly couple of ounces consumed by today's average American. The rest of the population, presumably, had to wait for weddings and holidays to indulge in expensive foods such as chicken and eggs spiced up with ginger and cinnamon.

Or did they? Did they really use spices (other than pepper) as infrequently as we serve cranberry sauce? Cost alone couldn't have been a determining factor. Some grades of ginger were actually cheaper than pepper, and you could buy clove stems for much the same price. If spices were eaten so infrequently, why would the cookbooks have dozens and dozens of recipes calling for pepper, cinnamon, and ginger? More than likely what actually happened was that special occasions called for pulling out all the stops, but that did not mean that everyday food was entirely devoid of spice.

The food of the time was different from contemporary European fare not merely in the way spices were used. Honey, and later sugar, along with dried fruit was combined with vinegar or verjuice (the sour juice of unripe grapes or apples) to produce a distinctly sweet-and-sour taste. A similar strategy is often adopted in contemporary cuisines in which spices are widely used. In Indian cooking, for example, spices often complement a dish sweetened by the addition of raw sugar and made sour from unripe mangoes.

The Italian food historian Massimo Montanari has described mod-

ern Italian and European cooking as predominantly "analytical" in char-
acter, by which he means that we like to distinguish between flavors. As a
result, we keep bonbons away from salami and segregate our spices into
sweet or savory ghettos. The idea that "cabbage soup should taste of cabbages, leeks of leeks, turnips of turnips," as one seventeenth-century
Frenchman would put it, was not a concept with much currency in the
centuries between the Crusades and the Reformation. To use Montanari's terminology, the cuisine of that era was "synthetic." Rather than
trying to keep flavors apart, the art of the cook required careful synthesis
so that, ideally, all the main flavors would be present in any given dish. In
addition, contemporary dietary beliefs emphasized the need to balance or
correct, as they would see it, the "natural" flavors of many ingredients.
Spices were considered highly useful in this respect, but, theory aside, the
people who got used to eating highly seasoned food would have found
cabbages that taste like cabbages a bit of a bore.

THE PRICE OF SPICE

Buried in the Venice State Archive, there is a court record that gives us a
clue about the price of spice (and incidentally, of cabbages) for upper-
middle-class citizens in the 1340s. Apparently, a certain Bernardo Morosini
had been charged with taking care of his younger brothers after his father's
death. Apart from his three young-adult brothers, he was responsible for
feeding a household that consisted of some three servants as well as an elderly former slave who had been freed in his father's will. Occasionally,
others had to be fed, such as a nurse hired to take care of Bernardo during a protracted illness, as well as the porters who would arrive with the
wine, wood, and grain.

Bernardo's carefully recorded purchases give us a somewhat surprising insight into the diet of an upper-middle-class Venetian on the eve of
the Black Death. (It's worth remembering that this was a time of increasing famine and population pressures, which made food more expensive
than it had been in centuries past or would be for the hundred years following the plague.) The register covers only the winter and spring months,
so it is naturally skewed toward foods available or permitted (in the case
of Lent). It should come as no surprise that meat would be more available

in the colder seasons (it wouldn't spoil and was relatively cheap); still, who would think the Morosini household would, in the three months preceding Lent, be consuming, on average, almost seven pounds of beef per day, over and above the geese, chickens, and fish they bought? And this for a paltry eight to ten people! During Lent, meat intake plummeted, but the fish, cheese, and egg purchases easily took up the slack. Wine consumption was similarly generous, with the household sopping up some sixteen liters daily! In other respects, the diet must have been dull, indeed. Cabbage is practically the only vegetable recorded for several months (it must have been cheap, even though exact figures are absent), only to be replaced by *le erbe*, most likely salad greens or radicchio. Intriguingly, pepper and saffron appear in the register, too, though it's unclear whether these were intended purely as medicine or whether some of that beef was turned into steaks au poivre (or the medieval Venetian equivalent). Still, it's obvious that for the Morosinis, pepper was no extraordinary luxury. Which is not to say that it wasn't expensive, but then eggs were, too.

What is striking when you look at food prices across Europe—and this is more or less the case right through the Industrial Revolution—is that many foods we take for granted were virtually unaffordable for all but a small slice of the population. In good years, working-class Europeans would be spending some 80 percent of their income on bread or its equivalent. When a bad harvest hit, that figure could top 150 percent.

In other words, they'd starve. They certainly couldn't afford imported spices; however, eggs, poultry, oil, and wine were also out of reach.

Somewhat surprisingly, when you compare the cost of spices to some of today's more commonplace foods, the relationship was more or less the same in Bernardo Morosini's lifetime as it is now. An ounce of pepper or the lesser grades of ginger was worth about a dozen and a half eggs. (Cinnamon and the most expensive grades of ginger were typically about twice that price.) And this is not an isolated case. That ounce was worth about ten eggs in Venice in 1225, a dozen or so in London in 1450, and much the same in Wroclaw (Poland) in 1506. Seventy years later in Vienna, eggs had gotten more expensive: you'd get only about nine eggs for your ounce. Compare that to today. My local supermarket charges around a dollar fifty to three dollars for an ounce of pepper, just about the same price as a dozen eggs. Similarly, when the *Ménagier* listed the prices paid for the wedding banquet, chickens were running about eight pennies a pound, while ginger could be had for six pennies an ounce. Compare the cost of a free-range chicken to ginger today. You'll find the ratio is roughly similar.

So you can see that when we look at the recipe books from the fifteenth century, it isn't merely the presence of ginger and saffron that distinguishes them as the cuisine of the well-to-do; it is also the abundance of poultry, sugar, and eggs. The spices stand out because we are not used to cooking with them, yet it would be hard to argue that they were extraordinarily expensive in relation to many other foods.*

What has changed, though, is how much people earn. In the late fifteenth century, a skilled employee of the Arsenale, Venice's shipbuilding works, would have needed to work something like an hour and a half to buy an ounce of pepper (and more like two and a half hours in northern Europe), while today, an employee of General Motors would earn that same ounce in a few minutes.

All this is to say that by the fifteenth century, at least some of the less expensive spices were affordable luxuries, less like a bottle of Dom Pérignon (two hundred dollars per liter) than a Starbucks latte (eight dollars per liter). Which doesn't mean that the average man or woman working at the Arsenale (women were employed as sailmakers) could afford them, but for the kind of people who could afford the occasional dozen eggs or a roast capon, pepper and ginger were not an especially big stretch. (Period cookbooks occasionally show that they are mindful of less than princely budgets, recommending cheaper substitutions so that your tastes would not outweigh the ducats in your purse.) By the time of Bernardo Morosini's death, pepper had become much more ubiquitous

---

* Admittedly, this sort of analysis has its limits. While the relationship of the price of pepper to the prices of poultry and eggs was much the same as today, red meat was typically cheaper. Bernardo Morosini could buy about 1½ pounds of beef for an ounce of pepper, while in northern Europe, you could get anywhere between 1 and 5 pounds, depending on the time and place. What's more, regional specialties were less costly closer to home, too, so that olive oil was affordable in Venice (about ½ liter per ounce of pepper) but relatively expensive in northern Europe, where a liter of oil could be worth between 4 and 12 ounces of the Asian spice!

outside the kitchens of the high and mighty than any other imported seasoning. This may explain why, when the fashion for spicy food among the
elite had passed, Europeans as a whole never stopped using black pepper.

Before that happened, though, increasing numbers of Europeans got
a taste for the more expensive Asian condiments. The fifteenth century, in
particular, saw a spectacular rise in the consumption of ginger (up 200 to
300 percent), while the following century was a boom time for cloves, nutmeg, and mace (up some 500 percent). In the meantime, the population
slowly recovered from its Black Death losses, rising some 60 percent in the
two centuries. In contrast, per capita pepper imports rose just a smidgen
in the fourteen hundreds and hardly budged during the next hundred
years. Then, in the seventeenth century, when a price war between the
Dutch and English sent the price of pepper to unprecedented lows, consumption doubled even as the overall population stagnated. It would
seem that the skyrocketing cost of basic foods (the fifteen hundreds were
a time of rampant inflation) made it necessary for the middle classes to
scrimp on superfluities such as pepper in the sixteenth century—the poor
just died of malnutrition—but when pepper got relatively cheap in the
next century, then they sprinkled it on.

Ironically, even as the price of basic foodstuffs was going up, the overall cost of living for the wealthy may actually have gone down. In the fifteen hundreds, the rich never spent much more than a quarter of their
income on food, while the well-to-do may have spent twice that. Most of
the rest of their money was spent on luxuries (arguably, many of the foods
they purchased would fit into that category, too). And it was precisely the
goods that you needed to keep up with the sixteenth-century Joneses that
got cheaper in those years. Books, fine clothing, and servants were more
affordable than ever. This was especially true in the Renaissance Italian
city-states, where the inflationary spiral was not as severe as elsewhere in
Europe. In sixteenth-century Florence, almost a quarter of all households
could boast two or more servants, surely a pretty good indication of who
could afford the newly popular spices. In Venice, if anything, the standard
of living was even higher. Wages certainly were, and this in a town where
wheat was often cheaper than on the mainland. Here, a master builder
earned enough in a day to buy some thirty pounds of bread or about ten
or more pounds of beef. At this wage scale, he could certainly afford the

occasional ounce of pepper or ginger, costing about the same as a half pound of beef. Architects and bank managers were earning perhaps two to three times that amount, so you would imagine that, at least once in a while, they could splurge on an ounce of nutmeg or cinnamon at twice the pepper price. But this was Venice. In far-off England, where spices were easily two to four times as expensive in comparison to the normal wage, lordlings didn't have it this good.

This may in part explain why pepper, ginger, cinnamon, and nutmeg were so widespread in Italian Renaissance cooking. But any economic explanation surely tells only part of the story. Luca has the most succinct answer to the popularity of spices in the glory days of I Antichi and the other *compagnie de calza*. "Fa più figo," he says. (Spices were "cool," he translates.) They were trendy. Everybody who could afford it wanted ginger and cinnamon in their food. A given fashion has many explanations, but to a certain extent, it also has a life of its own.

CELEBRITY CHEFS, THE NEW MEDIA, AND THE RISE OF THE PARTY TOWN

The Renaissance has been credited for cultural advances of all kinds, but one of that remarkable era's lesser-known innovations may be the invention of the celebrity chef. "What a cook you bestowed, o immortal gods, in my friend Martino of Como," bubbled the bookish Bartolomeo Sacchi (better known by his pen name, Platina) in his bestselling cookbook based on his friend's recipes. One of the changes that came with the Renaissance was that craftsmen who had long labored in the shadows now stepped into the limelight. This phenomenon is well documented among painters, who morphed from anonymous blue-collar workers sprucing up palaces and churches into household names like Leonardo and Raphael. The same thing happened (admittedly on a much smaller scale) in the culinary arts. Not that we actually know all that much about Martino, "the chief cook of our age" (again, according to Platina), other than that he was probably born in Como, in the foothills of the Alps. He may have had red hair, since he was also known as Martino de Rossi.

Yet even if it were not for the cookbook author's accolades, you can see from the chef's résumé that he was in high demand at Italy's most glamorous courts. He appears to have worked for aristocrats in Milan and

Naples. But his most prestigious assignment came when he arrived in Rome in the middle of the fifteenth century and took on the job of running the kitchens of Cardinal Ludovico Trevisan. The cardinal was one of the richest members of the papal court and was famous for his appetites for gambling, horses, women, art, dogs, and fine cuisine. He was reputed to spend some twenty ducats a day on food alone. (That was the yearly wage of our laborer at the Arsenale!) He obviously snatched up the best cook in town, and it might have been at his house, around 1463, that the talented chef met the erudite Platina. Soon enough, they came up with a book of recipes. The fruit of their collaboration, *De honesta voluptate et valetudine* (On Honest Pleasure and Good Health), was to be the most widely read cookbook of its time. Where Martino was clearly a practical chef—or *scalco*, as these culinary maestros were known—Platina was an academic, employed as the Vatican librarian. Platina was part of a Roman circle of Humanists who appear to have divided their time between quoting Virgil and planning dinner. Similarly, the book is divided between scholarly references to long-dead Romans and recipes for roast piglet and Sicilian macaroni.

Of course, Martino would have been nothing without his highbrow publicist. Martino's recipes had been collected before this, but without the prestige of someone like Platina writing in polished Latin, it's unlikely the book would have been read outside the peninsula. And it was. There were at least eight Latin editions before 1517, but the collection became even more popular when translated into the vernacular. All told, there were some fifteen French, seven German, five Italian, and even a Dutch translation by the late fifteen hundreds. Moreover, Martino's recipe collection was plagiarized and bastardized under an assortment of disguises in dozens of editions in the two hundred years following its publication. As a result, cooks in Elizabethan England (and elsewhere) were stuffing their pies with fillings seasoned in the Italian style as much as Shakespeare was packing his plays with Italian characters.

So what did gourmets eat on the eve of Columbus's and da Gama's voyages in search of the spiceries? It's clear from the beginning that Martino's cookbook is not for the budget-conscious. There is plenty of pricey poultry and game. Eggs, meat, and fish of all sorts are common. And the majority of recipes include at least some spice. The most popular by far is saffron, closely followed by cinnamon, ginger, and pepper. Cloves, nutmeg, and melegueta make a token appearance. Gone, however, are all of the more obscure spices of the earlier collections. You will search in vain for long pepper and galingale, to say nothing of cubebs and zedoary. In that sense, at least, it is a more bourgeois cuisine, using the more restricted palette of seasoning accessible to bankers and architects, not just to princes and cardinals. If we look at Martino's original recipe for the *fior di ginestra* sauce (the one Sergio uses at Bistrot de Venise for his sea bass), it is actually a model of simplicity. Martino instructs you to make an almond milk–based sauce, which is then "tempered" with verjuice, thickened with egg yolk, colored with saffron, and scented with ginger. Presumably, salt would have been added as well. So here, at least, the seasoning is relatively austere. More typical, however, is a recipe for eel *torta* (a sort of pie), flavored with ginger, pepper, cinnamon, and saffron as well as a little sugar and rose water. As in so many cookbooks of the late Middle Ages, you just can't tell how much of any of these spices went into the food, since neither Martino nor Platina thought to include quantities. If you look at slightly later Italian cookbooks, such as the 1549 edition of Cristoforo Messisbugo's *Banchetti* (Banquets), the quantities of spice seem roughly commensurate with the *Anonimo Veneziano;* one to two teaspoons of spice per pound of meat are the norm.

Overall, though, the chef whom you meet in Platina's popular book (as well as in Martino's own earlier manuscripts) is a cook at the top of his game, using a broad battery of cooking styles and seasonings to create a complex and sophisticated cuisine. And yet, although the cooking is decidedly more refined than the recipes we find in earlier Italian or French cookery manuals, its flavor structure is still largely Byzantine and Arabic. Sweet is blended with acid and balanced with spice, even if sugar has mostly replaced honey. The earlier medieval penchant for ginger is beginning to shift somewhat to cinnamon, and the use of pepper is much more explicit than it was in some of the earlier sources. But the cosmopolitan approach of the earlier cuisine is also still there, with Catalan and French recipes right beside dishes from Italy. In other words, this is no culinary revolution. Among Roman foodies, Martino may have been more famous than Michelangelo, but he was no iconoclast like the ceiling painter down at the Vatican. Yet even if Renaissance Italian cooking

A late-Renaissance banquet, as illustrated in Cristoforo da Messisbugo's Banchetti.

didn't invent the culinary equivalent of perspective, it was just as influential in the kitchens of northern Europe as the radical Italian picture makers were in Flemish and German artists' studios.

In the two hundred years or so between the last Crusades and the arrival of the all-too-worldly popes of the late fourteen hundreds, the centers of fashion had drifted away from the French-speaking world. In part, this was simply a matter of a shrinking French sphere of dominance. The Franks were ejected from Outremer, the Gallic kings of the house of Anjou lost southern Italy, the English ruling classes stopped speaking

French, and the popes returned to Rome from a long sojourn in Avignon. Then there was the cataclysm of the Black Death, the pandemic that wiped out somewhere between a quarter and a third of Europe's population. The fleas that carried bubonic plague apparently first arrived in western Europe in 1348 in the same way as the fork: on Venetian ships from Constantinople. The routes that transported pepper to Paris and cloves to Cologne turned out to be an all too efficient vector for the disease. This is not to suggest that the Black Death was a consequence of the spice trade; however, the same network of exchange that had encouraged the diffusion of a cosmopolitan cuisine among the elite now facilitated the spread of the bacterium among the population at large. Trade suffered enormously as a result of the plague, not merely because, in some urban centers, half the customers were dead but also due to the onerous restrictions placed on travel in the following years.* This constriction in exchange made every town a little more provincial in the next few years, Paris included. France, however, had the additional tragedy of over a century of more or less continuous carnage, the so-called Hundred Years' War, which would peter out only in the middle of the fourteen hundreds. This made room for Italy to become the undisputed capital of style for the continent.

The recovery from the Black Death was patchy and slow, and Europe as a whole did not recover its preplague population until perhaps 1500. Venice was especially hard hit by the epidemic, though her moneymaking prowess, even if not her residents, recovered relatively quickly. It was Florence and Rome, however, along with a number of other minor northern Italian cities that would first play host to the phenomenon for which German nineteenth-century historians invented the term *Renaissance*. By this time, Florence was in her twilight as the manufacturing and banking center that had made her a world player in the preplague years. Rome was

---

* A Flemish reporter describes the arrival of the plague in Genoa: "In January of the year 1348 three galleys put in at Genoa, driven by a fierce wind from the East, horribly infected and laden with a variety of spices and other valuable goods. When the inhabitants of Genoa learnt this, and saw how suddenly and irremediably they infected other people, they were driven forth from that port by burning arrows and divers engines of war; for no man dared touch them; nor was any man able to trade with them, for if he did he would be sure to die forthwith."

crusty and corrupt but full of people trying to make a name for themselves. Hiring the top decorator of the time to paint your chapel and the finest chef to cater your banquets was essential if you wanted to stand out from the crowd. Elsewhere in Italy, the petty princes did their best to keep up. Consequently, celebrity chefs were in high demand.

Still, to call Martino a chef barely begins to do justice to his job description. Sure, he had to make certain that the cooks didn't arrive at work drunk and that breakfast was served on time like any professional today, but he also had to supervise extravaganzas that would test the skills of a circus impresario. While medieval banquets had always been a feast for all the senses—with a vaudeville revue of music, dancing, and other entertainments interspersed with the courses—the impression given by the descriptions of Italian Renaissance feasts is that you've stepped out of an off-Broadway variety show into a Busby Berkeley extravaganza.

The wedding dinner thrown by Giovanni II Bentivoglio in Bologna in 1487 to celebrate the wedding of his son Annibale to Lucrezia d'Este is typical of this kind of over-the-top spectacle. Our reporter at the event, Cherubino Ghirardacci, describes a supper that started at eight at night and lasted until three the next morning. The dinner opened with a selection of sweet, spiced wines and antipasti of various little birds, including partridges "with sugared olives and grapes." The servants then brought in a castle of sugar "with artfully constructed battlements and towers" packed with live birds, which were set loose to careen across the dining room, "to the great pleasure and delight of the diners." A seemingly endless procession of meat was then paraded into the hall. Deer and ostrich surrounded by pies, veal, capons, goats, sausages, and partridge, cooked in all sorts of ways, each with their own sauce, presumably seasoned with cinnamon, pepper, and ginger as Martino instructs; then peacocks "dressed up in their own feathers as if spreading their tails," one for each guest; then mortadella, hares, and stewed venison re-formed into its skin so skillfully "as to appear alive"; then doves and pheasant "from whose beaks issued flames," accompanied by citrus and spiced sauces; then sugar and almond cakes, cheesecakes, and biscotti; then more meat and game birds as well as "a castle full of rabbits," who ran out among the diners' feet; then rabbit pies and dressed capons; then an "artful castle" imprisoning a large pig, which grunted and snorted within its crenulated cage; then the waiters arrived with whole, golden-brown, roasted suckling pigs, various other roasts, wild duck, "and the like." Finally came sweets made from milk, jellies, pears, pastries, candies, marzipans, "and other similar favors." And just before leaving, the guests were given spiced confections and "precious wines" on their way to bed.

As exhausting as all this sounds, it's worth pointing out that most of this spectacle was just that, an impressive performance. The diners were not able to sample most of the food, if only for logistical reasons. But even if they could, they might not have found everything to their taste. In this respect, the Renaissance feast was the equivalent of one of those obscenely lavish buffets found on cruise ships: vastly too much food for the number of diners but also enough variety so that everyone will find something he or she likes. Also, much as on the *Queen Mary,* the guests were offered a different selection depending on their status. Medieval maître d's saw it as part of their job to send the fanciest morsels to the VIP tables. All the same, everybody did get to watch the show.

In the coming years, the literate classes everywhere could read about these fantastic occasions in books such as Platina's but even more explicitly in the likes of Messisbugo's *Banchetti,* a kind of how-to guide on throwing a Renaissance feast published in 1549. The enduring but widely disparaged myth that Catherine de Médicis, when she married the French king in 1533, brought a fashion for all things Italian to the Parisian court isn't without a grain of truth. Her arrival at the royal court certainly must have reinforced a trend that was already in full swing. The taste for spices had long been a feature of aristocratic cooking throughout Christendom; however, these new Italian cooking guides also made it trendy. The brand-new medium of the printed book spread the vogue for Italian seasoning to every corner of Renaissance Europe.

Venice was particularly well placed to take advantage of the communication revolution that swept across the continent after Gutenberg came up with movable type. While the Republic's spice traders were increasingly shut out by the Portuguese and then wiped out completely by the Dutch, the city's role as a world information hub blossomed. Venice had always been a communication center, if only because her pepper and silk merchants traveled the world and intelligence on everything from the

price of rice in China to the latest harem coup in Istanbul was worth hard
cash to the traders on the Rialto. Little wonder that four Venetian nobles
once removed part of the roof of the Ducal Palace in order to listen to a
confidential report from Istanbul. When rumors about Indian spices arriving in Lisbon reached Venice in 1501, the reaction of the government
was to send an agent to Portugal to discover what was up. His report still
survives. When Antonio Pigafetta of Vicenza returned from his voyage
round the world with Magellan, he visited Venice, where the bureaucrats
charged with the spice trade heard his account of India "with the utmost
attention." Even more than a consumer of data, however, Venice was Europe's preeminent distributor of information. This only increased with
the arrival of printing in the city.

The technology came to Venice early because of the pepper routes
that long connected her to central Europe. The first printers to arrive
were the German brothers Johann and Wendelin von Speyer, who set up
shop in the city a little before 1469. They had apparently learned the new
technology in Mainz, where Gutenberg had started his printing business
some fifteen years earlier. By 1500, about twenty-five German printing
firms had opened in Venice. The city had two distinct perks for a printer:
one was the ready supply of paper, and the other was that the church censors left you alone. Until the nineteenth century, Europeans made paper
out of cotton or linen rags, and Venice was well supplied with both, and
given the Republic's mostly antagonistic relationship with Rome, the
press was generally free of religious meddling. This, at least in part, accounts for the fact that there were more books printed in fifteenth-century
Venice than in any other city in Europe (perhaps as many as 4,500 titles
accounting for some 2.5 million copies), and while, in the next century,
the city began to lose its lead over other centers such as Paris, it still managed to produce some 15,000 to 17,500 titles during the following one
hundred years. These books were set in Latin, Greek, Hebrew, Arabic,
Slavonic, German, French, and Spanish as well as various Italian dialects.
Their subject matter ranged from theology to geography, from military
treatises to handbooks on table manners. There were a good number of
cookbooks and dietary manuals, too. It was only natural that the first
cookbook ever published, Platina and Martino's *De honesta voluptate et vale-*

tudine, was set in type in Venice in 1475. At least five subsequent editions were printed here over the next thirty years.

There were, in fact, a great number of cookbooks published in Venice, including the first printed edition of *Apicius,* the sole surviving ancient Roman recipe collection. However, the majority were contemporary Italian food books by the likes of Cristoforo Messisbugo and the Venetian-born Bartolomeo Scappi, which were snapped up by trendy diners all over Europe. It's clear from the many translations that cookbooks were in high demand, but the medical and dietary guides were even more popular. Many came out of Venice's university at Padua, widely recognized in the fifteenth century as the Harvard Medical School of its day. Diet books, especially when endorsed by medical professionals, were as profitable for publishers then as they are now. It's amazing to realize how quickly these Venetian books ricocheted across Europe. To give just one example, Girolamo Ruscelli's *Secreti,* a collection of recipes and remedies, was first published in Venice (1555), then in a French translation (Antwerp, 1557), in English (London, 1558), Latin (Basle, 1559), Dutch (Antwerp, 1561), and German (Basle, 1575)—and this is the list only of those copies that survive in American collections!

This information revolution had an immense influence on the dissemination of culture. As books rolled off the presses in hundreds and thousands of copies, many more people could glimpse the culinary fireworks long hidden behind palace walls.* The wives of merchants in Bordeaux and investment bankers in Augsburg could try to replicate the dishes served at the feasts of princes and popes. Undoubtedly, this was often as successful as some of the famous chefs' dishes I have tried to reproduce from the pages of *Gourmet* magazine, but, however muddled the results, the middle classes did get the idea that spices were necessary, even if a little expensive, if you wanted to keep up with the Medici. The popular diet manuals must have had a similar effect. The literate public could

---

* The reading public was remarkably broad. One survey of fifteenth- and sixteenth-century private libraries in France indicates that the majority were owned by lawyers and churchmen; however, 66 out of 377 book collections belonged to haberdashers, weavers, drapers, tanners, shoemakers, hawkers, locksmiths, coach builders, skinners, dyers, grocers, cheese mongers, and pastry cooks!

now prattle on about the need to balance the phlegmatic characteristics of sturgeon with the addition of a little cinnamon, all on the learned authority of esteemed doctors from Padua.

The Italian interest in food wasn't always appreciated. The visiting French writer Michel de Montaigne was clearly fed up with all the food lectures he had received on his 1580 visit to Italy when he penned a portrait of the obsessive head cook, or *scalco:*

> I asked him about his job, and he replied with a discourse on the science of guzzling, delivered with magisterial gravity and demeanor as if he had been expounding some great point of theology. He spelled out to me the differences in appetites: the one we have before eating, the one we have after the second and third course; the means now of simply gratifying it, now of arousing and stimulating it; the organization of his sauces, first in general, and then particularizing the qualities of the ingredients and their effects; the differences in salads according to the season, which one should be warmed up and which served cold, the way of adorning and embellishing them to make them also pleasant to the sight. After that he entered upon the order of serving, full of beautiful and important considerations.

Hand in hand with a desire to ape the sophisticated Venetian, Roman, and Florentine fashions came a reaction against the decadent ways of the Italians. For every courtier trying to flatter Catherine de Médicis by having his cooks re-create dishes from Messisbugo's *Banchetti,* there was another who wanted to return to an idealized French simplicity. Venice, in particular, was both admired and reviled. Like New York, the city was considered the paradigm of sophistication and the incarnation of sin. Also a little like New York, its role as fashion center came somewhat late in the day.

When we look at Carpaccio's paintings from the late fourteen hundreds, we see a society dressed to the nines and ready to party. While perhaps not the most cultured city in fifteenth-century Europe, Venice was the continent's wealthiest. Its position as international entrepôt made it the best place in Europe to shop not only for spices but for every other ornament to wealth as well. The Milanese priest Pietro Casola noted the abundance on a visit in 1494:

> Something may be said about the quantity of merchandise in the said city, although not nearly the whole truth, because it is inestimable. Indeed it seems as if the whole world flocks there, and that human beings have concentrated there all their force for trading. I was taken to see various warehouses, beginning with that of the Germans—which it appears to me would suffice alone to supply all Italy with the goods that come and go—and so many others that it can be said they are innumerable. . . . And who could count the many shops so well furnished that they also seem warehouses, with so many cloths of every make—tapestry, brocades and hangings of every design, carpets of every sort, camlets of every colour and texture, silks of every kind; and so many warehouses full of spices, groceries and drugs, and so much beautiful white wax! These things stupefy the beholder, and cannot be fully described to those who have not seen them.

That the city was fantastically rich is without question. The wealth, however, was increasingly settling in the purses of fewer people as the moneymen turned away from buying and selling. At the height of the spice trade, everyone made at least something, from the rowers on the galleys to the wealthy widows who invested their gold ducats in pepper. But now that profits were more often sunk into real estate and manufacturing than commerce, a smaller fragment of the population benefited. In this climate, the old, powerful, but not always flush families became especially prickly when the nouveaux riches and even the middling classes began to flaunt their affluence by building great big mansions on the terra firma and throwing lavish bashes at their canal-side palazzi. So laws were passed over and over in a vain attempt to limit conspicuous consumption. Excessive expenses for weddings and banquets organized by the *compagnie de calza* were specifically singled out in legislation passed in 1460, then again in 1466. The government set a maximum limit of half a ducat per guest, and anyone breaking the rules would get nailed with a hefty penalty of two hundred ducats, or worse.* Informants got to keep half the fine, and if the snitch happened to be an indentured servant or slave, he would get his freedom, too. Then, since the monetary limit didn't seem to be working, the grumpy bureaucrats started to set rules about just what could be cooked. Doves, peacocks, partridge, pheasants, and other game birds were inscribed on the forbidden-food index. No more than three dishes were to be allowed, not counting confections, and the gilding of food was outlawed. (That spices don't show up on this list of banished delights seems to reinforce Luca's contention that they were not considered especially luxurious.) Dinners in public, the kind of parties today's I Antichi regularly throw on the Campo San Maurizio outside of Jurubeba's house, would also no longer be tolerated: "rather only private ones in the chambers as the ancients were accustomed to do, and only with small sweets [served]."

In 1489, a special commission of "three of our honorable gentlemen, ready and enthusiastic" (later elevated to the rank of magistrates), was specifically charged to pursue spendthrift malefactors from its offices at the Rialto. The legislation must have been observed about as much as speed limits are today. You get a hint of this from a 1526 legal note: "And truly, those who would act so dishonestly as to throw bread or oranges at [the commission's] employees, or push them or kick them out, will fall subject to a penalty of fifty ducats."

The impression that Venice had been transformed from the hungry, hard-bitten merchant republic of Doge Dandolo's time into a flabby, complacent party town by the early years of the sixteenth century would certainly be overstating the state of affairs. After all, the city had long had those prolonged periods of *Carnevale*, when indulgence temporarily replaced bookkeeping as the city's main pastime. And business was still the city's fountain of wealth in the sixteenth century. But changes both within the city and without presaged the twilight of its golden age.

THE BITTER END

In spite of the masks that Venetians are so expert at creating, it is still possible to peer behind the marble façades topped with cell phone antennae

---

* A half ducat would be on the order of several hundred dollars today.

Venice developed many dry crispbreads, which wouldn't spoil on long sea voyages. The taste persisted even as the port withered. Here, eighteenth-century vendors sell bussolai, *a ring-shaped breadstick that is still sold in the city's bakeries.*

and find clues that point to an earlier Venice, a city that was once Europe's spice emporium without peer. Among the edible hints and whispers that recall that glorious past, there is a dark cookie known as a *peverino* that maintains a tenuous connection between the city of Saint Mark and the pepper woods of Malabar. This throwback to the spice-laced cuisine of the Renaissance is about the size of a hockey puck, studded with almonds and raisins, and faintly bitter with molasses. How much black pepper it contains depends on the baker. Some of the cookies burn the tongue with peppery pungency, while others are almost bland.

There are few as obsessed with these confections as Franco Colussi, whose bakery is tucked into a long alley off the Campo San Barnaba. As you open Colussi's shop-front door, you are enveloped with the aroma of butter and spice, and yet the space and the selection here are simplicity itself. Modest baskets hold *baìcoli,* the crisp little biscotti that go back to the days when baking ship's biscuit for sailors was a thriving industry. Panetoni of all sizes sit on a shelf like an army of Russian nesting dolls. *Peverini* are displayed in orderly pyramids. Above all, though, the narrow room is dominated by a large oven and the irrepressible Franco. When he hears of my interest in peppery sweets, he skips from behind his marble slab, a jaunty chef's hat perched on his rosy head, all bubbling with enthusiasm about the subject. His *peverini* are laced with nutmeg and cumin as well as pepper, he confides. But he doesn't make them as often as he used to. Apparently, the demand just isn't what it once was for these or other traditional Venetian pastries. With the passion of an archaeologist discussing a long-forgotten civilization, Franco describes a confection he now seldom makes called *bussolà di Murano*, a kind of super-*peverino* that is in the form of a ring almost a foot across and weighs more than two pounds. It, too, is spiced with pepper, and cinnamon this time. "It is a savage thing," he whispers, and then shakes his head, "But today, even the Venetians don't recognize it. It [the island of Murano] is only five minutes from here, only five minutes, but they don't know what it is!" Yet he insists on making his pastries the old way, because who knows if anyone else will? Though he hardly looks it, Franco is a grandfather, and despite all his best efforts, he can find no one to take over the store. Young people no longer want to stay in Venice, he tells me, launching into the standard complaint about the city's decline. In the end, I thank the white-haired baker and close the door behind me. And as I walk away, loaded down with a panetone, a bag of *peverini*, a satchel of *baìcoli*, I wonder if he really is the last of his line and if the little storefront will still be there when I next return.

Everyone in Venice complains about the disappearing stores, a result of an all too evident demographic collapse. Venice isn't unique in this sense: Italy has the lowest birthrate in the world, and the country's population is shrinking. As Luca points out over and over, Venice's population always went up and down. Throughout the Middle Ages and Renaissance, plague would hit, wiping out enormous numbers of people, but others would quickly arrive to take advantage of the opportunities the city offered. But when the plague of 1575 laid waste to the vain city, it never quite recovered. It has been estimated that Venice hit its peak of about 180,000 in that fateful year (a census of 1581 showed only 134,000), a number it would not reach again until the 1950s. Since 1980, the slow trickle of exodus has turned into a flood. The city has lost more than a third of its inhabitants, and there are fewer people now than there were at the time of the Fourth Crusade.

The path to decline became inexorable in 1453, when Constantinople fell to the Turks. Venice had succeeded in great part by taking over the maritime appendages of the Byzantine Empire but, in the process, made the fatal mistake avoided by all successful parasites—that you do not so weaken your host that it dies. The Venetians had so enfeebled the Byzantines that when the Ottomans arrived, the ancient realm gave up its last breath. From that point on, it was just a matter of time before Venice lost her empire in the Aegean.

By 1500, the geopolitical constellations that had long favored the Republic's fortune were beginning to predict a not-so-happy future. The fall of Constantinople made the strategy that had been so effective since 1204—to protect and secure Venice's route to the Orient—no longer feasible. Vasco da Gama's arrival in Calicut in 1498 seemed as if it would throttle the spice trade at its very source. Even in its own neighborhood, the city couldn't muster the resources to police the Adriatic Sea, where thugs and pirates now lay in wait to mug unsuspecting traders as they passed by. As the mercantile empire withered, the city shifted its gaze from the eastern Mediterranean, where it had been firmly fixed since the first Venetians loaded salt onto their galleys, to western Europe and the terra firma.

In this new climate, what was a young Venetian with money to do? Trade, and especially the still-lucrative but increasingly less predictable spice trade, now seemed too risky. As a result, more and more Venetian profits were pumped into real estate as well as into new luxury industries. Better to sink your money into growing grapes or making glass or setting up a publishing business than risk your shirt, or worse, by chancing the voyage to Alexandria. Venice was abuzz with stories of its citizens abroad abducted by Barbary corsairs (mostly, though not exclusively, Arab pirates from North Africa), sold into slavery, and forced to work under the most inhuman conditions for their godless captors.

All the same, Venetian merchants did not retire en masse from the spice trade to stay home eating contraband gilded pigeons. After a brief collapse of the Mediterranean spice business in the early sixteenth century—more a result of the wars against Turkey than the incursions of the Portuguese—Venice regained a huge portion of the spice trade for most of the remaining hundred years. (Both the Turks and the Venetians realized soon enough that it was better to exchange profitable trade goods than deadly volleys.) Partially as a result of the renewed fashion for spices that had been, to some extent, fueled by modish Venetian cookbook publishers, the Europe-wide demand for spices kept growing. Even while Lisbon was bringing in some 2½ million pounds of pepper a year directly from India, the Venetians were still able to sell more than half that amount picked up from their usual suppliers in the Near East, even if fewer merchants were willing to run the increased risks.

It wasn't the Portuguese but the Dutch who wiped out Venice's role as spice merchant to Europe—not so much because they cut off the supply but because they lowered the price so much that spices bought in the Middle East were simply not competitive. Even the Ottomans mostly found it cheaper to buy spices from the Dutch and English rather than get their supplies by way of Persia and Arabia (even though some continued to arrive by the ancient caravan routes well into the eighteenth century). Consequently, by the first decades of the seventeenth century, the flow of spices through Venice had shrunk to a bare trickle. But the Rialto traders might still have been able to recover if it hadn't been for the Thirty Years' War (1618–48), which had sucked in almost all of Venice's most profitable customers in central Europe and thereby wiped out what remained of a market north of the Alps. Even as the opening salvos of the long conflict were fired, it was clear that the merchant republic was out of the spice business for good.

In the wake of the first collapse of the spice business after 1498, the number of young nobles who, like Alessandro Magno, were still willing to follow the old Venetian pattern of a few years in trade followed by a political career began to dwindle. In part, it explains why groups such as I Antichi were such a draw. Venice, always a gerontocracy, offered no system for young men to clamber up the political ladder, and now that their traditional jobs as apprentice merchants had shriveled away, what were they supposed to do? One option was to organize public parties to show off to their peers and, along the way, make friends and influence people. It's worth mentioning that unlike today's I Antichi, the original confraternities were bachelors' clubs. The demise of the commercial culture in Venice had resulted in a peculiar custom that discouraged all but one son from marrying so that the inheritance would not be spread too thin. Obviously, there is a close connection here to the widespread prostitution for which the city was renowned. I also wonder, though, about the effects of venereal disease on sapping the vigor of the population. This was the era when syphilis was first epidemic in Europe, and Venice would have made the perfect petri dish for STDs.* Whatever the explanation, the young aristocrats of Venice had plenty of time, and inclination, for wine, women, and song.

Art, literature, food, and music were the talk of Venice by the late fifteen hundreds. By the sixteen hundreds, when the city definitively lost her place in the pepper trade, visitors to Venice came as much to gamble at the card tables as to risk money on commerce. By the seventeen hundreds, Venice had become Europe's Las Vegas, a city of brothels and casinos, a gorgeous vacation getaway where tourists would buy expensive trinkets and return home with postcard views of *La Serenissima* cranked out by the deft studios of painters such as Guardi and Canaletto. The Venetian aristocracy began to look to French chefs for inspiration, and spicy cuisine, which had characterized the Republic almost from the beginning, was relegated to just a few traditional specialties: the *peverada,* a pepper-laced sauce found mostly on the terra firma; the gnocchi still occasionally sprinkled with cheese and cinnamon in out-of-the-way villages in the Alpine foothills; the still-ubiquitous *sarde in saor,* the sardines smothered with a vinegary mix of raisins and onions, even though they are seldom finished with cinnamon as the more old-fashioned cookbooks suggest.

When Mark Twain visited in the late nineteenth century, there was little left to remind the visitor of the famed pepper fleets:

> Today her piers are deserted, her warehouses are empty, her merchant fleets are vanished, her armies and her navies are but memories. Her glory is departed, and with her crumbling grandeur of wharves and palaces about her she sits among her stagnant lagoons, forlorn and beggared, forgotten of the world. She that in her palmy days commanded the commerce of a hemisphere and made the weal or woe of nations with a beck of her puissant finger, is become the humblest among the peoples of

---

* In sixteenth-century Venice, interested visitors could buy an inexpensive pamphlet containing the "tariff of all prostitutes in which one finds the price and the qualities of all courtesans of Venice." According to two contemporary sources, there were about twelve thousand official prostitutes in the city at the time, or about one in three adult women. The figure is certainly an exaggeration, but it does point to the scale of the sex industry.

the earth, —a peddler of glass beads for women, and trifling toys
and trinkets for school-girls and children.

Even so, visitors continue to be seduced by the well-practiced charms
of the dowager of the lagoon. And as a rule, the Venetians don't complain about the tourists; they understand how important foreigners have
always been to the city's economy. No, they complain about the shopping.
"This transformation is ruining our lives," says Luca when I mention that
bakers such as Franco Colussi can't find anyone to take over their business. In Venice, there is little alternative to shopping on foot, and as the
stores disappear, you have to walk farther and farther. From a transportation standpoint, the city makes absolutely no sense unless you are traveling by boat. If you look at Carpaccio's painting of the Rialto, you notice
that the crossing is a drawbridge, designed for the easy passage of cargo.
It was replaced by immovable stone between 1588 and 1591. Early depictions of the city show floating bridges, one-piece flying bridges, pivot-
ing bridges, and, of course, the usual kind of drawbridges that allowed
sailing ships free passage. Every single one of these was gradually replaced
by permanent footbridges, transforming a city of sailors into a town of
boatless pedestrians stranded on sinking islands in the middle of a lagoon.
The reality of Venice's maritime patrimony became as insubstantial as all
her other myths.

There is at least one holiday, though, when thousands of Venetians
still sail out onto the sea. The city's loveliest celebration is the *Festa di
Redentore* (the Feast of the Redeemer), the party held to commemorate
that most demoralizing plague of 1575. This particular plague hit the city
at its precarious peak, just four years after the rout of the Turkish navy at
Lepanto. It soon became evident that while the Venetian ships may have
won the battle, the war against the Turk was lost and Venice would once
and for all be shut out of the riches of the Orient. Soon after, the Ottomans took her colony of Cyprus, with its sugar and cotton plantations,
and then the fluttering flags of Saint Mark started falling like dominoes
across the remaining Aegean Islands. Meanwhile, back in Venice, many
thought the plague had come as a punishment for the city's ungodly ways,
and a wave of newfound piety swept the population. As a result, the government, so long resistant to the power of Rome, was convinced to let in

the Inquisition. The city's university at Padua, the home to independent thinkers such as Galileo, now succumbed to the Jesuits, and the Queen of the Adriatic became a foot soldier in the Counter-Reformation.

Today, the sociopolitical details of the holiday's origin are mostly forgotten, as half the population of Venice clambers into boats and paddles into the lagoon to picnic and wait for the midnight fireworks that mark the date. For the occasion, the members of I Antichi dress in radiant white and perch like seagulls on their banner-bedecked boat, the *Manissa*. As they drift in the lagoon, they spread the decks with fine damask and dine on a meal of *bigoli in salsa*, the sweet-and-sour *sarde in saor*, roast duck, and baked peaches filled with almonds, butter, and amaretti. Luca stuffs his duck with cinnamon, cloves, pepper, and rosemary, among other seasonings. "Fantastico!" he exclaims as he details the menu from last year's event. "The Venetians always say how beautiful this year's holiday was." He laughs. "But the next sentence—and they just have to say it—is always the same. They murmur, 'Beautiful, beautiful, yes. But last year, it was more beautiful.' "

Luca tells me this last story as we finish our long meal, which began with the *canoce* and *bigoli* at the old Zancopè house on Campo San Maurizio. For dessert, we spread creamy mascarpone and *mostarda veneta* on *baìcoli*, the crisp little biscotti from Franco Colussi's pastry shop. The sweet and spicy *mostarda* is reminiscent of a Martino recipe ("Grind . . . together mustard, raisins, dates, soaked bread and a little cinnamon"), except that here the mustard is combined with pears and quinces instead of dry fruit and bread. The condiment comes from the last *spezieria*, or spice shop, in the city, the Drogheria Mascari, just over the Rialto Bridge from the once great spice emporium at the Campo San Bartolomeo. These stores once specialized in the spices and other "drugs" of the Orient, but gradually, as spices became less prized, they branched out into other foodstuffs. Still, this is where the grandmothers go shopping for their spices and *mostarda*. Jurubeba confides in me that she is planning to open another spice shop, "the old-fashioned Venetian kind," on the Campo San Maurizio with an American friend, a longtime resident of the ancient city. To supply her shop, though, she needs to turn to a wholesaler on the terra firma, who, no doubt, is getting his spices from a trader in Rotterdam. The members of I Antichi work hard for their whiff of authenticity.

As our dinner in Jurubeba's dining room moved from one course to the next, the group of diners slowly grew. We were joined by Mizue, Luca's Japanese tutor and onetime lover, and then by Jurubeba's half-Brazilian, half-Venetian son. I was reminded of a description by a seventeenth-century French visitor who commented on the "mighty concourse of strangers" in the city. Jurubeba insists that there are people moving to Venice: Brazilians and Japanese and Americans. She maintains that the city remains a magnet as it has been since Turk and German and Jew negotiated the price of pepper on the Rialto. But when I ask Luca, the only full-blooded Venetian here, what he sees of the future, his giant's shoulders droop. "Son vecio . . . ," this vigorous forty-three-year-old says in Venetian dialect, only half in jest. "I am old. . . ."

"On the other hand,"—he takes a final swig of Prosecco as the distant bell of San Marco rings midnight—"there is this feeling of resistance. The Venetian has become more determined to go on existing, *fino alla fine*—until the bitter end."

PART 2

·

Lisbon

THE CARAVEL

From across the pier, the *Vera Cruz* seems no bigger than a toy sailboat, her masts no more than two chopsticks poking the air; she looks like a little dinghy next to the hulking freighter chained up at the adjacent berth. Up close, the small craft is about the size of a Greyhound bus with masts and spars rendered of modest tree trunks crocheted together by a web of fasts and stays. She lies bound to an anonymous concrete jetty on the Lisbon waterfront, her black hull glum now that her sails have been furled. Yet even when her triangular sheets are raised and puffed out with the ocean breeze, there is still something awkward and even homely about this ancient sailing ship, this caravel. It seems all too incredible that sailors from such a little country, navigating unassuming vessels like the *Vera Cruz*, crisscrossed the Atlantic to scout the path for a sea route to the spice coast of Malabar, that these short and sinewy seamen were the leading edge in Europe's conquest of the world.

When the Venetians, the Genoese, and even the independent Catalans went sailing to procure their aromatic cargo in the Middle East, they traveled over routes that had been amply documented for a couple of thousand years. The winds, the shoals, the rocky shores were the same as Odysseus had endured on his long trip home. But when the Portuguese pointed their prows south and east into the Atlantic gales, it was another matter altogether. Experts debated whether it could even be done. There was concern that great beasts would swallow ships whole; that sailors, as they entered the torrid zones to the south, would be incinerated; that the vessels, as they rounded the curve of the earth, would simply fall right off into oblivion. In fact, the real-life obstacles were probably worse. Yet in spite of all of this, thousands went willingly to die of scurvy and of thirst, to perish on alien rocks and on foreign spears. Historians have filled many exhaustively footnoted volumes with their explanations of why this chronically impoverished fleck of a nation achieved so many improbable feats. And their theories have great merit, I'm sure. Still, I figured if I wanted to make sense of it all, I would do better to ask a sailor.

To get to the *Vera Cruz* dock, I had to dodge the thick morning traffic that sputtered fitfully along Avenida Infante Dom Henrique (named, appropriately enough, after Prince Henry "the Navigator," who is popularly credited with encouraging the voyages that eventually led the Portuguese past the Cape of Good Hope). Across the asphalt and past the chain-link fence, a dusty trailer serves as the command center of Aporvela, an organization that might be described as a sailing club for time travelers, navigating ships that haven't seen salt water for five hundred years. Inside the cramped trailer, Hernâni Xavier greeted me in his office, hemmed in by high shelves crammed and spilling over with charts and books. He rose from his old office chair, looking more like the Portuguese Ford executive he used to be rather than the sailor he has become. "My original plan was to join the codfish fleet, but then I met my wife . . . ," he would later tell me, dismissing the memory of corporate servitude with a shrug. Even while he was with the automobile company, he began making antique ship models—first plastic, then wood, and finally this: he points out the window to the black hull. Hernâni is squat, burly, and dead serious, much like the caravel itself. He knows just about everything there is to know about the little ships and a great deal about naval history in general. "I have fourteen thousand books on history, sailing, and navigation," he notes, pushing a wayward volume back into its place.

Hernâni's stubborn humorlessness seems to break down only when he espies the vast horizons of my ignorance. To make it simpler, he draws me pictures to explain the difference between a round ship (the one with square sails) and a caravel (with triangular sails) and then draws a simple chart to explain how the caravels could practically sail into the wind, where the square-rigged ships had to tack back and forth a dozen or more times. This is how the caravels could skim south along the African coast all the way to the Cape of Good Hope. He pulls out his pencil again to draw a diagram to show why the much larger square-rigged pepper ships had to go all the way to Brazil in order to make the same journey.

"But you must see the caravel to understand." He summons me to follow him across the ramshackle waterfront. "It was exactly to have a

The Vera Cruz, *Aporvela's re-creation of a fifteenth-century caravel.*

glimpse of how it worked, how it stood on the sea, how it was navigated—
because none of this was known—that thirty years ago, we founded
Aporvela to study this." A curt motion indicates the tethered black hull.
Up close, the vessel's deck gleams with finely polished wood, but even
standing on deck, you feel cramped. The original crews consisted of some
dozen sailors, if for no other reason than that there wasn't enough room
to store food for more. Hernâni indicates the shallow hold. "The *Vera Cruz*
draws only 330 centimeters [about 11 feet], so it could go up the African
rivers." But, because of space considerations, that same shallow hold
meant that they could bring back only the most precious African cargo. In
the fifteenth century, that meant gold, melegueta pepper, and slaves. "We
didn't capture the slaves," Hernâni reassures me; "we traded for them
with the natives"—a distinction I find even more technical than his explanation of fifteenth-century rigging.

The very first caravel built by Aporvela, the *Bartolomeu Dias*, was financed by the Portuguese community in South Africa to commemorate
Dias's famous trip round the Cape of Good Hope. Naturally, the club's
volunteer sailors had to sail it there. "Up until then, there were only theories. Now we built one, we navigated it, so we know how the maneuver
of the sail was." Then two more ships were built. Hernâni's attention to

the practical details is reminiscent of the early Portuguese navigators, who got to where they were going by trusting the experience of their weathered companions, while other explorers (a certain Genoan comes to mind) trusted armchair geographers whose ideas of the world came from Ptolemy and Mandeville.

Aporvela's weekend mariners have sailed their feisty vessels from the Baltic to Brazil, to South Africa, to the Azores. Hernâni Xavier allows himself a hint of a smile. "In all, we've sailed them over seventy thousand miles!"

You have to wonder how many of those first sailors risked life and limb just because they were similarly curious and obsessed. Perhaps more than historians would have us believe. Human beings often behave in ways that make more rational types question their reason. But even reasonable people must have been swayed by the wealth that was off-loaded on Lisbon's docks—at first, in a precious trickle of African gold in the fourteen hundreds and then in a fabulous flood of Indian spice in the following century. So when you add up the curious, the bored, the impoverished, and the greedy, it's no wonder that there were plenty of men willing to board the little caravels to gamble their lives on the treacherous seas.

Portugal, then as now, was a poor, small country situated at the western extremity of Europe. It takes up no more than 15 percent of the continent's westernmost peninsula, but even that sliver has little to recommend it when it comes to making a living. The sharp cliffs that rise from narrow valleys make lovely backdrops in tourists' snapshots, but try tilling the soil. Getting from place to place used to be a wretched affair. It is only quite recently that a decent highway system has connected up the country. For most of its history, any industry or commerce depended on the sea.

This was all too evident to the medieval Portuguese king João I as he surveyed his army of armed and hungry knights with nowhere to go and nothing to do. In the early Middle Ages, conquistadores from northern Portugal had gradually annexed the country from the Muslims in a move that mirrored the Christian expansion in next-door Castile. By 1385, the kingdom was secured from the greedy encroachments of the Castilians and consolidated under João I. But now that there were no more Moors to slaughter or Castilians to fight, what was a king to do? The sensible

João, "having no one to conquer on land," to quote the Portuguese national poet Luís Vaz de Camões, "attacked the waves of the ocean."

Or to put it more prosaically, in 1415, he dispatched a fleet of his restless conquistadores just across the narrow Strait of Gibraltar for a looting spree at the wealthy Muslim port of Ceuta. It was just a logical extension of the Christian campaign in Europe. "The Portuguese kings were very keen on the idea of *guerra justa*, a 'just war,' " is the way Hernâni explains it. Which is to say that Christian legal scholars could always rationalize fighting (and enslaving) Muslims. And if the infidels happened to occupy a town bursting with grain and gold, so much the better. Ceuta had become wealthy because it was the outlet for caravan routes that delivered sub-Saharan gold, melegueta pepper, and slaves to the Mediterranean coast. These were then sold to Arab, Genoan, and Catalan merchants, who exchanged them for grain but also for Asian spices brought in from the Levant. Though João's greedy troops had been more or less aware of the loot behind Ceuta's gates before their battering rams splintered them to pieces, they had had only a vague glimmer of where the riches came from. After some unsubtle interrogation of the residents, they now knew. It's worth noting that among the desert-dusted knights who rode into Ceuta were the king's own sons, including the young Henrique, the one later dubbed "the Navigator." The prince, who was subsequently made governor of the colonized city, seemed especially keen on the details of the caravan route.

Hernâni tells me there were no caravels during that first African incursion, but they came into play very soon afterward. Their voyages down the African coast started shortly after the Ceuta conquest, no doubt stimulated by the riches the conquistadores had found, and some of these trips, at least, were under the auspices of Henrique. In many ways, these excursions were just an extension of what Portuguese mariners had been doing for uncounted generations. Lisbon merchantmen had long been sailing the rough Atlantic waters north to Flanders and the Baltic ports with cargoes of olive oil, salt, and oranges. To the south, Portuguese fishermen had traced the African shore for hundreds of miles. Hernâni scoffs when I remind him that the Venetians and Genoans, too, delivered spices to the northern ports. "They stayed by the shore," he corrects me. "We sailed direct across the open sea."

Yet despite the impression given by Aporvela's historian-in-residence, the Portuguese did not discover everything. The Genoans, Catalans, and even the Castilians had sailed out into the broad Atlantic and certainly discovered at least the Canary Islands and Madeira. The very idea of going round Africa to reach the spiceries most likely originated with the Genoese, who were trying to pull one over on the Venetians. Still, however daring, those earlier trips never led to much of anything. It was only when the Portuguese rediscovered the uninhabited islands of Madeira and the Azores far out in the Atlantic that they came to be colonized and exploited on Lisbon's behalf. Extensive sugar plantations were carved into ravines between Madeira's craggy slopes in the early fourteen hundreds. A hundred years later, the Azores became essential for provisioning armadas sailing back and forth from the Americas. In the meantime, as the caravels were sent south past the desert shore and farther south to the jungle coast of Guinea (as most of sub-Saharan Africa was called), they discovered riches only hinted at by the caravans that crossed the dunes.

There is no question that the caravels' main objective was the gold that flowed down West African rivers. But other "goods" were picked up along with the precious cargo, too—most notably, enslaved Africans, ivory, and the "pepper" collected in the backwoods. Melegueta pepper, also known as grains of paradise and Guinea pepper, had been imported into Europe for centuries, mostly via North African ports such as Ceuta. The French, in particular, had an especial fondness for *les graines de paradis*, as fourteenth-century cookbooks such as the *Ménagier de Paris* make abundantly clear, but the African spice was used in other parts of northern Europe, too, mostly to flavor beer and wine. According to medieval physicians, the spice was "hot and moist," and perhaps because of this, it was much appreciated in colder climates. The little grains were, at least for a time, more expensive than Asian black pepper. In Ceuta, melegueta was even used as a local currency (much like peppercorns in Europe), and prices were quoted in gold and melegueta, much as we might say dollars and cents. When caravels replaced camels, the profits from the melegueta trade poured into the Portuguese treasury. The West African spice imports would generate a steady flow of cash well into the sixteenth century, even if the profits never approached the fabulous wealth of the later black pepper imports.* All the same, in Prince Henrique's day, the Portuguese were still only dabbling in the spice trade.

Just when the idea of turning those profitable little trips down the African coast into a concerted effort to round the Cape of Good Hope occurred is unclear. Hernâni insists that it was the Navigator Prince who came up with the idea; still, even he will agree with most other historians that it was Henrique's great-nephew, King João II, who really made reaching Asia by sea a national priority. It was under his watch and with his often-direct supervision that the scheme of circumnavigating the Muslim world for a direct path to India's pepper coast was put into action.

With twenty-twenty hindsight, it's easy to admire the audaciousness of João's plan, the relentless drive down the coast, the investment of enormous treasure to secure a goal that was perhaps a generation in the future. A Venetian of the time would most likely have dismissed the idea as unaccountably reckless, but then no merchant of the great trading republic could have assembled enough investors for this kind of risky adventure— or, for that matter, sacrificed the lives of thousands of his employees to secure such an ephemeral prize. The Portuguese approached the spice trade much as they had the attack on Ceuta, flailing their battle lances and yelling out the war cry *Santiago e a elles!* ("Saint James and at them!"). They could justify every raiding party as an assault against the Moor, each trip up an African river as a scouting party for potential Christian allies. This kind of reasoning might not have cut it in the boardrooms on the Rialto, but at the royal palace in Lisbon, suffused with the ideology of chivalry and holy quests, who could argue with a king whose stated goal was to defeat the infidel and free Jerusalem? To further these ends, each caravel was charged with searching for Prester John, the fabulous Christian ruler who supposedly waited in the Muslims' rear. Of course, it didn't hurt the king's cause that money was pouring in from gold, melegueta,

---

* In the 1620s, Portuguese traders were importing some 140,000 pounds of melegueta, more than any spice other than black pepper and ginger. By the late nineteenth century, some 200,000 pounds were still exported from Ghana alone, though by the First World War, exports from West Africa had virtually ceased. In Ghana and Nigeria, where the spice is still grown, the seeds continue to be used. Not only do they flavor food, but they are also chewed on cold days to warm the body.

and, increasingly, sugar. All the same, João II and his men needed the foolhardiness of conquistadores to stay the course, given all the hardships along the way.

Yet why India? Why pepper? João's kingdom was already profiting handsomely from melegueta, so it could be argued that black pepper was just another lucrative item to add to the product line. For many years, historians asserted that the motivation for Portugal's expansion could be explained by a rise in pepper prices at the end of the fifteenth century. But the numbers do not bear this out; prices actually slid. Moreover, it does not naturally follow that a small maritime nation at the westernmost edge of Europe would decide to expand its trading sphere from the middle Atlantic to India, a spot more than five thousand miles in the opposite direction (and that's as the bird flies, not as the caravel sails).

There's no doubt that the king needed more money for the treasury. The court soaked up mountains of African gold just to keep up appearances: to purchase Florentine woolens, Oriental silks, and Venetian spices. Whereas the royals' relatives in Castile, Burgundy, and England could depend on the receipts from their vast estates and to some degree taxes, the monarchs in Lisbon grew increasingly dependent on their income from overseas to make ends meet. As it was, they were always living beyond their means, needing to borrow money from Italian bankers to pay the bills.

It's worth remembering that Lisbon was directly on the Italian route between the Mediterranean and Flanders. Venetian ships, loaded with spices, would pull up to docks only a few hundred feet distant from João's harbor palace to pick up supplies before continuing north. The king could literally open his window and sniff the precious cargo as the pepper galleys passed by. Hernâni Xavier points out that the Italians, however, had no use for the salt and olive oil that were Portugal's stock-in-trade, so when the royal court needed pepper or cinnamon, it had to pay for the spices with precious African gold.

As in the rest of Europe, the Portuguese elite used to eat food seasoned with saffron, ginger, cloves, and pepper, and especially cinnamon. The earliest Portuguese cookbook that has come down to us apparently traveled with the household of the Infanta Maria, João II's great-niece, when she married into an Italian family. The manuscript, *O livro de cozinha,* has a scattering of recipes that call for the usual medieval masala. To make a dish of lamprey eel, for example, you sauté it and then "add a very small amount of water and vinegar, and sprinkle on cloves, pepper, saffron, and a little ginger." However, the Renaissance *O livro de cozinha* had many fewer of these well-spiced recipes than its Italian and French counterparts. Quite a number of the recipes use no spices at all, and others confine themselves to a finishing sprinkle of sugar and cinnamon. This last touch can probably be credited to the Moorish influence, as is hinted by a recipe for *galinha mourisca* (Moorish chicken).* The fact that the Portuguese had to pay hard cash for their beloved cinnamon may account for the relatively modest use of spices at the time; by the same token, it made the royal household aware firsthand how much money there was to be made in the spice business, a point that was brought home with every royal bite.

The thought must have occurred to João that if his merchants were already turning a neat profit from the melegueta (less expensive than pepper by now), how much more could be earned from wresting the pepper trade from those lagoon-dwelling, money-grubbing collaborators of the Moor. He must also have heard more than one whisper in his ear from the Genoese who had flocked to the Lisbon court. The Venetians' archrivals had long been active across Iberia as bankers, merchants, and mariners. They had also once provided Atlantic Europe with a good portion of its spices, but as the fifteenth century wore on, the Rialto merchants gradually pushed most Genoans out of the spice business. What sweet revenge if Portugal would snatch the spice monopoly from their Adriatic foes! And the Genoans weren't the only Italians to smell opportunities at the Lisbon court. The Florentines were there, too, ready to invest in the lucrative trade at the first opportunity. Yet I wonder if João's men would have made the sacrifices for a more ordinary commodity, for the alum

---

* Moroccans still finish off some main dishes (most famously the pigeon pie called *bisteyaa*) with a sprinkle of cinnamon and sugar. Of course, all medieval European cuisine was heavily indebted to the Arabs, but in the Iberian Peninsula, the influence was much more direct. Portuguese is full of Arabic food words, from *beringela* for eggplant to *açafrão* for saffron, *laranja* for orange, *limão* for lemon, *arroz* for rice, *amêndoa* for almond, *espinafre* for spinach, and *açúcar* for sugar. The sugar and rice cultivated in the southern province of Algarve were another Arabic import.

(used as a mordant in dyeing wool) that made the Genoese piles of money in those days or the barrels of herring that funded the early Dutch republic. Did not the stench of Eden so long associated with spices make them more worthy of the conquistadores' quest?

The idea of circumnavigating Africa must have dawned slowly on the king as Portuguese caravels moved steadily down the Guinea coast, but at some point, the initial motive of the voyages—the search for gold and Prester John—was joined by a concerted strategy to reach the pepper coast of India. To further the plan, João sent spies across the Sahara to Alexandria and as far as Malabar to report what they found. But mostly, he sent the nimble little ships farther south to find their way under unrecognizable stars, past unknown coasts, in search of the southern passage to the Orient. Finally, in early January 1488, two caravels captained by Bartolomeu Dias rounded the cape that João would call the "Cape of Good Hope" for the promise it offered.

During these decades of exploration, Lisbon's state-of-the-art shipyards refined and enlarged their vessels. A document from 1478 mentions a *caravela de descobrir* purpose-built for the voyages of discovery, while a tubbier version called *caravela redonda* became popular for its larger hull capacity. (Columbus's *Niña* and *Pinta* were both *caravelas redondas*.) Eventually, a much larger ship—the *nau*, or carrack—was designed. The *nau* had even more cargo space, thereby making the trip to India worthwhile.

The knowledge of those consummately skilled shipwrights hasn't been entirely lost, or at least not yet. Aporvela was able to build modern-day caravels because there is one remaining shipyard that builds fishing boats much as they have been built for five hundred years. The sailors still sail them as they did in the heroic days of Prince Henrique and Bartolomeu Dias, Hernâni tells me as we clamber off the *Vera Cruz* and say our goodbyes.

A CITY RISES

In the Alfama, the district that rises across the road from Aporvela's trailer office, the smell of grilling fish penetrates every alley and tilted square, especially at lunchtime, when restaurants set up impromptu grills on the sidewalks and the working-class residents jostle elbows at the small tables that spill out onto the streets. The neighborhood gives you a sense of the rather modest place medieval Lisbon must have been before the profits from the black Indian gold transformed the city: a Lisbon of fish-wives more than of God-possessed explorers. Today's local restaurants, however, give virtually no clue as to Lisbon's history as the capital of a spice empire. The fish is exquisitely fresh, the portions are abundant, but as far as spice, it is almost entirely absent, even if there is something vaguely medieval in the buckets of salt the Portuguese use in their cooking. But maybe I shouldn't be looking for remnants of a world-spanning empire in my lunch of fat and delicious sardines. I would do better to look about. The harvest of Lisbon's pepper ships is all around me, in the pink, brown, and black faces of the men at the next table; in the inter-twined light and dark fingers of the couple next to me; in the kinky hair and sea gray eyes. This is where you can see the Christian Portuguese conquerors, the Jews who had fled Isabella's Spain, the North African Moors, and sub-Saharan slaves. Sailors and fishwives still rub shoulders here (and not only shoulders, I expect) as they did when they came back from Cochin and Malacca.

In the fifteen hundreds, Lisbon was one of Europe's greatest cities, a magnet for shipwrights, bankers, and merchants as well as seamen and working girls. It was a metropolis of ornate churches and sumptuous palaces that towered above another city of crowded tenements. Yet, today, that vision of gilded cloisters, tile-covered mansions, and twisting streets of teetering pastel houses is no more in evidence than the Asian aromatics that once used to season *Lisboetas'* fish. Unlike Venice, which continues to float like a mirage from the distant past, or even Amsterdam, where the solid mansions built on the profits of the spice trade still stand to remind you of the Dutch city's glory, the Lisbon you see today was built in a later, shabbier time. The resplendent city built of pepper and gold was almost entirely destroyed by an earthquake on the feast of All Saints on November 1, 1755. Ironically, the neighborhood that survived the earthquake was one of the city's poorest. It is only in the upper reaches of the Alfama—on the steep slopes of the hill where the Romans first built their fortress, where the Moors set their citadel, and where the Christian kings spawned their schemes—that there are still hints of the gilded city that was.

When you look up from the *Vera Cruz,* the medieval houses of the Alfama tumble down the hill without, somehow, managing to look picturesque. In the ancient neighborhood's lower reaches, the buildings are as mangy and unkempt as the cats that lounge in deep pools of shadow. Climbing up the narrow lanes strung with celery green undershorts and custard yellow tank tops, it's all too easy to imagine dodging the foul consequences of women yelling "Àgua, vai!" (Water, go!), as they used to before throwing the contents of their chamber pots out the window.* The crooked passageways of the lower Alfama have always belonged to the city's working poor. Even in the heyday of the Portuguese spice trade, chances are that the grilled fish here never saw most of the Asian seasonings that provided jobs for the locals. Pepper might have been an exception. Hernâni Xavier makes the intriguing suggestion that Lisbon's working classes were able to buy third-rate pepper (ruined on the return voyage) on the cheap, and so it is perfectly conceivable that it was more common then than it is now. What is certain, though, is that up the hill, the aroma of cooking fish would have mingled with cloves and cinnamon.

As you climb the ever-wider stairways toward the crowning citadel of the castle, you leave the leaning tenements behind. The alleys become tidier and larger. Concealed behind some of the old walls, there are clues of the wealth that poured in with the *Carreira da Índia,* the annual convoy that arrived packed with pepper, ginger, cinnamon, and cloves. Through the open door of the Church of Santiago, a single gilded altar that escaped the earthquake's fury still glimmers like a faded beacon from that earlier Midas-touched era. A half-open gate offers a tempting glimpse of a palm-shaded courtyard, the ancient tiled walls a florid tangle of blue, white, and gold. Out in the street, the steps take you higher, past mansions and boutiques filled with antique ceramics.

At the top of the hill, the tallest of Lisbon's seven-odd peaks, the citadel, the Castelo de São Jorge, towers over the skyline. The castle itself is fake, constructed in the 1940s by the fascist-leaning government of the time in a postcard-perfect, medieval style that Prince Valiant would be

---

* João II should not be remembered solely for his efforts to secure the spice route. In 1484, he ordered that measures be taken against the "overturning of chamber pots." The contents of these were supposed to be disposed of in "reserved places," such as the beaches. He even ordered the construction of a sewage system the same year Bartolomeu Dias sailed for the Cape of Good Hope, though with little result. A hundred years ago, many of Lisbon's poorer districts still lacked indoor plumbing, and the cry "Àgua, vai!" still echoed through the alleys.

proud to call home. The current structure completely obscures a succession of older hilltop fortresses built by the Romans, the Muslims, and the conquering Portuguese. As you pause atop the crenellated towers with the other out-of-breath tourists, you can see why this would be the perfect place to build a fortress. Below, the river Tejo forms an estuary as it approaches the Atlantic Ocean, which makes it an almost ideal port. It is shaped like a bottle, the neck facing the Atlantic and the city occupying one of the shoulders. The Phoenicians called it "Ubis Ubbo" (Gentle Bay) when they settled here. Under the Romans, that turned into "Olisippo" or "Olissipum" (thus, Lisbon). They called the natives Lusitanians, a name later revived by the poets of the Renaissance.

The last invaders to take the hill were a force of northern Portuguese conquistadores in 1147, led by King Afonso Henriques and assisted by a Frankish band of Jerusalem-bound Crusaders (described by one Christian observer as "plunderers, drunkards and rapists . . . men not seasoned with the honey of piety"). Given its ideal location, Lisbon soon became the country's main market, then, in 1260, its capital. From their hilltop aerie, the kings could overlook the sails multiplying on the wide green Tejo and peer down to see growing mountains of merchandise loaded and unloaded on the docks below.

Under the Christian monarchs, the city grew beyond the confines of the castle hill as ad hoc streets and squares spread across the surrounding peaks and valleys. Between 1400 and 1600, the city's population more than doubled. Not that the rest of Portugal saw much benefit from the yellow and the black gold that was unloaded on Lisbon's docks only to be immediately reloaded onto ships headed to London or Antwerp. Lisbon was increasingly the shining city on the hill surrounded by a country of shantytowns. But that only made it more of an attraction for the peasants and artisans who flocked here. Naturally, it wasn't merely needy agricultural laborers and skilled craftsmen who were lured by the city's wealth. Clerics, squires, and sycophants milled around the tiled courtyards by the castle walls to sniff out any opportunity of advancement. *Fidalgos* bowed and preened to train for any potentially lucrative appointments.* The

---

* *Fidalgo* derives from *filho d'algo*—literally, the "son of somebody"—though it later became a generic term for nobility.

path to fortune was different here than in Venice or any of the Italian merchant republics. Here, everything depended on royal favor. If you wanted to advance your career as a soldier, merchant, or priest, you needed the monarch's blessing. For the king, it was an expensive proposition. By 1500, Manuel I was providing for some four thousand retainers at his court alone. It's no wonder the Portuguese royals were always on the lookout for a new revenue stream.

As profits from African gold and Indian pepper increasingly flowed up the Tejo, it was more than symbolic when Manuel moved his residence down from the *castelo* to the riverbank Paço Real da Ribeira, right in the middle of the harbor. Just east of the palace, a broad beach swarmed with longshoremen off-loading foreign slaves, sugar, spices, and gold even while boats were packed with domestic oil, dried fish, and salt. A few hundred yards to the west were giant dry docks, where the groans of bending timbers and the pounding of hammers kept the monarch's windows rattling from morning to dusk. The kings, who prided themselves on their crusading zeal, now lived much like shopkeepers who set up house above their store to keep an eye on the merchandise. King François I of France had a point when he dismissed his Portuguese counterpart as "le roi épicier" (in French, *épicier* means both grocer and spice seller). The jibe must have stung, though, and it explains, at least in part, the Lusitanian rulers' chronic need to mix a judicious dose of evangelism into their commerce, to search for Christians as well as spices.

BEYOND GOOD HOPE

Looking down from the *castelo,* it would appear no more than a quick scramble to the Praça do Comércio, where the king's harborside palace used to stand. In fact, it is a long, circuitous descent down winding alleys and precipitous stairs. These days, the vast, charmless square is mostly desolate except for the occasional camera-toting visitor and the itinerant street peddler hawking fake Armani sunglasses. Under the grocer king and his immediate successors, this used to be the royal residence's busy front yard and was accordingly referred to as Terreiro do Paço (literally, "Palace Grounds"). Old illustrations show grand parades in honor of visiting potentates filling the field. Temporary grandstands were erected here to give a better view of heretics burned alive at the frequent and well-attended autos-da-fé. I've been told that visitors occasionally comment on the resemblance of the Praça do Comércio to the Piazza San Marco. It is true that both are more or less right on the water, both have monotonous three-story neoclassical façades defining three sides. There are no famous cafés here, though, and no pigeons. Nevertheless, it's worth noting that Lisbon, just like Venice, turns her back to the mainland to greet the sea. And in much the way the doge's palace stood guard over the Adriatic harbor, the king's palace stood sentry at his realm's front gate.

But the Portuguese monarch was a different sort of creature than the CEO of Venice Inc. It's almost as if the local topography reflected the way decisions were made in each town. Like Lisbon's tumbling vertical façade, here, all the power and the glory cascaded down from the king, while in Venice (and Amsterdam, too, for that matter), wealth and influence spread horizontally, much as the watery city spread across the lagoon. But that may just explain why the Portuguese pioneered the direct route to India. It's hard to see how anyone but an absolute monarch could have mustered the resources necessary to get the job done.

At Lisbon's Museu de Arte Antiga, there is a series of fifteenth-century panels that might as well be a family portrait. Here is Henrique, the Navigator Prince, doughy and wry. Nearby is his nephew King Afonso V in a fabulous tunic of purple and green velvet with his wife, Isabel, in a gorgeous scarlet dress. (It makes you wonder how many shiploads of melegueta paid for those fabulous outfits.) Their son, the future João II, is just behind his father—a pudgy preteen with tousled hair. His almond eyes show no hint of his later Machiavellian streak. Yet who knows how far the Lusitanians would have gone if it hadn't been for this ruthless and determined young man? At the time, not everyone in Portugal thought the Atlantic explorations were a good idea. King Afonso, for one, was never much interested in the Indian project. João, though, had none too subtle ways of convincing his opposition. Once he assumed the throne in 1481, he beheaded his most prominent opponents. An uncooperative bishop perished in a cistern. João personally stabbed to death one of his detractors. Even before he sat in his father's seat, he was, by all accounts, fixated with reaching India. The obsession was apparently born some years earlier when, as crown prince, he secured the African spice and gold monopoly from the king. Then, once he held the reins of power, João II pursued the search for a southern passage to India with all his resources. And finally, when Bartolomeu Dias rounded the Cape of Good Hope, the way to India's perfumed riches was clear.

Among the many hangers-on at Paço da Ribeira during João II's rule was a Genoese navigator named Christopher Columbus. He had married into a Portuguese family* and had his own ideas about reaching the Spice Islands. Contrary to what you may have been taught in elementary school, educated people did not think the world was flat in the Renaissance. There was, however, no consensus about just how big the globe was. According to one eminent Florentine geographer of the time, the earth was some ten thousand miles around the equator. (The actual distance is closer to twenty-five thousand.) Using this number, Columbus made the perfectly reasonable calculation that you could get to the Indies much faster by sailing west than by going south and east. There is some indication that João didn't cotton much to the Italian adventurer on a personal level, but what eventually damned his proposal in Portuguese eyes was the preposterousness of the numbers. The frequent trips down the coast of Africa had given Portuguese navigators a pretty good sense of how big the earth was from pole to pole. If Columbus's numbers were to be believed, the earth would have the improbable shape of an upended football. All the same, the king apparently took the idea seriously enough to have a commission look into it. They gave it a thumbs-down.

There may have been another reason why João was none too interested in going west. He may already have known what was there. Hernâni Xavier, for one, is convinced that two Portuguese maps show Brazil as early as the 1430s. But even if those maps are discounted, other circumstantial evidence all but proves that the Portuguese had at least some idea of the Americas before Columbus's voyage. Portuguese sailors certainly spent the years between Dias's discovery of the cape route and da Gama's epochal voyage exploring the southern Atlantic, and given the currents and winds, it's almost impossible that they didn't at least sight South America. This is the likely reason why, in the 1494 treaty of Tordesillas,

---

* In a book called *The Portuguese Columbus: Secret Agent of King John II,* a respected Portuguese academic has made the assertion that Christopher Columbus was in fact Portuguese rather than Italian. However, this is distinctly a minority view.

which divided up the world between Portugal and Spain, João fought tooth and nail to have the dividing line moved west. This just happened to place Brazil in the Portuguese sphere—six years before Brazil was officially discovered! But, at least for the moment, João knew that he did not have the resources to simultaneously explore a new world and pursue the pepper project in the East.

Spurned in Lisbon, Columbus went knocking on Isabella's door in neighboring Castile, talked the queen into backing his plan, and the rest, as they say, is history. It all seems inevitable now, the partnership of Columbus and Isabella and the subsequent Spanish conquest of the New World, but at the time, it seemed an unlikely scenario. The Castilians had never been especially interested in the Atlantic, busy as they were with conquests back home. But once Dias had shown the feasibility of the cape route, the Spanish monarchs must have felt a certain urgency to act so that they wouldn't lose out to their neighbors in any potential spice bonanza. This insecurity, this need to keep up with the Joãos, must have helped convince the queen next door to invest in the Genoan's scheme. Columbus, in the meantime, was so convinced of his numbers that even after several trips to the West Indies, he would never admit that he had not found the fabled East. Not only did he insist on calling the indigenous peoples "Indians" and their islands the "Indies," he came back with spices that he called pepper (*pimienta*), which were in fact capsicums and allspice. (The Spanish continue to call the latter *pimienta dulce* or *pimienta de Jamaica*.) Isabella was not impressed. When she found out that Vasco da Gama had returned from Calicut with the real thing, she sent for Columbus, who was on his third voyage to the Antilles at the time. Subsequently, the Genoan was brought home in chains and stripped of his titles and income. As far as the Castilian queen was concerned, his voyages were failures, the route to the Indies and their aromatic riches now in firm possession of the Portuguese. In Lisbon, Vasco da Gama would receive precisely the same titles (in imitation of the Castilian model) that Columbus had lost: those of admiral and viceroy of India.

Vasco da Gama set sail from the Lisbon suburb of Restelo on July 8, 1497, with a small flotilla of two *naus*, the *São Gabriel* and *São Rafael*, and a caravel, the *Bérrio*, dispatched by the king, according to an anonymous chronicler of the voyage, "to make discoveries and go in search of spices."

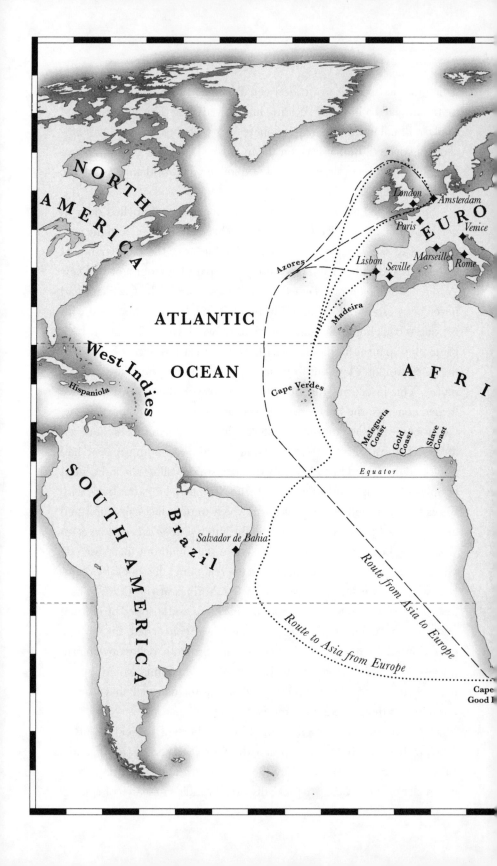

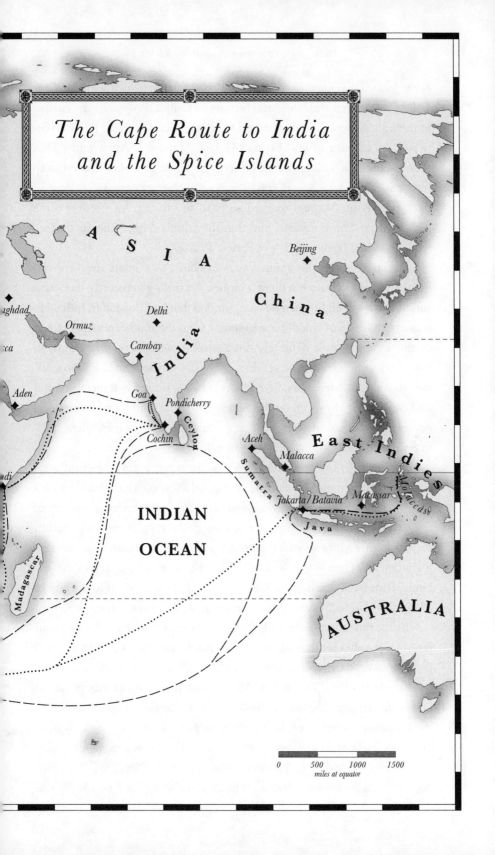

The Cape Route to India
and the Spice Islands

King João II was fated never to see those sails emblazoned with the Crusaders' cross swell with the Atlantic wind. He had died two years earlier, at the age of forty. The day he had been planning for all his life was witnessed by his cousin and brother-in-law, Manuel I. Apparently, João didn't think much of his wife's brother (he made an aborted attempt to have his illegitimate son declared heir), which may explain, at least in part, why King Manuel worked so hard to outstrip his predecessor's legacy. It must have rankled him that they dubbed him "the Fortunate" while João had been called "the Perfect Prince."

We know quite a lot about Vasco da Gama's fortunate royal patron, but the young explorer is a bit of a cipher. According to records, da Gama was only twenty-eight when he commanded that first mission to India. He was a middle son of middling aristocracy from the southern seaport town of Sines. While most definitely not a professional seaman, he seems to have had some experience serving in coastal missions under João's administration. In later years, he had a reputation for being temperamental and capricious. However, on this first journey, the young captain-general comes across as so cautious as to verge on paranoia—at least when dealing with the locals in the Indian Ocean.

Da Gama's ships carried provisions for three years, guns and gunners, interpreters, musicians and priests, and a few convicts (death-row inmates who had their sentences commuted to naval service) for some of the riskier tasks. The commander also carried a royal letter addressed to Prester John. Oddly, given its ostensible mission, the armada was surprisingly devoid of trade goods. The ships set course straight across the Atlantic, then back down to the Cape of Good Hope, and up to the city of Malindi, about halfway up Africa's eastern coast in what is today's Kenya.

By the time they reached Malindi on the eve of Easter 1498, more than nine months after setting sail, da Gama's sailors had been suffering weeks of dehydration and dying of scurvy left and right. Several close calls with none-too-friendly natives along the East African coast had convinced them that no one could be trusted, so even in Malindi, where their reception was cordial, the Lusitanian adventurers kept a wary distance. Here, they took on fresh food and water, and equally important, they hired a Gujarati pilot to guide them across the Indian Ocean to Calicut. The pilot, though Muslim, supposedly even spoke some Italian! The rest of the trip was thankfully un-

The Portuguese did not make a great impression on the locals when they arrived in India.

eventful. The fleet reached Calicut in a mere twenty-six days on May 18, 1498, arriving just in time to be drenched by the southern Indian monsoon.

What came next was more farce than high drama. After his close shaves along the African coast, da Gama had no intention of putting himself at risk. That's what the onboard convicts were for. So the first Portuguese conquistadores sent out to meet the legendary Indians were a couple of jailbirds. When they finally tracked down someone they could talk to, they also turned out to be foreigners—mainly, two Tunisians who just happened to speak Castilian and Genoese. Not surprisingly, the Arabs were none too pleased to see these all-too-familiar infidels. "May the Devil take you! What brought you here?" was their unsubtle greeting. To which the cons offered the oft-quoted reply "We come in search of Christians and of spices." That first Calicut visit was not terribly successful on either account. Later visits would prove much more lucrative—at least, when it came to the spices.

The following weeks saw the Portuguese slogging back and forth through the rain-soaked streets between the harbor and the royal palace. During their first visit, they could barely move because of the thick crowds who had come to gawk at this novel species of foreigner. Early on, the local ruler, the zamorin, had been quite favorably inclined toward the newcomers. He even granted da Gama a long interview, in which the potentate punctuated his sentences by expelling great gobs of betel juice and saliva into a royal-sized golden spittoon. But subsequently, the zamorin thought better of it and had the Europeans detained. Then he changed his mind and released them, and then once more locked them up. Da Gama spent several intermittent weeks fuming under house arrest, at a loss to figure out what was going on. He had arrived with the firm belief that the zamorin was a Christian, and now he wasn't going to let mere facts get in the way. The Portuguese were so convinced they had found their longed-for coreligionists that they took the Hindu temples for churches. These "churches," according to the chronicler, were decorated with "saints" wearing crowns and "painted variously, with teeth protruding an inch from the mouth, and four or five arms." Naturally, the only explanation for the zamorin's behavior could be that it was caused by his malevolent courtiers, the perfidious Moors.

You need not be a religious bigot to understand why the Muslim traders ensconced in Calicut wanted to get rid of the Europeans. Still, the conquistadores didn't make it any easier for themselves. While it's hardly surprising that courses in comparative religion would not be part of an aspiring *fidalgo*'s curriculum, it also seems that neither were the ABCs of business etiquette. The zamorin's commercial representatives reportedly burst into peals of laughter when they saw the presents the Europeans had brought for their master. "The poorest merchant from Mecca, or any other part of India, would give more," they sniggered. (The Portuguese chronicle of the voyage itemizes twelve pieces of cotton cloth, four scarlet hoods, six hats, four strings of coral, six washbasins, a case of sugar, two casks of oil, and two of honey as the sum total of the gifts for a ruler who used gold even for his cuspidor.) The Hindu potentate was not amused.

In the end, though, the two sides reached a compromise, no doubt aided by the fact that the Portuguese grabbed a few hostages of their own. So for the last few weeks, da Gama could supervise the trading operation from the safety of his own cabin. His men took advantage of this time to rummage through their chests to find anything and everything that they could hock in the Calicut spice market. The sailors went so far as to literally sell the shirts off their backs in order to buy pepper and cloves. The sweaty linen tops were apparently worth a lot less money here than back home, but then spices were even cheaper. The captain-general got to hold on to his clothes, but he did part with his personal supply of silver cups and other tableware, which he traded in for a hefty cargo of spices and precious stones.

All in all, this first European expedition to Asia didn't make much of an impression on the locals. Just to make sure the foreigners would be less confused in the future, the zamorin sent them off with a letter spelling out just what he wanted to see next time they arrived: "My country is rich in cinnamon, cloves, ginger, pepper and precious stones. That which I ask of you in exchange is gold, silver, corals and scarlet cloth." Future visitors, including da Gama himself, got the message. In the interim, though, the Portuguese had to survive the return voyage home. Not many did.

When da Gama's ships finally limped back to the quiet waters of the Tejo in the summer of 1499, they were down to 55 men of the original crew of perhaps 170. Just how much spice they brought home is impossible to say, since most of it was in the hands of the officers and crew. There must have been at least several thousand pounds' worth of pepper, ginger, cinnamon, cloves, and nutmeg on board—enough, at any rate, that the king awarded da Gama a bonus of more than a ton of spices while the surviving sailors received a couple of hundred pounds each. Still, it's unlikely the crown made a profit on this particular voyage. But at least King Manuel now had plenty of firsthand intelligence. He knew that a hundred-pound bag of pepper selling for sixteen ducats in Venice could be had for two in Calicut, and what was perhaps even more important to the heir of the Crusader kings, he also had eyewitnesses (however deluded) who swore that India was crawling with Christians.

The king embraced the returning mariners as heroes. They were paraded through the streets, and Vasco da Gama was the toast of the town. Manuel "the Fortunate" quickly dispatched the news to courts across Europe. In a jubilant letter sent a bare forty-eight hours after the India fleet's return, the Portuguese ruler announced to Isabella and Ferdinand, the joint monarchs of Castile and Aragon, the Portuguese "discovery" of the (real) India, where his men had found great quantities of cloves, cinnamon, and other spices, to say nothing of "rubies and all kinds of precious stones." (No wonder Isabella got so ticked off at Columbus just then.) He bragged that he would sweep the Indian Ocean clear of the infidel and, with the help of the Indian Christians, take over the spice trade. He even had the chutzpah to give himself a new title, "Lord of Guinea [that is,

Africa] and of the conquest of the navigation and commerce of Ethiopia, Arabia, Persia and India." That would stick it in the eye of anyone who thought he wasn't good enough to succeed João II!

In the following ten years or so, Manuel actually came close to living up to the terms of his boastful title. As soon as da Gama came home, preparations were made for another expedition, this one much bigger, better armed, and most important, better supplied with the silver that Indians wanted in exchange for their black gold. This was the 1500 armada led by Pedro Álvares Cabral that just happened to discover Brazil during a brief stopover on the way to India. But Cabral was even less of a diplomat than da Gama. When he finally reached Calicut, he quickly got into an altercation with the local Muslim merchants. This escalated into an all-out bombardment of the zamorin's capital. Needless to say, Calicut was not very receptive to trading with the Portuguese after that. However, the attack endeared Cabral to the zamorin's enemies.

In Cochin, the Europeans were greeted with open arms and allowed to buy spices by the ton: mostly, the local pepper, but also cinnamon brought in from nearby Ceylon and cloves and nutmeg from the distant Spice Islands of Indonesia. This second trip showed even more promise than the first. After all, the fleet returned home with some half million pounds of spices aboard (presumably, mostly in the form of pepper), and it did discover Brazil. But at what cost? Manuel couldn't have cared less about the beaches of Ipanema. His concern was those blessed Christians, and Cabral came back with the truth this time. Now the king knew that the longed-for fifth column in the Moor's rear was an illusion. What's more, Cabral had lost half the fleet along the way. Hundreds of men had died, and it wasn't even clear that the crown made a profit on the trip. Manuel complained to the Venetian ambassador that he had lost eighty thousand ducats on the venture—though, admittedly, that figure should be taken with a grain of salt, given his audience. Still, to put this into context, that half million pounds of spices brought back by what remained of an original fleet of fifteen ships was roughly equivalent to the average load of a *single* Venetian galley returning from Alexandria at the time. Whatever the actual numbers, Manuel was not pleased and never gave Cabral another commission. There were apparently many at court who thought the whole project should be abandoned. But Manuel had staked too much on it to give up just yet.

The next two trips—in particular, another large expedition led by da Gama—proved so fabulously profitable that from now on, an annual fleet left Lisbon for India's Malabar Coast. In many ways, the Portuguese modeled their approach on ideas developed by Venetians in their spice trade. There was the same thuggish behavior, the same brutal enforcement of the spice monopoly. Nevertheless, though the design may have been similar, Manuel and his men were drawing on a much larger canvas. The Portuguese set up fortified *feitorias* (trading posts) at strategic points from West Africa to the Moluccas. Unilaterally, Lisbon declared a monopoly in trading pepper throughout the whole Indian Ocean and proceeded to seize or sink any ship that wouldn't cooperate. Along the way, the sea-hardened conquistadores seized Ormuz, the critical lump of rock that controlled the entrance to the Persian Gulf; captured Goa, about halfway up India's western coast; and took Molucca (near present-day Singapore), which commanded the sea-lanes between the East Indies and points west.

With their paltry resources, at least six months' and perhaps seventeen thousand miles' journey from home, that the Portuguese more or less succeeded seems nothing short of miraculous. King Manuel's men certainly thought so and credited their God. More objective observers might note that the Europeans also had other things going their way. When the Portuguese arrived in the Indian Ocean, most of the spice trade was in the hands of loosely organized merchants, mostly Muslim, North Indian Gujaratis. A good part of northern and central India was in the process of being overrun by the Moguls sweeping down from central Asia, while Egypt was succumbing to the Turkish Ottomans. Both of these ascendant powers were vastly more powerful than the underresourced kingdom on Europe's western promontory. However, they were almost entirely land-based empires with no navies worthy of the name.* The masterful Lisbon shipwrights had no competition to speak of on the open seas, and Por-

---

* It's tempting to speculate what might have happened if the Portuguese had arrived seventy-five years earlier, when the Ming admiral Cheng Ho was leading Chinese armadas of one hundred to two hundred ships to Southeast Asia and Ceylon, and the Chinese maintained an official network of trade relations from Malindi to Japan. For reasons that are not entirely clear, Beijing not only decided to stop the expeditions in the 1430s but imposed a blanket ban on overseas trade by Chinese nationals. Even the building of new oceangoing ships was forbidden.

tuguese gunnery was state-of-the-art in its day. The Muslim merchants' ships carried no heavy artillery. They were less maneuverable, and their all-wood construction made them crumple up like balsa wood when smashed by Portuguese cannonballs. In 1513, the adroit Portuguese admiral Albuquerque boasted to his king that "at the rumor of our coming, the native ships all vanished, and even the birds ceased to skim over the water." In point of fact, plenty of smuggling went on, especially in the later years, more often than not with Portuguese collusion.

While Lisbon's caravels, galleons, and *naus* rode unchallenged on the waves, on land it was another matter. Here, the Portuguese never established anything even vaguely resembling an empire along the lines of the Spanish land-based conquests in the Americas. In Asia, the Lusitanians wrested a few square miles here, a couple of acres there—little more than supply stops for their spice armadas.

All the same, the arrival of the *naus* didn't just gum up the works of Muslim commerce in the Indian Ocean. It had serious repercussions for the Arabs' main trading partners in the Mediterranean, the Venetians. At first, the traders on the Rialto were nonplussed, reassured by the fact that what was now referred to as the "Calicut voyage" had been a financial bust. The Cabral voyage seemed only to confirm their theory that it was just a matter of time before the Portuguese monarch would give up on the Indian money pit. Others were less sanguine. Girolamo Priuli, himself a spice trader of note, wrote in his diary only weeks after Cabral's return, "I can clearly see the ruin of the city of Venice, because without the [spice] trade the city will lose its money, the source of Venice's glory and reputation."

Above and beyond the dispatches from Lisbon, the Venetians had more immediate, and probably more serious, concerns closer to home. While news of da Gama's return to Lisbon trickled back to Italy, war had broken out between the Republic and the Ottoman Empire. This was a disaster for the spice trade, which depended on those very ports—Alexandria in Egypt, Aleppo in Syria—that were now (or would shortly be) under Istanbul's rule.* Before the war, the Venetians' annual spice

---

* The Ottoman takeover of Mamluk Egypt in 1516–17 seems to have been aided and abetted by the massive fall in Egyptian revenue derived from taxing the spice trade that occurred when the Portuguese enforced their spice monopoly in the early years of the century.

convoy averaged some 1.5 million pounds of pepper (a little more than
half the total spice cargo), but ten years after da Gama's first trip, Venice's
combined spice imports were a bare third of what they had been before.
The difference was now made up in Lisbon, which was bringing in something like five times as much spice as the city of Saint Mark. As a final hu-
miliation, in 1515, Venice had to sail up the Tejo to buy spices for her
customers. Things eventually got so bad that in 1527, the Venetian senate
offered to buy the spice monopoly of the Portuguese crown, a proposal
that was looked into with at least some seriousness at the Paço da Ribeira,
though the two sides could never agree on the terms.

Venice's Italian competitors were chortling with glee to see the
mighty Queen of the Adriatic put in her place. A Florentine resident in
Lisbon at the time smirked that the Venetians would be reduced back to
catching fish for a living. The opinion among historians has gone back
and forth over the years as to whether the Portuguese blockade of the
Indian sea route or the war in the Middle East had the more severe impact on Venetian trade, but however you weigh the causes (everyone
agrees that it was a mixture of both), the result was that the Republic of
Saint Mark seemed to be all washed up in the spice trade. Or so it appeared to observers in the first couple of decades of the sixteenth century. Yet, by the 1530s, Istanbul, Alexandria, and the Levant reopened to
the Europeans, and the Rialto traders were back in business. The Portuguese had never really been up to the job of controlling all the shipping in the Indian Ocean. They had not managed to plug up the Red
Sea route. And while they had a more or less tight grip on the Malabar
Coast, they had virtually no say in what went on in Java, Sumatra, or the
Spice Islands. As a consequence, tons of pepper slid through their fingers
(often as a result of well-greased palms) on their way to the eastern
Mediterranean. By the end of the final years of the sixteenth century, al-
most as much pepper was sailing past the Lido as was unloaded on the
Lisbon waterfront.

Still, the Portuguese king was making a tidy profit, at least for a time.
The half dozen or so ships that arrived yearly on the *Carreira da Índia* (the
flotilla from Cochin) unloaded millions of pounds of spice—somewhere
on the order of 2 to 3 million pounds in the early years and at least twice
that later on. More than 80 percent of this would have been pepper, with

cinnamon, ginger, cloves, nutmeg, and mace making up the bulk of the rest.*

Commentators often remark on the smallness of Portugal and the enormity of its achievements. But that's just it: it's only when you take that very smallness (and poverty) into account that you can begin to understand why the Portuguese were so willing to risk their shirts—it's all they had. To the kings of France, with a population (and tax base) ten times that of Portugal, the profit rung up in the pepper trade would have amounted to only a small percentage of their takings. For the Mogul emperor ruling more than a hundred million Indians, it would have been chump change. However, for the impecunious country of Portugal, spices became even more valuable than African gold. King Manuel I was making twice as much money from the spice trade as from precious metals. When his daughter Isabella was betrothed to the Hapsburg emperor Charles V in 1521, her dowry was paid largely in sacks of pepper. In the case of Manuel's son João III, fully one-half of his revenue came from reexporting the African and Asian spices that his father's men had fought so hard to purloin. For the Portuguese kings, it was worth mobilizing all the resources of their little kingdom to secure the shriveled black berries for which Europeans were willing to pay good money. As a result, pepper became the currency that paid for the Lusitanian empire. Yet it wasn't just emperors who were paid off in pepper. Captains, officers, and even cabin boys received part of their wages in the form of spices.

The Caixa

Lisbon is full of sailors. Still, I had not expected that my official tour guide at the Museu de Marinha would greet me at the entry of the naval museum decked out in the glimmering white of a Portuguese navy uniform. Despite his outfit, it turns out that the navy does not pay Lieutenant Bruno Gonçalves Neves to serve upon the roiling seas but rather to dig through dusty archives. I soon realize that the young officer's polite, mili-

---

* We have the details of a cargo from 1518, which, out of a total of close to 5 million pounds, included some 4.7 million pounds of pepper, 12,000 pounds of cloves, 3,000 pounds of cinnamon, and about 2,000 pounds of mace. The amount of pepper is likely accurate, since its traffic was tightly controlled, though a great deal more of the other spices must have arrived in sailors' personal chests.

tary demeanor has done nothing to discipline his fascination with bizarre detail that is every historian's stock-in-trade. As he leads me into the gallery devoted to "the age of discovery," he makes sure to point out the location of the storerooms and kitchens on the elaborately detailed ships' models—mostly, it seems, so that he can expound (with barely a flicker of amusement in his earnest brown eyes) on the rats and ship's biscuit worms that must have made up a good share of common seamen's protein ration after several months on board. Lieutenant Neves has made the *Carreira da Índia* his specialty, and he is more than happy to share its every grisly detail.

He steers me past the display cases full of Lilliputian *naus* and caravels to a large, ornate wooden crate, about the size of an old-fashioned telephone booth set on its side. It was these *caixas de liberdade*—these "liberty chests," he notes breezily—that really kept the East India fleet afloat. "You see, the Portuguese kings could never afford to pay their sailors a decent wage," he explains, "so instead of an adequate salary, they got to fill these boxes with spice." He searches for the right word. "It was like a tip or a bonus." Crown employees could transport what they wished in the *caixas*, free of duty or freight charges, a little like the duty-free allowance that overseas tourists have today. The chests were a regulation size, and seamen were awarded one or more *caixas* depending on their rank—a nice little bonus if they came back filled with pepper but a princely gratuity if they returned packed with cinnamon. The finely carved crate at the museum must have belonged to an officer and could hold close to a ton of pepper, worth some six hundred ducats on the Lisbon market, or more than twice that value if it held cinnamon.* A captain was entitled to almost ten tons of spice, while a common sailor could bring home about three hundred pounds, an amount worth several years' wages if his *caixa* was filled with one of the more expensive spices. A big wooden box full of cloves at least begins to explain why someone would endure the hardships involved in the passage to India.

In the words of an Italian Jesuit who made the trip in 1574, the *Carreira da Índia* was "without doubt the greatest and most arduous [journey] of any that are known in the world." It was more difficult by several orders of magnitude than anything Italians engaged in the Mediterranean

---

* Skilled craftsmen would have to work about eight years to earn that kind of money.

spice trade had to endure. An earlier Portuguese historian had boasted that the navigation of the ancients was as child's play compared to what the Portuguese accomplished. As far as he was concerned, the legendary Argonauts were barely better than weekend sailors, traveling a mere three hundred to five hundred leagues, "dining in one port, supping in another, consuming many refreshments, and stopping frequently for water, with the result that their voyages were more of a pastime than toil." Though the comparison is a little over-the-top, Lieutenant Neves assures me that you could hardly overstate the perils of the India route.*

There are plenty of firsthand accounts of the miseries of the *carreira*, but ask a Portuguese navy historian to suggest a good source on the cape spice route, and he will inevitably point you to a book written by a Dutchman. The little Iberian kingdom never produced enough sailors to man every spritsail and ratline in its navy, and as a result, it had long been common for other nationals to join up—though, in this case, if the higher-ups had known the consequences, they would never have let this particular foreigner on board.

The book was written by Jan Huyghen van Linschoten, a Netherlander who had grown up in the little port town of Enkhuizen in the north of Holland. The sixteen-year-old Jan left home to seek his fortune in Seville, where his brothers had relocated earlier. He arrived in 1580, just in time to witness the Spanish annexation of Portugal. A couple of years later, with the help of one of the brothers, he managed to find a position in the entourage of the newly appointed archbishop of Goa and sailed for India. Then, after spending some nine years abroad, he returned home, where he wrote down his observations. The resulting exposé of the Estado da Índia turned out to be a bestseller, not only in Holland but in England and France, too. The book was full of information that Lisbon considered state secrets. Any Portuguese who wrote what Linschoten did would have been quickly relieved of his head. And with good reason. The Dutch later used Linschoten's book as an instruction manual on how to beat the Portuguese at their own game.

---

* There were inevitably dissenting opinions on this matter. The Italian merchant Filippo Sassetti, arriving in Cochin on the *carreira* in the 1580s, wrote home that it was less dangerous to travel from Lisbon to India than from Barcelona to Genoa. No doubt he was thinking of the pirates swarming in the Mediterranean in his day.

There is more to the book, though, than just the dry data of the secretive spice trade. The twenty-eight-year-old Dutchman managed to combine a shopkeeper's attention to detail with a social scientist's curiosity, so that even while he gave his readers a comprehensive catalog of hardheaded business information, he also included an almost anthropological survey of foreign lands and cultures. And, for good measure, a dose of sex seasoned the mix. He explained the commodities needed to buy pepper (gold), the best places to buy spices (Cochin and Malacca), but then he also revealed, in intimate detail, the libidinous escapades of Goa's mestiza women.*

His description of his outward voyage to India is delightfully informative. Not only does he give the breakdown of the wages paid to just about every one of the five hundred men on board, he tells us what they got to eat and drink. (The translation dates from 1598.)

> All the officers and other persons which sayle in the ship . . . have for their portion every day in victuals, each man a like, as well the greatest as the least, a pound and three quarters of Biskit, halfe a Can of Wine [probably the Portuguese *canada*, equaling 1.4 liters], a Can of water, an Arroba which is 32 pound of salt flesh the moneth, some dryed fish, onyons and garlicke are eaten in the beginning of the voyage, as being of small valew, other provisions, as Suger, Honny, Reasons, Prunes, Ryse, and such like, are kept for those which are sicke: yet they get but little thereof, for that the officers keepe it for themselves . . . as for the dressing

---

* Linschoten gives the impression that he had done firsthand research in this particular field. But then the Hollander wasn't alone in noting the Lusitanians' sexual mores. In 1550, a scandalized Italian Jesuit missionary wrote from India that "the Portuguese have adopted the vices and customs of the land without reserve, including this evil custom of buying droves of slaves, male and female. . . . There are countless men who buy droves of girls and sleep with all of them, and subsequently sell them. There are innumerable married settlers who have four, eight, or ten female slaves and sleep with all of them, as is common knowledge. This is carried to such excess that there was one man in Malacca who had twenty-four women of various races, all of whom were his slaves, and all of whom he enjoyed. I quote this city because it is a thing that everyone knows. Most men, as soon as they can afford to buy a female slave, almost invariably use her as a girl-friend (*amiga*), besides many other dishonesties, in my poor understanding."

[cooking] of their meate, wood, pots, and pans, every man must
make his owne provision.

The ships of the *Carreira da Índia* were a far cry from the little caravels
that had slipped in and out of African coves. They were vessels of five
hundred, six hundred, even one thousand tons that were constructed like
giant wooden warehouses with a modest-sized town perched on top. On
the outgoing trip, they might hold anywhere between five hundred and a
thousand people in a space about the size of a large American suburban
house. The upper-class passengers, officers, and clergy could count on
proportionately more room, leaving the rest packed even tighter. Yet on a
ship swarming with six hundred people, no more than a quarter were
likely to be involved in sailing the ship. The rest had a half year or more
on their hands: months of boredom, seasickness, malnutrition, and
stench ("stinking ayre, and filth," as Linschoten puts it). There were usually lots of priests and friars aboard, on their way to save the unbelievers,
and at least some of them tried to make sure the Devil did not find too
much work for idle hands on the long voyage to India. The way Lieutenant
Neves explains it, priests acted a little like the entertainment directors
aboard cruise ships. They put on pageants and organized processions, to
say nothing of keeping the passengers occupied attending frequent
masses. Nevertheless, gambling seems to have filled much of the time between prayers—in spite of priests' efforts to quench it. There were very
few women on board—a dozen or less was typical—and given the Portuguese penchant for sequestering their wives and daughters, they must
have been cooped up even more than normal. The sexual climate on
board ship would have been much like what you'd find in a twenty-first-
century American penitentiary. Cabin boys reportedly tied their trousers
with a stout rope if they did not wish to wake up sodomized to the tropical dawn.

As weeks turned into months, conditions worsened. In the first few
weeks, the food must have been plentiful and even rather elaborate for the
upper classes. We have several accounts of food brought aboard by Jesuit
priests. One clergyman brought with him some seventy-five liters of wine,
a whole smoked pig, fifty (live) chickens, fifty sides of pork ribs, seventy
pounds of beef, seventy hakes, a hundred dogfish (all presumably salted),

sweets, dried fruits, olive oil, butter, and "one pound of each spice"—and this covers only part of the list. Cages filled with several hundred squawking birds and glum rabbits were tied down by the mainmast so they wouldn't be blown away by the first gale. There were enormous stoves that were lit in the early morning by the ship's boys and kept going the whole day as the boys, along with the personal servants and slaves of the gentry, prepared at least two meals daily. Naturally, mountains of wood had to be stocked aboard. They must have had quite the feasts in those first weeks, eating well-spiced fricassées and fish pies finished off with a sprinkle of cinnamon and sugar.

By the time the ship had crossed the Atlantic, any fresh meat and live chickens would have been gone. The water began to stink in the barrels. At this point, both nobles and crew turned to the preserved meats and fish they had brought aboard. The Portuguese had not yet discovered salt cod, their beloved *bacalhau* (which today is supposedly prepared in more than 365 ways), but hake was prepared much the same way: split open, heavily salted, and air-dried. Sardines were packed in barrels between layers of salt. Hernâni Xavier tells me he has tasted these *sardinhas de barrica* in the North. "Blaagh," he says when asked to describe the taste. "It smells too much." The preserved fish were soaked in seawater before cooking (to decrease the salt content!), though when pitching waves made it impossible to use the stoves, or once the firewood had run out, the fish were often eaten raw. Another preparation of the time that is still current uses pork instead of sardines to make *conserva*. This is a little like the goose confit of southwestern France. To make it, small pieces of pork are fried, then layered with lard or oil. Today's recipe is more lightly spiced than those sixteenth-century Jesuit missionaries would have liked. Nevertheless, it uses plenty of black pepper, cloves, and chilies, especially if it is intended for long keeping. Today, *conserva* is typically eaten as a sandwich or occasionally grilled. Linschoten's sailors would have had to use hard ship's biscuit to make their sandwich—before it, too, began to spoil.

By the time the ships reached the Cape of Good Hope, the hardtack was likely to be crawling with worms, and the water in the barrels was fetid. On at least one vessel, some of the sailors apparently turned to eating the dogs and cats aboard so that they wouldn't have to eat the infested ship's biscuit. Crew members began to suffer from scurvy, the disease caused by vitamin C deficiency. At first, the affected sailors became lack-luster and pale. Then their limbs would swell, and their gums began to bleed. Finally, bloody sores covered the body. High fever was followed by convulsions and then death. The cure was perfectly well known at the time, but the fresh fruit that would have nipped the illness in the bud didn't last long enough in the tropical heat. The smell emanating from the ship, where five hundred unwashed men had been eating, sleeping, and relieving themselves of every bodily fluid (seasickness was all too common) in extremely close quarters for at least four months must have been astonishingly putrid as it sailed up the African east coast and into Moçambique harbor to restock. If lucky, a ship would lose no more than 10 percent of its human load on the outbound voyage. The remainder of the trip across the Indian Ocean was usually uneventful, discounting storms, shipwrecks, and the like.

The ships typically called first at Cochin, made their way up to the capital at Goa, and returned to load up with pepper at ports down the Malabar Coast, returning home about a year after they had left Lisbon.

Whereas, on the way to India, the ships were relatively empty, laden mostly with ballast and provisions for those on board, on the return trip, they were so overloaded that they were dangerous to sail. Two entire decks of each *nau* were specially constructed with compartments to hold pepper. Once they were sealed, their lids were caulked and each one carefully numbered under the watchful eye of the king's officials. All the other cargo—including the sailors' and officers' *caixas;* the bundles of cinnamon imported from Ceylon; the bales of cloves, nutmeg, and mace from the East Indies; all the provisions necessary for the return trip; and even the odd rhino or elephant—were placed anywhere there was room.* The survivor of one wrecked *nau* in 1554 recalled that there had been "about seventy-two boxes and so many bales and boxes stacked that they equaled the height of the castles." Others report that there was so much cargo, it might be hung on the outside of the hull, supported by ropes. No wonder

---

* Manuel I reportedly used to saunter through Lisbon accompanied by a menagerie of several elephants and a rhino. The rhino was later sent as a present to Pope Leo X, though the poor creature was shipwrecked on the way. The Holy Father did eventually get his promised pet, though, by this point, it had been embalmed and stuffed.

there were so many wrecks on the return trip! Between the trip there and back, the losses amounted to some 25 percent.

If you think it completely irrational that an ordinary person would undergo such hardships and risk his life to fill that *caixa* with pepper, think back to the conditions in Lisbon's slums. Here, the narrow lanes were open sewers, which, during the long, dry summer season, would remain unflushed for months. Dysentery was common, malaria endemic, accommodations not much more spacious than aboard ship, and the chances of social advancement almost nil. In the countryside, the peasants were starving. A single *caixa* could set you up for life (though given contemporary life spans, that didn't necessarily amount to all that many years).

Like rich people everywhere, the upper classes succumbed less often to deadly diseases than the people in the Alfama, yet they, too, had their reasons for the risky passage to and from India. The junior sons of nobility—the knights, squires, and *fidalgos* with little or no inheritance—saw the same kind of opportunity as the impoverished laborers. They, too, could come back with a fortune that would enable them to dine off Ming china and sip spiced wine from flagons of Venetian glass.

The motivations weren't always monetary, though, or at least, simple greed is only part of the explanation. If we can believe all the contemporary plays, poems, and songs that oozed with medieval chivalry, the spirit of the Crusades was still very much alive in the fifteen hundreds. "You, Portuguese, as few as you are valiant . . . Through martyrdom, in its manifold forms, you spread the message of eternal life . . . Heaven has made it your destiny to do many and mighty deeds for Christendom," writes Camões in the middle years of the century, when, admittedly, the chivalric ideals were no longer what they used to be. Nonetheless, in the early fifteen hundreds, the greatest honors could still be earned only by swinging your sword on the battlefront, and in those days, the greatest field of glory was India (as it was loosely defined). When it came to the risks involved, it was a win-win situation. Like jihadists today, and like the Crusaders who had battered down Jerusalem's gates, the early-sixteenth-century Portuguese conquistadores, I'm sure, genuinely believed that if they died in the pursuit of holy war (and the conquest of India was at first defined as such), they would garner all the rewards of heaven. And if they didn't die, they'd return home filthy rich. This sincere belief in the spice trade as just one part of the great crusade against the infidel must at least in part explain the crazy risks the Portuguese were willing to take.

Of course, the many priests sent annually to India were putting their lives on the line with no promise (at least theoretically) of worldly reward. Even if they were not all saints, most must have departed from Lisbon believing they were on their way to do God's work in saving the heathens and stamping out the heretics. Later in the century, a Jesuit missionary would write, "If there were not merchants who go to seek for earthly treasures in the East and West Indies, who would transport thither the preachers who take heavenly treasures? The preachers take the Gospel and the merchants take the preachers."

THE MONASTERY

Tram number 15 begins its route to the suburb of Belém just a few steps from Terreiro de Paço, the old front yard of the Portuguese kings. It makes a sharp turn at the waterfront and heads due west—past the ferry terminal of Cais de Sodré, where commuters pack the vessels that ply the waters of the Tejo; then alongside the riverbank, past the clamorous docks of the Porto de Lisboa lined with engorged tankers and overgrown passenger liners; past schools of sailboats skipping across the green and gentle waves. Once you've reached Belém, the Mosteiro dos Jerónimos is unmistakable. The monastery stretches the length of three football fields. If you miss one tram stop, you can get off at the next one and still be in front of it.

It may be huge, but at least from the outside, the Real Mosteiro de Santa Maria de Belém (Royal Monastery of Saint Mary of Bethlehem), as it is officially known, is disappointingly plain. Yet step inside and you enter another world. The cloister is like a fantastical garden where all the inhabitants have been turned to stone. A population of gloomy saints and grinning griffins is held up by twisting trunks of a hundred different species of column. Flowered vines wind and weave up treelike pillars where fishes and dragons hide, and up above, birds cavort amid limestone foliage. Inside the church, the forest of columns soars up some seven stories to the graceful arching branches of the Gothic vaults. Architectural historians have named this hyperornate style the Manueline, after the reign of the fortunate king when this late-Gothic exuberance flourished. At first glance, it would appear that the rational ideas of the Renaissance had made no inroads here whatsoever, that this petrified Eden is as medieval as the Lusitanians' quest against the infidel. And yet, if you look carefully, you will notice the vaults turn into ropes, and hidden among the wondrous menagerie are carvings of navigational instruments, the so-called armillary spheres made up of interlocking ribbons of steel that were the GPS devices of their day. Looking up, you can see the same tension between the ancient and the modern, between religion and science, between God and Mammon, that led the Portuguese kings to try to run a spice-importing business as a way to pay for gilded churches half the world away. The Mosteiro dos Jerónimos itself was built to pay off God for helping the kingdom attain the peppery riches of the Orient. Manuel pledged to build the monastery in gratitude for Vasco da Gama's epic voyage with money made in the spice trade, dedicating all the profits accrued from a crown investment of twenty thousand cruzados in a private trading company to the building project.

On entering the church, you find the tomb of Vasco da Gama just on the right and the remains of Luís Vaz de Camões, Portugal's great epic poet and da Gama's self-declared publicist, on your left. Belém was traditionally the last landfall before the outbound trip to India, and one of the jobs of the Hieronymite monks sequestered here was to look after the spiritual needs of the sailors before their long and perilous voyage. Vasco da Gama and his men went to Mass here (it was a modest chapel then) before clambering aboard the *São Gabriel* and the *São Rafael,* their two ships named—not by happenstance—after archangels.

Academic historians of the last hundred years or so get all stiff and tweedy when you suggest that people will go to all ends for the sake of their religion. They'll assure you that religion is just a cover for other, more "rational" motivations. They would prefer to explain the world in terms of economic self-interest, of class warfare, or of dynastic imperatives. But has not the early twenty-first century made it catastrophically clear how many people (and not just the desperate, either) are ready to leap over the brink in the name of their religion? The same was certainly true of "the age of discovery." While greed should certainly be given her due, there is no reason to think that da Gama was not perfectly sincere when he said that he came in search of Christians and spices. Certainly, the grocer kings spent piles of money to promulgate Christianity around the world, often using cash they didn't actually have. Portuguese viceroys in India regularly complained that money was being spent on gilding altars while their cannons rusted. Letters dispatched from the Paço da Ribeira overseas would typically begin with "Forasmuch as the first and principal obligation of the Kings of Portugal is to forward the work of conversion by all means in their power" or some such thick and pious phrase. And this idea was not limited to the kings. Portuguese of every class considered themselves as "the standard-bearers of the faith," chosen above all Western nations to spread the Catholic creed.

The way Europeans saw it in those days, the obstacle that stood in the way of Christianity was Islam. As far as the spice trade was concerned, it was simply a bonus, a gratuity that could be collected by the conqueror of the infidel—much as it had been during the Crusades. It's clear from the record that the Portuguese monarchs were on the lookout for Christians long before they got it in their heads to look for spices. And the Christian who was at the top of their list was, of course, Prester John. As everyone knew, he was the powerful ruler of a Christian kingdom somewhere in "India," a place that was vaguely indicated as anywhere to the south and east of Europe in most medieval conceptions of the world. Popular books written by the likes of John Mandeville described the mythical monarch's fabulous riches in tantalizing detail. In his land, precious stones were supposed to be so large "that men make of them vessels, as platters, dishes and cups." And what was even more enticing to the Lusitanian kings, the legendary ruler could field an army of more than one hundred thousand—according to Mandeville, at least. To give the court of Lisbon some credit, Prester John's kingdom wasn't entirely wishful thinking, since in the high plateaus of Abyssinia (today's Ethiopia), a Christian enclave had, in fact, withstood Muhammad's armies—though the modest mountain kingdom could hardly live up to the English knight's fantasy.

The Europeans had good reason to drool over a potential ally in the infidel's rear. Things weren't going so well for Christendom in the fifteenth century. Admittedly, Catholic Portugal and Spain had consolidated their possessions in the Iberian Peninsula and had even made some successful forays into North Africa. But elsewhere, the situation was grim. To the south and east, Christian armies were crumbling at the onslaught of an expansionist Turkish superpower. In the years before their 1571 defeat at Lepanto, the Ottomans seemed unstoppable, gobbling up the Orthodox Christian Balkans and ready to gulp down Catholic Vienna.

Because they had so successfully muscled into Muslim territory— admittedly, their opponents were the ninety-pound weaklings of North Africa's beaches—the Castilian and Portuguese monarchs figured it was their responsibility to venture out farther and save Christendom. Accordingly, the search for Prester John became a strategic imperative and the circumnavigation of the Cape of Good Hope a military maneuver designed to get behind the enemy lines. Prince Henrique even went so far as to send out an open letter to the European rulers to join him in his pursuit of Prester John so that they might all band together in a great Christian army to march on Jerusalem. (They turned him down.) João II's enthusiasm for the African project was also, in large part, motivated by the search. All those caravels were sent up the Senegal, the Niger, and the Congo rivers with the idea that they might connect with the Nile, which would take them to Prester John's kingdom. When that idea came to naught, Bartolomeu Dias was dispached to find an alternate route. At the same time, another expedition was sent overland with the same goal. That there was money to be made along the way simply made the project more attractive.

Unlike the Venetians, who considered business an estimable occupation, the European nobility—and the court of Lisbon was no exception— shuddered at the idea of making money through trade. Da Gama's knightly order of Santiago, for instance, specified that not only could Jews, Moors, and heathens not be admitted to the order but neither could money changers, merchants, their employees, or anyone who had at any time "exercised any art, craft or occupation unworthy of our knightly Order, and still less should any entrant ever have earned his living by the work of his hands." There was an out, however. While, under normal circumstances, knights would lose their standing if they became mere merchants, the act of buying and selling was considered okay if it was in connection with war (or with the holding of land). In holy war, which could potentially weaken the infidel, trade and plunder were even a

Christian duty. According to the same rationale, the king could build an empire based on trade as long as it was seen as an ongoing crusade. It was why King Afonso V named the coin minted from African gold the cruzado ("crusader"). Not everyone saw it this way. After all, when the king of France called Manuel "the grocer king," it had been an obvious put-down.*

The Renaissance popes—who were, at any rate, too busy poisoning their enemies, begetting children, and decorating chapels (at least, according to the Protestants)—were perfectly happy to let the Portuguese and Castilians take the fight to the enemy. To make the line of control crystal clear, the Spanish-born pope Alexander VI split the world between the two in a papal edict that began "Inter caetera." This was later finessed in the famous 1494 treaty of Tordesillas, which gave Castile all of the New World with the exception of Brazil, while granting most of Asia to Portugal. Over the years, various agreements forged in Rome gave the respective Iberian kings the right to exercise almost complete religious control over any conquered lands. As a result, as long as the ships departing Belém were filled with priests, the king could retain a clean conscience about the holds that returned packed with pepper.

Opinions on the Lusitanian record when it comes to evangelization are sharply divided. (We're talking about religion, after all.) Hernâni Xavier, for example, would point out that the missionaries sent by Lisbon were far less violent in imposing their religion in Asia than the Castilians were in the New World. In fact, official policy supposedly forbade forcible conversion, and the Portuguese methods did tend to be more subtle— if hardly less coercive—than was typical of the time. But perhaps more important, once Lisbon discovered that Eastern Christians were few and far between and Prester John had neither the means nor the desire to help conquer the infidel, the lure of India's black gold shoved the proselytization effort to a sputtering back burner. The Christians just couldn't keep up with the spices. A group of newly arrived clerics told the scandalized

---

* It's interesting to contrast this antibusiness sentiment to the attitude of Muslims. Muhammad, who started his life in the camel-driving trade, is quoted as saying, "The merchant enjoys the felicity both of this world and the next," and, more pointedly, "He who makes money pleases God." The Christians had to go through all sorts of doctrinal contortions to legitimate moneymaking through trade.

vicar of Malacca in 1514 "that the chief reason why they had come out to the East was to amass a fortune in *cruzados;* and one of them said that he would not be satisfied unless he had secured 5,000 *cruzados* and many pearls and rubies within the space of three years." Even if they were not all this greedy, the quality of the average clergyman did not improve until the arrival of the Jesuits in 1542.

Unlike the Spanish in America, where slaughtering the heathen simply facilitated the looting of temples, the Portuguese in India couldn't be so cavalier. (Lieutenant Neves, who, like every Portuguese, will find any opportunity to put down the Spanish, adds the telling detail that the looting Castilians referred to their cargo as "treasure," while Lisbon-bound pepper was always referred to as "merchandise.") Unlike their Iberian neighbors, the Portuguese needed the Hindu and Muslim spice merchants alive to deliver the goods. Consequently, non-Christians in most Portuguese possessions were allowed to practice their religion more or less unhindered during the first thirty years after da Gama's arrival. This, however, was to change as the winds of the Counter-Reformation propelled the foot soldiers of a newly proactive Rome to the eastern empire.

The Catholic Church in Europe had taken several decades to react to its Protestant critics, but by the mid-sixteenth century, a sweeping retrenchment was in full swing. The so-called Council of Trent, which met on and off throughout the middle years of the century, set a take-no-prisoners policy toward anyone who wavered from the rule book. Partly as a result of this uncompromising approach, Europe would be embroiled in a century of religious wars. In India, the new emphasis on toeing the Vatican's line led to a much more aggressive policy of intolerance. In Goa, the Hindu temples that had previously been allowed to stand were burned to the ground. New, highly discriminatory laws were put in place, making the practice of religion and livelihood onerous for any non-Christian. Orphans were forcibly taken from their relatives and raised as Catholics. On alternate Sundays, Catholic enforcers rounded up Hindu families and corralled them in nearby churches, where they were subjected to interminable sermons. Non-Christians, arrested for breaching the religious laws, often sought to evade punishment by asking to be baptized. But, lest they go back on their word, the Jesuits "invited" the quaking Hindus to lunch. For a Brahman, to eat a meal prepared by untouchables was tantamount to being excommunicated from his religion. The practice is recounted in a letter to the queen in 1552, in which a crown official describes the Jesuits' forcibly shaving their Hindu victims and compelling them to eat beef. Not that the correspondent found the practice itself particularly reprehensible; his complaint was that so many of the locals had fled due to this overzealous behavior that no one was left to work the fields! Obviously, not every Jesuit considered force-feeding heathens part of his job description, and, at least among the lower castes, many Indians came willingly to Christianity. They, after all, had nothing to lose by abandoning Hinduism with its discriminatory rules. What's more, no matter how involuntary were the original converts, by the second and third generation, their descendants invariably turned into devout Catholics.

In Portugal, many Jews had also converted under duress, and there, too, most became sincere practicing Christians. Nevertheless, enough tried to hold on to the vestiges of Judaism that the Inquisition wouldn't let them be. Much like the Brahmans forced to eat their sacred cows, the so-called New Christians were compelled to eat pork sausages to prove the authenticity of their conversion.* Refusal to do so could land you in the clutches of the Holy Office. This would result, at best, in a life of disgrace and, at worst, in a fiery death at the stake.

Needless to say, food is used to constrain as well as to unify the members of many faiths. Most religions meddle in the day-to-day culinary habits of their adherents. The Christian rules could never compare to the thicket of Talmudic jurisprudence that grew up around the laws of kashruth, nor the tangled hierarchy of dietary strictures of the Hindu caste system. Even so, there were plenty of regulations that obedient Christians were supposed to observe. The most notable restriction was on the consumption of warm-blooded animals. Birds, mammals, and their by-products—eggs, milk, butter, and so on—were restricted for something like a third of the year by the time you added up Lent, Advent,

---

* One of the dishes that resulted from the persecution of crypto-Jews was called *caldo verde com torah*, which was the usual Portuguese potato kale soup but with a pork sausage floating in it. You had to eat the sausage, "the Torah," to prove your Christian credentials. Apparently, one technique devised to fool the prying eyes of neighbors was to eat a sausage made of bread, chicken, duck, and so forth made up to look like regular pork links. A similar sausage is still made with a mixture of bread and meats, but these days, it includes pork.

every Friday, and a basketful of other ecclesiastical fast days. Fashions in canon law and the practical considerations of the Vatican meant that there were usually plenty of exemptions made for certain individuals (the infirm and soldiers come to mind) and even for whole regions of Christendom. After 1365, parts of northern Europe were exempted from the no-butter rule on meatless days. (It continued to be banned during Lent.) But even in Europe, caste also played some part. Many of the religious orders, for example, had to adhere to more restrictive rules than laypeople. Much like several Indian religions, Christianity put great stock in the mortification of the body, and fasting was seen as a particularly effective tool for spiritual enlightenment. Peasants, on the other hand, made do with a mostly Lenten diet year-round, whether they liked it or not.

All this might be worth no more than an esoteric footnote in a history of medieval Europe if it weren't for the fact that these religious rules and restrictions had an enormous impact on national economies and international trade—to say nothing of what ended up on the dinner table.

The church's diet rules, like the religion itself, were invented in the Mediterranean, with its gracious weather, olive groves, and abundant coastline. An Italian would hardly take it as hardship that she was forced to cook with olive oil and eat fish one day in three. In the north of Europe, however, it was another matter. Here, cooks had only animal fats to cook with, and fishermen were at the mercy of months of miserable weather when they could hardly go fishing at all (notably during the winter months of Advent and Lent). One result of the fasting rules had been to encourage fishing where it was possible and fish-farming where it was not. In part, the Dutch were aswim in capital to invest in the spice trade because they had made a fortune off the herring fishery. To preserve the perishable catch, tons of salt had to be shipped across seas and up rivers, subsequently followed by a return cargo of the preserved fish themselves. The Portuguese, despite their renown as fishermen, imported dried fish from northern Germany. Along with the salt, thousands of barrels of olive oil made the trip north as well, accompanied by smaller quantities of almonds (to make almond milk) to provide a substitute for lard, butter, and milk. Southerners didn't necessarily export their best. The English expression "as brown as oil" is noted as early as the fifteenth century and gives an idea of the quality of much of the oil arriving in the North. To add insult to injury, the imported oil could be at least double and some-times as much as ten times the cost of local butter (itself an expensive commodity). Portugal was especially well located to profit from this reli-giously required trade, since, by sea, it was the closest to the needy nations of the North. Long before Lisbon was outfitting *naus* for the East India route, her merchants were already making a tidy profit sending salt, olive oil, and almonds to London, Bruges, and Hamburg.

Spices came into this religious framework rather indirectly. Since most pepper, ginger, cinnamon, and their like were considered "hot" and "dry" according to medieval dietary beliefs, they were especially needed on all those fast days to temper or adjust the "moist" and "cold" humors attributed to fish. (A quick look at any medieval cookery manual makes it evident that fasting was in no way related to abstemiousness; some of the fish dishes are even more over-the-top than meat preparations.) In gen-eral, the church did not particularly approve of spiced food, especially when cinnamon and ginger were added purely for reasons of taste. As the early medieval saint Bernard points out, you could sin by "taking carnal pleasure in smelling spices or potions or flowers or herbs or foods or other things with a good scent, not out of praise to God, but for immoderate sensual pleasure." In a late-fourteenth-century diatribe, "Of Antichrist and His Followers," the proto-Protestant preacher John Wycliffe describes the minions of Beelzebub wolfing down foods "seasoned with hot spices and extra-hot with sauces and syrups." When taken for "medical" pur-poses, however, the use of spices was more excusable. Moreover, theolog-ical antipathy to the Asian imports waxed and waned. In the early Middle Ages, cinnamon and other aromatics were actually brewed up into an anointing oil used in church sacraments, but by Wycliffe's day, spices were more likely to show up on a bishop's pot roast than on his altar. The early medieval emphasis on mortification of the body was losing much of its appeal in those later years. Certainly, most of the Renaissance popes had no issues with pursuits of the flesh—culinary or otherwise. But then this is what led to the Protestant reaction, after all. To Martin Luther and his fellow travelers, the Roman church was a cesspool of corruption and moral turpitude; Christianity could be purified only by returning to its simpler origins. The abolition of pleasure, whether in the form of exotically spiced dishes or public baths where the genders mixed, was placed high on the new puritan agenda. Unfortunately, the Catholic reaction to this was to become even more puritan than the puritans, with sex and cooking falling as sacrificial lambs to the Counter-Reformation. Not that the religious reformers managed to ban fun entirely. People still licked their chops with pleasure, but now they worried more about going to hell for it.

Even more indirectly, the popularity of spices fell victim to the religious conflicts that wracked Europe during the years of the Reformation and its Catholic response. The split in Christendom affected life far beyond the limits of Sunday morning. Borders were sealed to foreign ideas. In Portugal and Spain especially, Catholic censorship eviscerated the local presses. The censors did not target merely nonorthodox religious material, they went after anything even vaguely scientific, which included diet books. Not only did the doctrinal divide encourage the rise of national churches, it also promoted the use of the English, German, and French vernacular, from the pulpit and the poet's pen as well as cookbook authors. What's more, the rift also meant that Protestants and Catholics would now follow different rules when it came to dinner. Protestant northerners dumped the Catholic fasting regulations faster than you can recite a Hail Mary. And though it might be overreaching to claim that the butter eaters of boreal Europe rose up against popish Rome just because they were sick of overpriced, rancid olive oil and months of salted fish, getting rid of the diet rules certainly didn't hurt the Protestant cause. Whereas once medieval Europe had adhered to a common Catholic religion, a common Latin language, and common well-spiced cuisine (at least, for the elite), the balkanization of the Christian world along national lines now meant that nations could no longer gather around the same table as easily as before. Even though it would take some years, the Europe-wide fashion for spices—as much as Latin—would be a casualty of Martin Luther's squabble with the bishop of Rome.

The irony of Europe's splitting asunder even while the Iberian voyages were bringing the world closer together was not lost on contemporary commentators. Camões excoriated his fellow Christians—the Germans, who, "devising a new pastor, a new creed . . . wage hideous wars"; the Ital-

ians "enslaved by vice"—bent more on mutual destruction than on unit-
ing to defeat the Turk. Accordingly, it was up to "this little house of Portugal" to carry the Catholic seed across the earth.

Many of the early sailors who prayed at the Mosteiro dos Jerónimos
before setting off halfway across the world sincerely believed this, yet if
you look around Asia, the impact of Portugal's evangelization effort is
thin on the ground. Today, in Goa and Malacca, great Catholic churches
rot in the tropical sun. But other reminders of Lisbon's conquistadores
grow and flourish. The Portuguese seeds that took root in Asia and Africa
had little to do with religion. One of the unremarked, yet most significant,
corollaries of the spice trade is the transfer of foods from the Americas to
the African and Asian continents. The pepper ships that passed from the
New World to the Old brought cashews, cassava, chilies, tomatoes, corn,
sweet potatoes, and other unknown foods along with the friars and the
fidalgos.

GOLDEN GOA

When you step out of the main gate of Lisbon's hilltop Castelo de São
Jorge, you can't help but notice a small restaurant on the square opposite.
With its timbered ceilings and racks of dusty wine bottles, Arco do Castelo
has that quaint, rustic look that is usually a sure sign of more *caldo verde*
(potato kale soup) and *bacalhau,* those ubiquitous clichés of the Portuguese
kitchen. Yet, surprisingly, a small sign above the door reads "Cozinha de
Goa," and a quick look at a menu listing shrimp curry and pork vindaloo
tells you that the chef is a long way from home. I had been invited to the
exotic bistro by Rui Lis, the childhood friend of a Portuguese naval archaeologist. He had commended Rui to me as a fascist, a raving lunatic,
and a very good person. A sound judgment, it would seem. It turns out
that Rui divides his time between defending local mob figures and working as a human rights lawyer. He often finds himself in Portugal's former
African colonies (the ones established in the wake of the pepper *naus*) taking unconscionable risks on behalf of political prisoners. Portuguese missionaries apparently still carry some weight in Africa. Totally deadpan, he
tells me how he used to dress up as a priest in order to dodge Angolan
guerrillas. I can see it, too. He looks the part of one of those rotund Jesuits
sent to convert the heathen, though I somehow can't see him force-

feeding hamburgers to recalcitrant Hindus. Filet mignon, perhaps. In Lisbon, the renegade lawyer's enthusiasm for tossing rhetorical Molotov cocktails is exceeded only by the relish he takes in eating well.

Rui had promised me spice in a city that, given its history, is oddly devoid of spicy food. His eyes sparkle as he gestures to the platter of Goan *sarapatel* that arrives on the table. He assures me that it is simply a variation on a dish much like you'll find in his hometown in the southern Portuguese province of Alentejo before he dips naan lustily into the (mildly) spicy sauce and spears the meat with his fork. I haven't the heart to tell him that Goans don't eat Indian flatbreads like naan, they eat *pãozinhos*, fluffy Portuguese rolls, with their curry, and that an Indian would have no use for all the flatware that clutters the table; like medieval Europeans, Goans eat with their hands. Nevertheless, when it comes to the *sarapatel*, I concede Rui his point. Portugal does in fact have several variations on the dish. In the Alentejan version, pork or lamb, with their respective offal, go into a stew seasoned with a small quantity of garlic, bay leaf, paprika, peppercorns, cloves, cumin, and vinegar—a mixture that, apart from paprika, could come from the medieval *O livro de cozinha*. The Goan version, which uses more spice, may be closer still to the lost Portuguese original. Even today, the state of Goa, which was incorporated into India only in 1961, remains as a remnant of Portuguese-influenced culture hemmed in by the multihued tapestry of the subcontinent. In Goa, only the tourists are sparing with the spice.

Sitting in Arco do Castelo while Rui riffed on Maoist paramilitaries and Portuguese mobsters, and eating the all-too-delicately seasoned chicken stew called *xacouti*, I kept thinking back to my last meal in Goa earlier that same spring. There, a basket on the table was piled high with fluffy *pãozinhos*. I had insisted that the chef season the giant prawns with as much chili as if he were eating them himself—despite the waiter's skeptical eyebrows. It was Fat Tuesday, and the tall windows of the grand dining room of the Hotel Mandovi shuddered with the techno-beat coming from one of the many parties that announced the end of Carnival in Panjim, Goa's capital. Earlier in the day, a parade of writhing naked abdomens had flowed along the reviewing stands just outside, one of the happier residues of colonialism as far as I'm concerned. Inside, the cavernous room, frosted with ornate blue and gold plasterwork like an elaborate gâteau, was almost entirely empty. I could just barely make out the whisper of Portuguese conversation emanating from a prim elderly couple seated in a secluded corner. Before long, the smiling waiter arrived with my order. The prawns were violently spicy, and delicious.

Panjim is reminiscent of a provincial town on the Portuguese seaboard. The architecture is more Mediterranean than South Asian, with window grilles of curlicues, and shaded balconies behind ornate metal balustrades. Here, though, the houses are dyed in colors of Indian intensity: the deep pink of watermelon; the russet of hot cinnamon; and, hotter yet, mango yellow and papaya orange. Red-tiled roofs top these confections, often supplemented by rusting sheets of corrugated metal. The colony's capital was moved here in 1760, when the viceroys finally gave up on the original disease-ridden location several miles up the Mandovi River.

There are excursion boats that will take you the five miles up the languorous river to the old capital, much as the local dhows once ferried cargo from the *naus* that had to anchor at the river's mouth. There is something oddly evocative of Lisbon in the way Goa Velha, "Old Goa," nestles among low-lying ocher hills on the bank of the broad river. When the Portuguese viceroy relocated his capital from the tropical jungles of Cochin to this semiarid site so reminiscent of southern Portugal, I wonder if they didn't settle here, in part, because it reminded them of home.

Today, all that remains of the city that gave the state of Goa its name is a carefully manicured tourist destination, a scattering of churches circled by stray dogs, day-trippers, and the vendors who supply the visitors with the requisite liquid refreshments, simulated silver crucifixes, and miniature chess sets. I suppose I had expected to stumble upon the crumbling remains of a colonial empire rotting in the jungle, but instead, I found a carefully embalmed collection of brilliantly whitewashed buildings isolated by primly manicured lawns burned brown by the dry season's sun. All the same, the churches are sensational. No wonder they called this place "the Rome of the East." The Sé Cathedral is vastly bigger than Lisbon's own, with a wildly gilded altar, outrageous chandeliers, and fantastically coffered chapels. The ceiling is denuded of its gold, but the red ocher sizing reminds you just how radiantly gaudy it must once have been. The altar of the Basílica do Bom Jesus remains an orgy of gilt with a giant relief of Saint Francis Loyola, like a giant gold egg, with arms upraised to another, smaller egglike orb that is supposed to represent the Divinity. The many other churches—São Caetano, São Francisco, São Augustin, Santa Mónica, Santo António, Santa Catarina, Nossa Senhora da Graça, Nossa Senhora do Rosário, and Nossa Senhora do Monte among them—are not as well preserved, with no more than a few gold flecks reminding you of the wealth that built the city the Portuguese called *Goa Dourada*, "Golden Goa." How much African and then later American gold was diverted from buying pepper and cinnamon so that it could be beaten into acres of imperceptibly thin sheets to cover all these altars and ceilings and walls?

Back in Linschoten's day, the city was much more than an ecclesiastical theme park. He describes a vibrant urban organism alive with the babble of barter and the chatter of a dozen nations: Persians, Arabs, Jews, Armenians, Gujaratis, Jains, Brahmans, and "all Indian nations and people." Streets were lined with shops selling everything from silks, satins, and damask to "a thousand sorts of clothes and cottons." You could buy "curious works of [porcelain] from China." Jewelers from the northern Indian port of Cambay specialized in "all sorts of precious stones." Gold-, silver-, and coppersmiths had a street unto themselves, as did the carpenters and the wholesale wheat and rice merchants. Others sold vegetables and spices. And just as in Indian markets today, all this was intermingled with dust and trash.

In 1534, the Portuguese made Goa the capital of the Estado da Índia, the network of forts and trading posts that extended from the city of Moçambique in Africa to the island of Amboina in eastern Indonesia. Yet "the Queen of the Orient" reigned over territories that could hardly be described as an empire, at least when you compare it to the vast territories the Dutch and English would later conquer in these self-same waters. Although their *naus* and caravels sailed unchallenged on the sea-lanes, the Lusitanian kings never held more than a few flecks of the Asian landmass—often just enough property to build a fort or a warehouse to protect the precious, peppery cargo.

Even on the sea, the Portuguese mostly just forced their way into routes that had been traveled for hundreds of years. Europeans had never

The decadent ways of Portuguese Goa are amply illustrated in this print from a Latin translation of Linschoten's Itinerario.

been the world's main customers for the pungent berries and seeds of southern Asia's jungles. Persia, the Middle East, North India, and China were all vast, populous markets for spice. It has been estimated that Europeans took no more than a quarter of the spices produced. My bet is that it was even less.

When Vasco da Gama arrived on the scene, the intra-Asian spice trade was mostly in the hands of Muslim traders from the northern Indian state of Gujarat. A contemporary Florentine reporter estimated that fifteen hundred "Moorish" vessels arrived in Calicut during da Gama's initial three-month sojourn. They brought their wares to China, too. At the end of the thirteenth century, Marco Polo had claimed that for every Italian spice galley in Alexandria, a hundred docked at the Chinese port of Zaiton (Quanzhou). And in the following centuries, Chinese demand for spices spiraled ever upward. According to one well-placed sixteenth-century source, China alone was importing three times as much pepper as the Europeans. Among the Ming elite, spices were as much a part of the

A Misericordia

Joannes à Dœtechum fecit.

dus

gerb.

Fori Goensis tabernarum mercium et mer-
catorum illud frequentantium aperta ex-
plicatio per N.Linschoten.

Claere opdoeninge vande merckt van Gou
met haer winckelen waren en dagelickse
Coopluyden door I.H.V. Linschoten

privileged lifestyle as they were in Baghdad or Barcelona. North India itself was an enormous market for South Indian pepper and imported
cloves and nutmeg as well. Here again, spicy food was associated with the
court—in this case, the Muslim Moguls, who had grown up with sophisticated Persian cuisine. It's worth remembering that spices were an exotic
import here, too. Great caravans of mules and oxen had to transport the
tropical spices across the high peaks of the Western Ghats to reach North
India's capitals; it is almost as far from Cochin to Delhi as from Alexandria to Venice.

Wherever the North Indian merchants loaded their junks and dhows
with pepper and cloves, they left behind their religion as well. The diffusion of Islam throughout Southeast Asia can be directly credited to the
spice route. (The story of the earlier spread of Hinduism is much the
same.) As the Muslim merchants established trading posts, they eventually put down roots, erected mosques, and married local women. Moreover, what is remarkable about the spread of Islam is how peacefully it

occurred here, especially in comparison to the violent methods employed by Muhammad's immediate successors in the Middle East or, for that matter, when compared to the Portuguese conquistadores.

In spite of Manuel's stated intention to wrest the Indian spice trade from these "Moors," the king's men never managed to achieve anything close to the wished-for monopoly. In the early years, they had some small successes in disrupting the old route when Admiral Albuquerque took Ormuz, the critical link between the Persian overland route and the sub-continent, but by the middle years of the century, realpolitik had made it necessary to placate the Persian shah in order to support the Portuguese against the Turks. As a consequence, Persian merchants, soon followed by Arabs and Venetians, were able to come to Ormuz to buy as much spice as they liked. And increasingly, the pepper wasn't coming from Portuguese-controlled territories at all. Once they had gotten over the initial shock of the Europeans' arrival, the Gujaratis had figured out how they could bypass the Estado's strongholds in India and ship pepper directly from Sumatra to Egypt. Among the Lusitanians, the crusading spirit that had launched the early voyages seems to have faded, too. The seek-and-destroy impulse toward any Muslim that had characterized da Gama's generation was eventually replaced by a grudging entente. By midcentury, trade within Asia itself had settled down to a pattern familiar before the Euro-peans' arrival. The Portuguese contented themselves with playing the racketeer, skimming a small percentage of all the trade that passed within cannon-shot of their vessels. The *fidalgos* had learned that there was more money to be made selling spices to local merchants than filling up the king's ships. As a result, long caravans loaded with aromatic cargo would trudge again across the dusty Arabian desert, and the warehouses of the Campo San Bartolomeo were filled once more with the sharp scent of Asian pepper.

Yet, while the Portuguese never achieved anything near a monopoly in pepper, it was a different story with cinnamon. In the sixteenth century, *Cinnamomum verum* ("true" cinnamon) was limited to Ceylon (Sri Lanka), and although it had been traded for at least a thousand years, only rela-tively small quantities ever left the island. What most of the world knew as cinnamon was actually a closely related spice called cassia (*Cinnamomum cassia*), which grows in numerous locales in southern Asia. Even today, most of the "cinnamon" sold in the United States is in fact cassia. True cinnamon is recognizable by its lighter color and softer bark. It has a more floral aroma hinting of incense and resin. Both spices are distinctly sweet, but cassia has a much more noticeable burn in its aftertaste. They are produced by stripping the second bark from either species' tree shoots. As the bark dries, it forms the characteristic stick. The spice grown on Ceylon was long considered superior. Writing in Goa in 1563, the Portuguese botanist Garcia da Orta noted in his vastly informative *Colóquios dos simples e drogas a cousas medicinais da Índia* (Colloquies on the Simples and Drugs of India) that, "as a fruit is better in one country than in another, so the cinnamon of Ceylon is better than all others. . . . They do not send any other cinnamon than that of Ceylon to Portugal." At the time, the aromatic bark was collected in the wild, while the Ceylonese monarch controlled its sale and distribution. The Portuguese, using their usual persuasive ways, convinced the king to grant them a monopoly, with the result that a ship was dispatched each year from Ceylon to meet up with the *Carreira da Índia.*

Lisbon had entered the spice trade at a time when Christendom's tastes were in flux. In southern Europe, in particular, the medieval fashion for sharp flavors dominated by pepper and ginger with the sour tang of vinegar or verjuice seemed to be giving way to a decidedly sweeter flavor complex by the middle years of the fifteenth century. By the sixteenth century, ginger had also been planted in the Caribbean and had now become cheap and commonplace. Documents record that Jamaica alone exported more than two million pounds of ginger to Spain in 1547! Other spices, such as turmeric and cardamom, disappeared almost entirely from the European repertoire. Pepper at least seemed to retain its previous popularity, though mainly in the north of Europe. The new fashion was to pair sugar with the sweet spiciness of cinnamon, whether on the Piazza San Marco or the Terreiro do Paço. Da Orta has the following to say about his countrymen's favorite spice: "One cannot eat any spice with pleasure except cinnamon. It is true that the Germans and Flemings eat pepper, and here our negresses eat cloves, but Spaniards [that is, Iberians] do not eat any of the spices except cinnamon."

He certainly overstates his case; moreover, he may not have been the best-placed individual to comment on mainstream Portuguese foodways given the fact that he was a "New Christian," one of the many nominally converted Jews who went abroad to escape the prying eyes of the Inquisition.* Nevertheless, he has a point. Infanta Maria's *Livro de cozinha* repeatedly instructs the cook to finish dishes with a sprinkle of cinnamon. A contemporary Catalan cookbook says much the same. But even the Italian sources, including the widely disseminated cookbooks of Scappi and Messisbugo, make it clear that cinnamon was the "it" spice of the sixteenth century. Not that cinnamon wasn't used earlier. The recipes of Martino/Platina, so popular in the latter part of the fifteenth century, use plenty of cinnamon, but they typically use it in concert with ginger and only occasionally sprinkle it on as a final garnish. It would be hard to prove that the increased availability of better-quality Ceylonese cinnamon brought about by the direct sea route between India and Lisbon had a direct impact on the tastes of the fashion capitals of southern Europe; however, it is a documented fact that the *naus* increasingly devoted more cargo space to cinnamon as the century progressed.

The taste for sugar increased in tandem with the fashion for cinnamon. Food historians who find medieval quantities of spice off-putting must be apoplectic when they read how much sugar was used in meat and fish dishes in the Renaissance. In a typical recipe from Cristoforo Messisbugo's trendy sixteenth-century cookbook, a fish pie made with some three pounds of fish includes more than a cup of sugar as well as cinnamon and rose water. The slightly earlier *Livro de cozinha* may not give quantities, but more than half the "savory" dishes include sugar. And while the Portuguese certainly did not invent the European sweet tooth, their plantations—first in the Algarve, then in the Atlantic islands, and finally in Brazil—went a long way toward creating the very idea of dessert in European cuisine. Even today, the Portuguese love their sugary sweets sprinkled with cinnamon. Moreover, the use of cinnamon as a final garnish, even for savory items, has never entirely left the Portuguese repertoire. In *Arte de cozinha,* a cookbook written by the royal chef Domingos Rodrigues around 1680, cinnamon makes an appearance in dozens of

---

* Da Orta managed to avoid the clutches of the Holy Office during his lifetime, but the church's inquisitors got to him a dozen years after he had died and was buried. He was condemned postmortem for the crime of Judaism, and his bones were exhumed and burned.

Portugal's favorite spice, cinnamon, in a somewhat fanciful print from Garcia da Orta's masterwork.

meat, poultry, and vegetable dishes as well as the expected sweets, typically sprinkled on at the end. Fish seems to be the exception; there, pepper is more popular. Rodrigues's book stayed in print until 1836, attesting to the recipes' popularity. At the turn of the last century, cinnamon was still used commonly in stews. Even today, it can be found in rustic main-course dishes in the mountainous enclaves in the Algarve as well as in soups in the Azores. Admittedly, these days, cinnamon appears much more commonly in Portuguese confectionary than in savory dishes, yet a popular culinary website still recommends cinnamon sticks for flavoring "chicken, lamb and stuffed vegetables."

Though the opening of the sea route to India made spices more widely available (albeit by no means cheaper) in Europe, Portugal's influence on the continent's tastes north of the Pyrenees can be considered only marginal at best. Elsewhere, however, this little country's impact on the way people eat was nothing short of transformational. Today, a brief walk through Panjim's central market reveals piles of cashews still attached to the yellow, plum-sized fruit on which they grow, papayas the size of watermelons, fat winter squashes, hillocks of tomatoes, straw baskets bristling with pineapples, galvanized metal tubs of white and purple sweet potatoes, woven trays of lumpy passion fruit—all foods brought from the Americas by the Portuguese. The transfer of foods between the New and the Old Worlds has come to be known as "the Columbian exchange," but at least in the Tropics, it would be more apt to describe it as "the Cabralian exchange," for the man who put Brazil on the map. It was the Portuguese sailors in their pepper *naus,* not the Spanish conquistadores, who brought peanuts to Africa and cashews to India.

Nonetheless, when we think of Indian cuisine, we tend not to dwell on cashews and sweet potatoes. The first thought that comes to mind is the spicy burn of red pepper. The produce aisles of the Panjim market have plenty of chili peppers both large small, but it isn't until you enter the ill-lit back section of the sprawling market, where row after row of vendors display their dry spices, that Cabral's stopover in Brazil hits home. As you would expect in this nation of curry eaters, there are bright plastic basins full of every indigenous spice, from fat yellow fingers of turmeric and loose brown curls of cassia to fine crystals of asafetida and wrinkled peppercorns. Yet as you breathe in (and I would recommend doing this gingerly, for even the locals go about sneezing), you do not smell the spices that Europeans risked their lives for. What you smell, what scrapes through your nostrils and lungs, what makes your eyes well with tears, is the fierce burn of chili pepper. For while the other spices occupy modest washbasin-sized containers, the chilies fill enormous chest-high burlap bags, color foot-high pyramids of ruddy masala powders, and flavor jars of spicy relishes and pickles. It is certainly the most delicious irony of the spice trade that the Portuguese, who had come to India to bring home black pepper, would be the ones to introduce red pepper to most of the world. It is widely accepted that New World peppers—which are, of course, in no way related to *Piper nigrum*—were carried to Africa, India, and Southeast Asia in Portuguese ships. What is less clear is just how this happened and when, and even more obscure is how capsicums got to Portugal itself.

THE PEPPER MYSTERY

In Portugal, until recently, people bought their fish, their fruit, their spices, in much the same sort of sprawling market as you still find in Panjim. But today, the customers who make the trip down to Lisbon's main waterfront market are getting older and fewer. Just as everywhere else in the developed world, almost everyone now shops in supermarkets. If you really want to know what people in Lisbon eat day in and day out, visit a Pingo Doce. The Portuguese are mad about their shopping malls, and it seems that nearly every one is anchored by a Pingo Doce, the country's largest chain of supermarkets. Most of these markets are upscale, antiseptic, and entirely generic. There is Coca-Cola by the case; you can stop by the sushi bar or buy vacuum-packed tortellini. But since this is Portugal, there are also counters of exquisitely fresh sardines and overtly odiferous *bacalhau*. So what can Pingo Doce tell us about chilies in the national cuisine?

You'll find plenty of sweet peppers in the produce section. In Portugal, these are called *pimentão*, and you'll find them grilled, slow-roasted in olive oil, and ground up into a paste that is used as a marinade. The spice shelf features jars of equally sweet peppers dried and ground into a paprika-like spice referred to as *pimentão doce*. When the locals want a bit of heat, they reach for cellophane packages of little dried peppers called *piripiri.* But just to confuse things, the Pingo Doce sells fresh hot chilies under the name *malagueta,* the same name once given by the Portuguese to grains of paradise. Out of this comes a misconception I hear stated more than once that chilies actually went from Africa to Brazil instead of the other way around. Yet this very confusion is illuminating, for it hints that the route that chili peppers took from America to Portugal was far from direct.

When João II sent Bartolomeu Dias past the Cape of Good Hope in search of a quicker route to those Christians and spices, there was no doubt about what spice his sailors were after. It was black pepper, *Piper nigrum,* the fruit of that leafy vine that still clambers up trees in the emerald jungles of India's Western Ghats. Columbus had much the same idea when he pointed his *caravelas redondas* west. Yet, in our time, the world's most widely traded spice is not *Piper nigrum* but the dried fruits of the *Capsicum* genus—what we call hot pepper, red pepper, chili, chilli, or chile, depending on just who is doing the cooking. And the world's appetite for this incendiary seasoning is growing by leaps and bounds.*

When we look back to 1492, the only cooks familiar with the spice were limited to the kitchens of the Western Hemisphere. Kashmiris had to make do with black pepper and ginger to give a little kick to their *rogan josh,* there wasn't a Thai curry that could make you break a sweat, and Korean kimchi wouldn't have been much hotter than sauerkraut. Yet fifty years later, chilies had circled the globe. How did this happen so fast? And just who brought the chilies from the "New World" to the Old, and why did they bother in the first place? Then there is the question of why they were so quickly adopted from Spain to Sichuan.

The broad outlines of the answers are reasonably uncontroversial. It is in the details that the story gets murky and promises to remain so until a cadre of fanatical graduate students scours all the unpublished sources and digs through Renaissance privies of five continents to find the undigested seeds that would provide more definitive answers. In the meantime, we have botanical clues, some scattered linguistic testimony, and the

---

* In fiscal year 2003–4, India alone exported more than five times as much chili as black pepper, some 86,575 metric tons of chili compared to only 16,635 tons of black pepper.

occasional eyewitness. Unfortunately, none of this adds up to more than circumstantial evidence.

Here's what we know. In Mexico, chilies had been cultivated as far back as 5000 to 7000 B.C.E. By the time Columbus made landfall, an assortment of cultivated varieties grew across most of what is now Latin America. In addition, many varieties must have grown wild, since chilies are widely distributed by certain birds that happily munch the fruit of these little tropical bushes. (Birds are apparently not sensitive to capsaicin, the chemical responsible for chilies' characteristic burn.) Chilies are notoriously promiscuous and will cross-pollinate with no more than the glancing touch of a passing insect's thigh. This makes them particularly hard to classify. There are nevertheless some four or five domesticated species (with hundreds of cultivars) that botanists can reliably identify.

Columbus and his crew mention chili peppers several times during those early Castilian visits to the Caribbean. "The pepper which the local Indians used as a spice is more abundant and more valuable than either black or melegueta pepper," he writes. Elsewhere, he notes that "there is . . . much *ají*, which is their pepper and is worth more than our pepper; no one eats without it because it is very healthy. Fifty caravels can be loaded each year with it on this Isla Espanola [the island of Hispaniola, today divided between Haiti and the Dominican Republic]." The misguided Genoan naturally called this newly encountered spice *pimienta*, after the Spanish word for black pepper, in much the same way as he called the islands he visited the Indies and the indigenous people, Indians. There's been confusion ever since. In South America, the term *ají* (from the Arawak *axi*) became a common name for the spice; in Mexico, *chile* (from the Nahuatl *chilli*) was preferred; while in Spain, *pimienta de India* ("Indian pepper") was gradually supplanted by the word *pimentón*. In most European languages, some variation on the word *pepper* is used.

Back in Castile, as we know, Isabella did not exactly leap off her throne in delight when she learned the details of Columbus's discoveries. Others were more intrigued. Within months of the *Niña*'s return, the spice was planted in several monastery gardens, the botanical incubators of the time. By 1564, the visiting Flemish botanist Charles de L'Écluse reports seeing peppers growing all over Spain. He adds, "The fruit has various shapes and is used both fresh and dry as a condiment." Five hundred years on, we can't be sure whether these peppers were of the sweet or hot variety, but it's a fair bet they were both. Later on in the text, he mentions coming across a hotter, yellowish variety at a Lisbon monastery. These were apparently so strong that they would burn the jaws for several days. Today in Spain, pungent and mild *pimentón* exists side by side, though the sweet type is much more common. We can infer from *pimentón*'s absence from Spanish cookbooks for the next couple of hundred years that it was a decidedly lower-class seasoning used by peasants to color as much as flavor their fare. Given the way ground red pepper is often used to tint food orange in today's Spain and Portugal, it may have replaced domestic saffron in the culinary ecosystem rather than imported black pepper. In other parts of Europe, capsicums were slow to take off, though botanists across the continent noted the new plant with great curiosity.

One of the earliest descriptions and illustrations of the capsicum plant comes from an herbal written in 1542 by the German naturalist Leonhard Fuchs. Here (in the hand-tinted versions, at least), we have peppers in shades of red and green. There were also little champagne-cork-shaped chilies and long peppers like lizards' tongues. You would presume that they made their way to Germany from the Caribbean by way of Spain. But just where Fuchs himself thought they came from is hard to decipher. The one he calls *Piper hispanum,* or Spanish pepper, is a no-brainer. But did he think the *Indianischer pfeffer* (Indian pepper) came from India, or was it just a translation of the current Spanish name? More intriguing is the *Calechutischer pfeffer* (Calicut pepper). Had capsicums already made the round-trip from the Americas to Malabar and back to Germany in the fifty years following Columbus's inadvertent discoveries? It's possible. Fuchs spent most of his career in German cities up the Rhine from Antwerp, the great spice entrepôt of its day. Literally tons of Portuguese black pepper were being shipped up the river in those days, so who is to say that a few capsicum seeds might not have made the trip, too?

But how did chilies arrive in India to begin with? In the West Indies, according to at least one Castilian conquistadore, Gonzalo Fernández de Oviedo y Valdes, European settlers were eating as many chilies as the natives by the 1520s at least. The hidalgo was particularly taken with the plant's healthful qualities. Because of its heating properties, it is most suitable for the winter, even better with meat and fish than "good black pepper," he writes. He also mentions in passing that the spice had been taken to Spain, Italy, and many other places, though, unfortunately, he doesn't spell out any specific itinerary.

There are two likely scenarios that sent the spice around the world, the first premised on boredom and the second on curiosity. While wealthy officers and passengers of the Portuguese *naus* boarded with plenty of fine spices to flavor their oversalted food, common sailors had fewer options. It's reasonable to think they picked up dried chilies as they stopped to provision the ship on the way to India so as to add a little zing to their dreadful diet. They then introduced the spice to new ports along the way. This dissemination could have occurred intentionally or perhaps inadvertently as the pepper seeds were deposited in dung heaps from Moçambique to Malacca. Another possibility is that members of the religious orders carried the seeds with them to gardens established in Portuguese forts along the spice route.

Where the sailors (or friars?) got the chilies to begin with is unclear. The *Carreira da Índia* made one, or sometimes two, stops on the way to the Cape of Good Hope: one in the Cape Verde Islands to pick up fresh water and provisions and occasionally another (though Lisbon discouraged this) in Brazil as the ships swung across the Atlantic to take advantage of the trade winds. Most likely, it was the semiarid Cape Verdes, ideally situated off the African coast, that were the first tropical beachhead for chilies' march around the world. Whether the peppers came from the Caribbean or Brazil is impossible to say. José de Acosta, a sixteenth-century Jesuit priest who spent many years in New Spain, claims that in his day, chilies were called *axi* (a variant spelling of *ají*) in India. Brazil was closer, though, and the so-called bird chilies grown early on in India and eastern Africa are closely related to their South American cousins. Both might have occurred—there was plenty of traffic between the African islands and the New World. As early as 1512, a letter from the Cape Verdes records "a large concourse of ships" arriving from Portugal, Brazil, as well as the nearby Guinea coast.

After the Atlantic islands, the next stop en route to India was the eastern African port of Moçambique, just down the coast from the Swahili-speaking cities in what are now Tanzania and Kenya. Across southeastern Africa, hot peppers would come to be known by their Swahili name *pili-pili* or *piri-piri*. Goans, too, use the term *periperi masala* for a mixture made especially spicy with the addition of hot chili peppers, though just when the African term came into use here is unclear.

In the Indian subcontinent, the first mention of the chili appears in the work of the southern composer Purandaradasa around the middle of the sixteenth century. "I saw you green, then turning redder as you ripened," he sang, "nice to look at and tasty in a dish, but too hot if an excess is used. Savior of the poor, enhancer of good food, even to think of [the deity] is difficult." A roughly contemporary Sanskrit work also mentions chilies. Nevertheless, it is surprising that the otherwise highly perceptive Garcia da Orta did not mention them in his 1563 opus, despite the fact that he was living right there in Goa. Were chilies first introduced into the south before reaching Goa? (Recall that Fuchs calls it "Calicut pepper," not Goan pepper.) Portuguese ships typically made landfall in the southern city of Cochin before going on to the viceroy's capital. Would it not be logical that the residents of the pepper coast would pick up the habit of using chilies before Indians to the north?

I put the question to Thomas Thumpassery, as we had lunch at his pepper plantation in the southern Indian province of Kerala. Thomas's mother had been sure to choose dishes that would not cauterize my delicate gringo palate. Accordingly, I was presented with a series of delicate vegetable dishes and mild meat preparations along with a sweet mango pickle that is usually served to children. The food was a delicious blend of smoke, coconut, and spice with a subtle interplay of chile, turmeric, cumin, ginger, and curry leaf. But where was the black pepper that grew just across the driveway? "We don't eat it," Thomas told me. One of the odd ironies of the black pepper trade is that the spice is hardly ever used in the local cooking. Just about the only exception, made mostly by Keralan Christians, is in so-called continental preparations, which are the local interpretations of European cooking. But very little is used in indigenous dishes. This is not true in other parts of India, where Keralan pepper is used much more commonly than in its place of origin. Even just across the Western Ghats, which separate Kerala from the state of Tamil Nadu, they use lots of black pepper. "I hate the taste," quips Thomas, confirming the point.

He reminds me that in India, outside of its native Malabar, black pepper was also an exotic import, which—while perhaps not so dear as in Antwerp—was affordable only for the well-to-do. The only part of India where black pepper was used as a seasoning by the common people would have been right here where they could go into the woods to pick it for free.

Coincidentally, just about the time chilies arrived in India, around 1500, the worldwide demand for black pepper (in China and North India as well as Europe) was going through the roof.* For the first time, black pepper began to be cultivated rather than just foraged in the woods. It became a cash crop. Put yourself in the place of a Keralan peasant. Would you sell your pepper crop for hard currency or crush it into your curry? The cheaply grown chilies must have made landfall at just the perfect time to replace the locally grown but now especially marketable pepper. There are other indications that chili was a poor people's spice—*pimento dos pobres,* as it was once known in Goa. Thomas explains that when it comes to ritual foods made by upper-caste Brahman monks in the south, only black pepper will do, even in preparations that commonly use red peppers. Yet despite these sorts of ritual exceptions, most of the population would have found it easy enough to incorporate chili into their cuisine. In Indian cooking, spices are used to correct or adjust other foods much as they were in the Europe of Vasco da Gama's time. Accordingly, capsicums not only made food spicy-hot in a way reminiscent of black pepper, they fit the same pharmacological slot.

From Malabar, chilies must have followed the same routes traveled by black pepper for hundreds of years: up the coast to Goa and then to North India, across the Himalayas to the interior provinces of China. (The Sichuanese were especially enthusiastic converts to the new spice.)

---

* In an odd mirror image of Europe, China was also undergoing a consumerist upsurge in the sixteenth century. This was stimulated in part by increased domestic manufacturing but also to some degree by American silver, which was eddying into China as it was into Europe. Here, too, a printing revolution had led to a new popularity for cookbooks, and the same kind of epicurianism you find in Renaissance Italy was in full swing.

Going west, Indian chilies certainly made it as far as Persia and even pos-sibly Turkey, though it is much more plausible that the Ottomans got their hot peppers from Spain.* It was also Portuguese (and Gujarati) traders who most likely brought chilies to Southeast Asia as well, though it is also perfectly possible that Spanish seamen sailing the Manila galleon route from Acapulco to the Philippines can be assigned the credit. But even in places where merchants and mariners were inadequate to the task, birds swooped in, scattering capsicum seed–filled droppings in even the most remote locations.

West Africa is a different matter altogether and adds yet another layer of haze to an already cloudy picture. In the years when Christopher Columbus was hanging around the Lisbon court, Portuguese caravels were shipping two kinds of "pepper" from what was known as the Guinea or Melegueta coast of Africa: grains of paradise, aka melegueta pepper (*Aframomum melegueta*), and also an African peppercorn (*Piper clusii*) related to cubeb pepper. Few people would mistake the spice called *pimenta malagueta* in Portuguese for black pepper (*Piper nigrum*). The seeds are much smaller, smoother, and lighter in color. They largely resemble the cardamom seeds to which melegueta is related, though, once it is ground, the spice has its own floral, juniperlike aroma with, admittedly, a distinctly peppery bite. The second pepper, which the Portuguese came across as they were nosing up the Niger in 1485, was dubbed *pimenta de rabo*, "pepper with a tail," because it looked like a peppercorn with a little stem attached. The Italian pilot aboard described it as especially pungent. "It is very similar to cubeb pepper in appearance, but in flavor an ounce of this [African pep-per] has the effect of a half-pound of ordinary pepper." These little berries, occasionally called Ashanti pepper today, actually are related to the Indian spice; they have a similar kind of pungency. However, their somewhat bit-ter flavor may explain why this so-called false pepper had a relatively short run in the European market.

The caravels weren't just shipping pepper, of course. One of the main "commodities" transported from the Guinea coast to Madeira and

---

* The sixteenth century saw an enormous migration of Spanish Jews to the eastern Mediter-ranean, and many of these had been active in the transatlantic trade. What is more, the Turk-ish name for chili, *biber aci*, clearly comes from the Caribbean *ají*.

southern Spain to work the sugar plantations was human beings. Then, after Columbus's famous trip, the Portuguese quickly got into the business of supplying slaves to the new Spanish colonies, and by the 1530s, they could count on customers in Brazil as well. Once again, the records are inadequate, but chilies must have arrived on the West African coast by way of the Cape Verde Islands, since this was the most common stopover for the slavers going in both directions. By the late sixteenth century, some Europeans are referring to chilies as "Guinea peppers," while Brazilians are calling their native chilies *malaguetas* or *pimenta de rabo.* Is it any wonder that historians as knowledgeable as Aporvela's Hernâni Xavier are convinced that chilies were native to West Africa and were being imported into Portugal long before Columbus set sail?

My guess is that chilies got to Portugal proper relatively late through several distinct if circuitous routes and were incorporated into the cuisine in a series of waves. Walk into any Portuguese deli and you're likely to bump into red-tinted *chouriços, linguiças, morcelas,* and *salpicões* hanging from the ceiling and filling the display cases—all sausages tinted to a greater or lesser extent with *pimentão.* Cooks will add *pimentão* to foods cooked at home as well but with nowhere near the frequency found across the border in Spain. All the indicators suggest that these mild chilies reached Portugal by way of its next-door neighbor rather than directly from the New World and that here, too, they replaced expensive saffron as much as black pepper.

When a *Lisboeta* wants heat, she reaches for a *malagueta* or for *piripiri.* Both words are used rather loosely for any hot pepper, though the latter is usually dried. At some point, chilies called *malaguetas* must have been brought in from both Brazil and the Guinea coast, probably long after *pimentões* arrived from Spain. They've become widely popular only in the past few decades when the *retornados,* colonials (and natives) who fled Portugal's newly independent former colonies in the 1970s, brought their African tastes back to the metropolis. The popularity of East African *piripiri* is of similarly recent vintage. Ask for *piripiri* in a restaurant (it is as common as ketchup in America) and you'll get a little jar of ground hot pepper in olive oil. You can slather the condiment on whatever pleases you (though you might see a few eyebrows raised if you use it on some very traditional dishes). Even today, hot pepper has a working-class (and gender) association. I have found that *piripiri* is by no means ubiquitous in Portugal. Rui Lis, the nonconformist lawyer who has seen his fair share of heat in Africa, insists that's because I've eaten at too many yuppie restaurants. When pressed, he admits that Portuguese women are also generally not fond of the condiment, but men, real men, need their *piripiri*.*

Of course, most contemporary *Lisboetas* give as little thought to the origin of *piripiri* as they do to the globe-spanning empire the capital once ruled. No wonder: the hot pepper is much more pungent than some dimly remembered history lesson about a little country whose long-gone wealth was once coveted by grasping hands from Madrid to London to Amsterdam.

Shipwrecks and Custard Tarts

Across the railroad tracks and the highway that now separate the Mosteiro dos Jerónimos from the Tejo River stands Lisbon's best-known monument, an ornate little tower that looks like nothing so much as a toy fortress put up so that children can play king of the castle in the radiant southern sun. Like the monastery, the Torre de Belém is constructed of shiny white limestone and decorated with graceful arches and proud shields bearing the Crusaders' cross. The whole thing is girded with a faux stone rope tied in a sailor's knot, as if the architect had decided to gift wrap his present to the king. Yet all this is disguise, an ornate blind with twelve-foot walls, a platform for the sixteen cannons pointed at anyone who would dare trespass into Lisbon's estuary. From the tower's highest platform, there's an unlimited view of the entire river—all the way to where it opens up to greet the Atlantic near Cascais. Any enemy ship arriving from the ocean would have had to sail past these cannons, but perhaps even more important, the lace-covered gun battery reminded any would-be smuggler not to mess with the king. When the pepper-laden ships entered the estuary, they were met by customs officials who followed the ships all the way to Lisbon to make sure none of the crown's spices were surreptitiously brought to shore.

The sea could be treacherous between here and the mouth of the bay. There, the unseen sandbanks shifted with every storm. Hundreds of

---

* It's amazing how foods still retain biases based on gender. Not that Portugal is in any way unique in this respect. In places like Texas, hot chilies have a decidedly macho association, too.

ships wrecked within sight of Belém. We know a great deal about one in particular thanks to recent joint American-Portuguese archaeological excavations led by Filipe Castro and Francisco Alves.

On September 15, 1606, the lookouts of the Torre de Belém saw the tall masts of the *Nossa Senhora dos Mártires* careening in the blowing wind, tilting and then crashing to the water as the massive hull struck an underwater obstacle and shattered, spilling cannons, *caixas*, sailors, and close to a million pounds of black pepper into the boiling waters. The next morning, *Lisboetas* awoke to beaches tinted black from the midnight tide of peppercorns. Witnesses report a mad rush to collect the costly cargo washed ashore before the king's officials could fish out the remainder. Even recently, when the marine archaeologists went looking for the remains of the great *nau*, they discovered them embedded in a layer of muck mixed in with peppercorns. Many of the artifacts were long gone, pilfered by amateur divers and swept away by four centuries' storms, but in the midst of the peppercorns, the fragments of the hull contained a sampling of the riches of the east—silver pieces of eight, gold jewelry, and Chinese porcelain—as well as the more common pewter plates and earthenware pots that are the bread and butter of the archaeology trade. You can go and see some of the finds at the Museu de Marinha. There's even a generous pile of peppercorns. Pepper does keep well, but not this well. Some of the team's members actually tasted the four hundred–year–old peppercorns. Not surprisingly, any trace of taste was gone. All the same, Professor Castro confesses that he detected a dim aroma when he dove down into the deepest of the muddy layers. Mostly, though, the peppercorns were just a flimsy outer layer with nothing inside. They had to be dehydrated in alcohol, then dried with a hair dryer in small batches, and impregnated with glue so that they would not turn to dust in the exhibit.

The breakup of the *Mártires* was just one more incident to add to a rising tally of shipwrecks that were a symptom of an empire that was increasingly as flimsy and hollow as the *Mártires'* peppercorns. You can blame the loss of Lisbon's spice trade on a long inventory of reasons, but the empire built on a shoestring—and held together with the spit and sealing wax of distant forts and factories—was just too wobbly to sustain the incompetence within and the assault from without.

Much of what went wrong, all my sailor historians are quick to point out, can be blamed on the Spanish. In 1578, King Sebastião I of Portugal (one of the more unhinged of the royal line) got himself killed on yet another crusade against the Moors. The result was that two years later, the Portuguese crown fell into the lap of the workaholic and fanatically religious Hapsburg monarch of Spain, Philip II, thereafter also Filipe I of Portugal. "We refer to those sixty years of Spanish rule as our 'Babylonian captivity,' " Lieutenant Neves informs me, lest I have any illusions about the love lost between Portugal and her pushy neighbor. Theoretically, the two kingdoms were supposed to stay separate under Philip, but it didn't work out that way for long. The Spanish ruler just couldn't keep his fingers off the profits from the spice trade, especially when he needed the money to pay for his religious wars. At the same time, the annual *Carreira da Índia*, which was already depending on too many slaves and convicts to man the sails, lost even more of its experienced sailors to the comfier and more profitable Spanish galleons that used to make the relatively quick passage to the Americas. When Philip sent his disastrous armada to punish England's Protestant queen in 1588, a good part of his fleet was actually Portuguese. "Those were our ships he wrecked!" Hernâni Xavier spits out. But the Spanish kings had their eyes fixed elsewhere—which meant that Lisbon's fleet withered and her empire shriveled from neglect.

Holland's entry into the spice trade—or at least, its timing—can also be laid at Philip's door. Portugal had had a long, cordial history with the Low Countries from the days when her kings married into Burgundian nobility and her merchants unloaded salt and oil on Bruges's medieval piers. Throughout most of the sixteenth century, Portuguese pepper was distributed through Antwerp, and Dutch middlemen regularly came down to Lisbon to fill their holds with melegueta, black pepper, and cinnamon. The Portuguese kings had encouraged this trade, granting the Dutchmen a package of privileges analogous to the Venetians' *fondachi* in Muslim lands. The crown even allowed the northerners to practice their heretical rites within their own compound. In 1580, though, Holland was in the midst of an armed rebellion against Spain (the Netherlands had fallen under Hapsburg rule some years earlier). Philip II reacted by closing all his ports to Dutch shipping and sending his shock troops north to bring the heretics to heel. It didn't work out quite the way he planned. The conquistadores experienced one humiliating defeat after another, and Holland's navy sailed right up to

Gibraltar and sank a Spanish armada a stone's throw from Andalusia's shore. With no pepper available to them in Lisbon, the Hollanders decided to go to the Asian source, looting and sinking as many of the enemy's ships as they could along the way. The poorly manned Portuguese ships were especially tender targets, particularly when compared to the heavily armed Spanish galleons that made up the silver fleet from New Spain.

Goa was always too well defended for the Dutch to take it by force, but Portugal's other redoubts in the Estado da Índia were picked off one by one. The spice islands of Tidore and Amboina fell in 1605, Malacca in 1641, Ceylon in 1656. Even Cochin, where the *carreira* had so long filled its ships to bursting with pepper, succumbed to Dutch assault in 1663. When, after the sixty years of Spanish captivity, a Portuguese king once again occupied the Paço da Ribeira in 1540, he could count on a mere eleven ships worthy of the name: eight galleons of Portuguese construction—of which, one was not fit to sail—and three other ships that had been seized from the French and the Dutch. In contrast, according to one contemporary estimate, the Hollanders could muster more than fourteen thousand vessels for war! Increasingly, the pepper fleet left India later and later in the season to avoid the Dutch (and later English) marauders, with the result that they missed the dependable winds of the monsoon and wrecked on the way home. The number of wrecks rose so precipitously in the early seventeenth century that in some years, Portugal had no pepper to sell at all.

Nonetheless, the Dutch could hardly be held responsible for every shipwreck. The Lisbon-bound ships were always chronically overloaded because of the crews' own allotments of merchandise, whether in the form of the official *caixas* or in contraband. Given their rotten salaries, it was the only way to make the perilous trip worthwhile. Incompetence at every level could also take a share of the blame. In Portugal, the job of captaining a ship was assigned as a royal favor to members of the high nobility. Knowing prow from stern was not one of the prerequisites. As a result, the actual practice of sailing the ships was handed over to the pilot. You can imagine what happened when captain and pilot disagreed. Beaches from Moçambique to Madeira saw their share of pepper tides. As if this weren't bad enough, experienced pilots were in short supply. In a meeting held at the viceroy's Goan palace in 1643, the local authorities realized that, back home, there wasn't a single pilot qualified to navigate a ship to India, since all those with adequate experience (all ten!) were stuck in Goa due to a Dutch blockade.

Sailors who had some idea of what they were doing were hard to find, too. Between the death toll on the *carreira* itself and the seamen who never returned from the Indies, the kingdom had been hemorrhaging sailors for years. Lieutenant Neves supplies a telling statistic, noting that in many years, there were more deaths on the return trip to India than there were mariners in the entire Spanish armada that sailed to America. Neves, like every historian of the spice route, repeats the story recounted by the royal chronicler Castanheda of the 1505 departure of the pepper fleet from Belém. The sailors were so green that the captain of one caravel nailed a braid of garlic to one side of the ship and an onion braid to the other so that they could tell right from left. Then, when he wanted to turn the ship to starboard, he shouted "Garlic," and to port, he yelled "Onion." The confusion wasn't limited to the sailors, though, for Castanheda mixed the two up as well. Just imagine the first storm they encountered! And the sailors didn't get better as the century progressed.

The Portuguese enthusiasm for promoting the faith, the very same fanaticism that had once led to the voyages of discovery, was now dragging the empire down. Not only was the king's purse being drained to gild the magnificent altars of *Goa Dourada,* the realm's policy of gunboat evangelism wasn't making it too many friends in the East. Meanwhile, back home, the jackboot tactics of the Inquisition were sending many of the "New Christians" packing to less hostile climes. The exodus of these formerly Jewish artisans, merchants, and professionals was a disaster for the Portuguese middle class, even as it did wonders for Amsterdam, Antwerp, and London, which took them in. What's more, the Counter-Reformation had insidious effects on the culture that were not as public as the autos-da-fé, where pork abstainers were burned alive. Compare the era of King João II, who authorized two French booksellers to import tax-free as many books as they chose because he believed "it is good for the common weal to have many books circulating in our kingdom," to the stultifying climate of a hundred years hence. By then, the dread of foreign heresies had imposed a totalitarian form of censorship on any books printed in or imported into the kingdom. Even masterworks by Portuguese authors such as da Orta were much more widely circulated abroad than at home.

In Asia, it used to be that the promotion of religion was every Lusitanian's business. Lieutenant Neves describes the early Portuguese mariner as a kind of multipurpose tool that could function as a sailor, soldier, merchant, and Christian enforcer, depending on the time and place. However, even before the years of Spanish rule, the religious campaign was firmly in the hands of a cadre of professionals, the Jesuits, many of whom were not even Portuguese. The Lusitanians once firmly believed that the reason their little country had conquered the waves was that they were doing God's will. Yet by the middle years of the sixteenth century, the crusading impulse had more or less evaporated in the rank and file who sailed out past the Torre de Belém, now wholly replaced by a quest to line their pockets.

Echoing the locals' low expectations, Linschoten mentions that when each viceroy arrives in Goa for his three-year term, he spends the first year redecorating, the second amassing as much treasure as possible, and the third covering his footmarks. Much the same could be said for every other crown official. The Dutchman writes, "There is not one of them, that esteemeth the profit of the commonwealth, or the furtherance of the king's service, but rather their own." This had direct consequences on the spice trade across the Estado da Índia. You could make a lot more money buying and selling within Asia than sending pepper and cloves to the king's agents, who were sending spices back home. Consequently, the trading system settled back to pretty much the same pattern that had existed before da Gama's arrival. It's been estimated that in 1515, the Portuguese were shipping some 30 percent of Malabar's pepper production. At the end of the century, this had shrunk to some 3 or 4 percent. (Admittedly, total production had increased in the meantime.) Once more, Gujarati merchants brought pepper to ports on the Red Sea and the Persian Gulf. And yet again, Venice became the Mediterranean's greatest spice emporium. The viceroys and the captains of forts across Asia were happy to cream off what they could from this trade and made sure that little was done to stem the flow that greased their palms. The result of this was that even before the Spanish takeover, and long before the arrival of the swift ships from Amsterdam, the Portuguese had been losing market share in Europe.

It's a wonder that the whole Lusitanian empire did not collapse like a half-baked soufflé at the crash of the first Dutch cannon. But maybe that's the wrong way to look at it. Rather than bemoaning the Estado da Índia's demise, it might be better to marvel at how long this improbable realm actually prospered, especially given the fact that it was based on nothing much more than the profits loaded into the half dozen ships that arrived yearly in the *carreira*. Amazingly, this rather impromptu empire survived, even if in greatly diminished form, until the twentieth century. Goa finally submitted to Indian troops as late as 1961. In the meantime, Lisbon found other revenue streams to build her palaces and gild her churches. As the Dutch slowly strangled the Portuguese spice route in the East, the monarchs in Lisbon turned west to their long-neglected territories in Brazil for a source of income. Sugar, not pepper, would be the lure of this new El Dorado.*

Whatever good and bad can be said of the consequences of da Gama's and Columbus's trips across the oceans in search of spices and paradise— and there is no shortage of either—they had the effect of undamming the flow of humanity and commerce across the earth. The silver that was mined in Mexico now influenced currency markets in China. An increase in the demand for pepper in Europe led to changes in production techniques in India. The labor requirements of Portuguese sugar plantations in Brazil had repercussions deep within Africa. People in Lisbon and Madrid made decisions that directly affected the lives of people halfway around the world. The Venetian ambassador to Manuel I had no illusions about the immensity of these transformations: "What is greatest and most memorable of all, you have brought together under your command peoples whom nature divides, and with your commerce you have joined two different worlds." The wheels of globalization were sent spinning by the wake of the great *naus* that took leave of the little white tower at Bélem.

Tell any Lisbon native that you are going to this historic suburb and her mouth will curl into a lip-smacking smile. Naturally, every visitor to

---

* Once they had lost nearly all their share of the spice trade to the Dutch, the Portuguese tried to cultivate spices in Brazil instead. In 1678, the king instructed his Goan viceroy to send pepper vines, clove trees, and the like to other Portuguese colonies, especially Brazil. At the time, the efforts failed, though the king would be vindicated in the end. Today, Brazil is among the world's five largest pepper exporters.

Lisbon must make a pilgrimage to Belém's national shrine. But don't think for a moment that what she has in mind are the Mosteiro dos Jeró-nimos and the Torre de Belém. "They are nice, of course," the *Lisboeta* sniffs regarding these architectural jewels, "but you really must go for the *pastéis de Belém.*" The citizens of Lisbon are impassioned about their sweets. A sweet muffinlike *bolo* is a typical breakfast; lunch might conclude with any one of a dozen variations of *pudim* (the term *flan* could hardly begin to describe the myriad variations in color and texture). Other desserts are so peculiarly Portuguese that the English language could not possibly do them justice. I am convinced that the city holds more pastry shops per capita than any other place on earth. A recent search of Lis-bon's Yellow Pages indeed turns up more than eight hundred *pastelarias* in the capital alone. (A similar search on much larger Paris yields only about 180!) Most Portuguese pastries use plenty of eggs, many are scented with cinnamon, and all of them are very sweet. All this comes together in what is the national dessert, the *pastéis de nata*, in Belém rechristened the *pastéis de Belém*. It is perhaps not entirely coincidental, then, that the high temple of this custard tart, the Casa dos Pastéis de Belém, should be located just between the president's pink-tinted palace and the nation's pantheon at the Jerónimos, where the country's greatest kings, heroes, and poets lie in-terred. On weekend afternoons, the pastry shop's bar is crowded four deep as visitors and locals alike wait for their turn to nibble the still-warm confection downed with a creamy espresso.

Today's Portuguese don't spend much time thinking about their his-tory. In this, they are much like people everywhere. Hernâni Xavier would like to blame the gays and communists who he claims run the Min-istry of Education, but even he admits that the sixteenth century is of lit-tle concern to his countrymen. Heroism is not in fashion in the European Union, and most of the citizens of what used to be called Christendom would prefer not to be reminded of the jihadist fervor that launched "the age of discovery." To most of his countrymen, Camões is just the name of a street, a square, an institute. When, in school, they read the great poet's epic account of their ancestors ("risking all / In frail timbers on treacher-ous seas, / by routes never charted, and only emboldened by opposing wind; / having explored so much of the earth / from the equator to the midnight sun [they were] drawn / to touch the very portals of the dawn"), it is no more than literature. You can hardly expect the descendants of those Lusitanians to make the connection between Camões's ancient, stubborn seamen sailing round an unknown world and the cinnamon on their *pastéis de Belém,* to remember the complaint of another Portuguese poet who lamented, "At the scent of this cinnamon, the kingdom loses its people."

And yet, the stories those little custard tarts could tell. You could distill Portugal's past into a single bite. The delicate flaky pastry that shatters on the tongue is a souvenir of the Moors who brought the technique of making phyllolike pastry to Iberia. The generous sprinkle of cinnamon is like so much aromatic dust, all that's left of the long-lost Asian empire. Then there's the sugar brought by the Portuguese to America, a memento of the continent found by accident on the way to the spiceries, a reminder of the sweet cane that sent helpless Africans to suffer and die across the sea and dispatched shiploads of the white crystals to pastry shops from Lisbon to Vienna. All this history bound up with creamy, cinnamon-scented custard.

I spotted the two *Zwarte Pieten* just in time, as they were getting ready to pack up and lug their sweet-filled sack across the canal. The black-faced figures were the only splash of color in the fading December light, the velvet of their red, yellow, and green tunics glistening from the interminable Amsterdam drizzle. Across the street, I could see little of their dark-painted faces except for the broad carmine grins and the flash of fine Dutch teeth as they watched me slip and slide across the slick cobblestones. I looked neither left nor right and made a dash for it—like the fool that I am. A hurtling bicycle almost sent me headfirst into the canal. Luckily, the grandmotherly bicyclist swerved her steed at the last minute, even though I think her expert maneuver was less out of concern for my safety than to keep the tower of pastry-shop cartons from toppling out of her basket.

It was December 5, the eve of *Sinterklaas,* the feast of Saint Nicholas. Dutch grandmothers mark the occasion by spoiling their grandchildren with all manners of sweets. Parents hide presents in wooden shoes and broom closets. And numberless blond, blue-eyed Netherlanders paint their faces black and dress up like Renaissance house slaves, as *Zwarte Pieten* ("Black Petes")—the name given to Saint Nick's "African" helpers. They hang out on street corners and in shopping malls, distributing *pepernoten* to every passerby. The spicy cookies, the campy blackface—they're as Dutch as windmills and wooden shoes. But they are also somewhat creepy souvenirs of the country's colonial history, of Amsterdam's once-great empire of sugar and spice.

Pepernoten are a kind of small, dark cookie made with brown sugar and a medley of spices that varies depending on the region and the manufacturer. Despite the name, and unlike Venetian *peverini,* they are unlikely to contain any pepper to speak of, but no matter what their flavoring— some are now even being dipped in chocolate, to the horror of purists—

they are as essential to Saint Nicholas Day as old Saint Nick himself and his swarthy sidekicks.

The white-bearded saint dressed in red would be familiar to any American child who has visited a mall in the weeks before Christmas. Our own Santa Claus is largely based on the Dutch original. In the Netherlands, though, he's supposed to represent a semimythical fourth-century bishop from the balmy city of Myra (in today's Turkey) rather than a frost-flushed elf from the wintry pole. In the Middle Ages, his claim to fame was as the patron saint of merchants and sailors, so it was only natural that the up-and-coming seaport of Amsterdam would appoint Nicholas as the city's official saint.*

Records as early as 1360 describe a *Sinterklaas* celebration for children. According to tradition he showed up in medieval Dutch convent schools, where he rewarded deserving pupils with spicy sweets and left behind a birch switch for thrashing ne'er-do-wells. Soon enough, the bushy-bearded visitor became associated with handing out presents, too. In medieval Amsterdam, the city's central Dam Square was taken over each year by a *Sinterklaas* market, where the booths overflowed with sweets like cinnamon bark, honey tarts, and *pepernoten,* all distinctly flavored with the sugar and spices imported from the bishop's home in the mythical East. All this fun was too much for the Calvinists when they took over during the Reformation, so they tried to ban the rotund saint, indicting him as an idolatrous Papist puppet. "The setting up of booths on St. Nicholas Eve where goods are sold, which St. Nicholas is said to provide, leads the children astray, and such a practice is not only contrary to all good order, but also leads the people away from the true religion and tends toward atheism, superstition and idolatry," ran the text of one anti-*Klaas* injunction from 1600. In town after town, measures were taken to ban the baking of spicy *Sinterklaas* cakes and setting out

---

* The Venetians, who never seemed able to keep their hands off any foreign saint they met, stole the remnants of Saint Nick's corpse from Turkey in 1100 and deposited them in a church on the Lido. These remains must have been especially miraculous because the same saint was supposedly also stolen from Myra a few decades earlier and set up in Bari. As a consequence, the ancient bishop is the patron saint of thieves. He is also the patron saint of pawnbrokers, presumably for helping out the "financially challenged."

shoes for presents. But it was to no avail. Old Saint Nick was just too popular.

Nowadays, *Sinterklaas* supposedly arrives a few weeks before the December 5 holiday on a steamship from Spain—an event that is widely covered by every TV network. The saint is accompanied by a white horse and one or more *Zwarte Pieten*. You will hear that *Zwarte Piet* is supposed to be a Spanish Moor, but that's a relatively recent idea. In earlier times, the black-faced Pete typically represented the Devil and was often shackled in chains. Today's Pete, with his frilly outfit and campy wig, looks like he stepped out of a nineteenth-century minstrel show. The look is hardly co-incidental. This particular incarnation of *Piet* was invented at about the same time as those racist cabarets, at just about the time Holland abolished slavery in its colonies in 1863—incidentally, one of the last European states to do so. The Surinamese government had no illusion about what *Zwarte Piet* represented when it gained independence from the Netherlands in 1975 and promptly abolished the black-faced figure. In the sugar plantations of Suriname (formerly Dutch Guiana), they had their own opinion of dressing up black men in shackles. All the same, *Piet* was so popular that he was reinstated in 1992.

Of course, back in Holland, the Dutch would be no more likely to associate *Zwarte Piet* with the horrors of the Middle Passage than they would think of the genocide their forefathers perpetrated in the Indonesian nutmeg isles as they nibble their spice-scented *pepernoten*. In this, they are much like the Portuguese, mostly oblivious to the loss of their sugar colonies in the Americas and their Spice Islands in Indonesia, though, again like da Gama's heirs, they remain adamant when it comes to their love of sweets. The Dutch sweet tooth has a taste for spicy sweets that is almost medieval when compared to the Portuguese—at least when it comes to the confections traditionally eaten around *Sinterklaas* and Christmas. If you can believe the statistics, the Netherlands' fifteen million people consume some sixty-two million pounds of spice cake every year!

Everyone needs *speculaas* for the winter holiday. My favorite version of this medieval cake wraps gingerbread spiced by the sweet heat of cinnamon and the gentle glow of ginger and nutmeg around a core of moist, sweet marzipan. But *speculaas* takes many forms. I was first introduced to this particular Dutch obsession by the food historian Peter Rose.* Peter (in Dutch, it is a woman's name) can list more varieties than a born-again preacher can count up sins. She has documented at least forty-seven different kinds of the gingerbread. She has even shared her recipe for *speculaas* with *Gourmet* magazine. That is more than most Dutch manufacturers will do. In Holland, the spices that go into gingerbread are something akin to a state secret. Without a doubt, the Dutch have a thing about *speculaas*. Typically, though, they buy their gingerbread ready-made. The supersecret *speculaas* spice mixture, however, can also be purchased, to be added to innumerable other recipes. Any supermarket will sell you a package of this sweet masala, which is likely to include cinnamon, mace, aniseed, cardamom, nutmeg, and cloves, as well as ginger.

This Dutch fondness for spice cakes—or *peperkoek*, as these sweets are generically known (whether they contain pepper or not)—is well documented as far back as the Middle Ages. You can look it up in a 1417 council decree from the eastern Dutch city of Deventer that prescribes just what could go into their compact honey and spice loaf. Anyone who made a *Deventer koek* that didn't conform was faced with an astronomical fine of 666 guilders. It turns out the fine burghers of Deventer knew they had a good thing going, for by the end of the sixteen hundreds, the city was exporting 715,000 cakes a year (and this from a city of a mere seven thousand souls!). More recently, gingerbread has been used as a morale booster for the troops: Dutch soldiers have been issued spice cake rations in much the same way as American GIs receive Hershey's bars.

In Amsterdam, the city's heritage of spice isn't just evident in December's *speculaas* and *pepernoten*. You can also see it on grand buildings by the old waterfront emblazoned with the logo of the Dutch East India Company. You can smell it in the old warehouses. Construction workers sometimes report the sweet smell of nutmeg and cloves seeping out from the beams when they tear apart former spice depots to renovate them into trendy lofts. Of course, spice scents Dutch kitchens, too, often in ways that would make other Europeans cringe. But that's because, in other

---

* Peter explains that not all *speculaas* comes filled with marzipan—it can just be a thick ginger cookie—and not all gingerbread is *speculaas*, which tends to be limited to the holidays. When gingerbread is made into loaves, it is called *zoete koek* and is eaten year-round.

places, tastes have changed. The penchant for spice cakes used to be shared well beyond Holland's borders; those Deventer cakes were intended as much for export as for the local sweet tooth. As the last of the great spice-trading nations in Europe, Netherlanders never gave up their love of spices in the way most other Europeans did with the waning of renaissance fashions. This is most obvious in the traditional sweets that accompany holidays, in treats like *Amsterdamse korstjes,* spice crusts from Amsterdam; in *Oudewijven,* a tangy, light-colored loaf flavored with aniseed; in the now rare *Kruukplaetje,* old-fashioned spiced griddle biscuits made in South Holland. But spices, especially the sweet spices so favored by sixteenth-century Italian cooks like Scappi and Messisbugo, show up not only in cakes but even in sausages and stews. Per capita spice consumption here is comparable to Morocco and easily double the American average. The Dutch, of course, who don't think much of, or about, their own food, are blissfully unaware of any of this as they shop at their local Albert Hein supermarket to buy a custom spice mixture for their evening chicken. In Holland, you find nutmeg sprinkled on asparagus, red cabbage scented with cloves, sausage rolls flavored with mace, and even eel topped with cinnamon. A visit to a butcher shop in a suburban shopping complex can unearth a treasure trove of Dutch culinary peculiarity. Hidden away among the preprepared schnitzel, Italian salami, and gloppy mayonnaise-dressed salads are blood sausages scented with pepper and mace, and a scrapplelike *balkenbrij* containing so much cloves it burns the tongue.

Even the cheese for which Holland is justly famous can be flavored with astonishing quantities of spice. If you need proof, walk west a few hundred yards from Dam Square to the *westelijke grachtengordel* (western canal belt), a district built to accommodate the mansions of spice and timber merchants in Amsterdam's golden age. Here, on a little strip of quaint shops, hidden behind one of the plain shop façades, is one of Amsterdam's cathedrals of cheese. Not that the Kaaskamer looks much like a high temple even when you've opened the front door. The modest space is more like a giant closet (*kaas kamer* means "cheese chamber"). Still, for Dutch cheese lovers, it is a place of devotion. Everywhere you look, the walls are lined with numberless wheels of cheese separated by plain pine planks. On the bottom layer are fat, yellow rounds of four-year-old *boerenkaas* (farm cheese), brittle and caramel-sweet with age. On the shelves near the ceiling are tubby, little red balls of creamy young Gouda. And in the middle are cheeses crammed with spice. Pepper, mild paprika, and hot chili season some of the *boerenkaas.* Cumin gives an almost Moroccan tang to cheeses both young and old. And perhaps most unexpected is the *nagelkaas,* packed with whole cloves, perhaps three or four in every bite. Oddly, the assertive presence of the cloves is tamed by the buttery cheese and the generally sweet undertone so characteristic of most Dutch cheeses. Admittedly, anyone who didn't grow up with wooden footwear would most likely think it weird, but I rather like it. What's more, a hunk of *nagelkaas* puts neatly to rest any skepticism historians of food might have about the amount of spice that Europeans could ingest, now or four hundred years ago.*

DINING IN THE GOLDEN AGE

Whereas the side streets of the *westelijke grachtengordel* are lined with modest brick shops topped with plain stepped gables, the canals that give the district its name reflect a procession of imposing limestone-clad mansions embossed with baroque curlicues. When the neighborhood was conceived in the first flush of Amsterdam's seventeenth-century golden age, it was specifically designed for the city's wealthiest merchant class, who were awash with money from the trade in spices and other foreign goods. Appropriately, the inner canal, the one intended for the most splendid palazzi, was named the Herengracht, for the *Heren XVII,* the enormously powerful directors of the Dutch East India Company, which had wrenched the spice trade from the Portuguese.

When the wealthy timber merchant Jacob Cromhout went looking for a place to build a new house around 1660, he naturally chose the Herengracht. The East India trade had been good to many people, but especially to those selling lumber to the thriving shipbuilding industry. Cromhout had done well for himself and wanted to let the world know it. He hired a fine architect who designed a gracious double-gabled town house some four stories high. The building gives the impression of a har-

---

* In its most common, and more subtle, rendition, *nagelkaas* is made with a mixture of cumin and cloves. Even so, you are still likely to get at least one whole clove in every bite.

monious pair of Siamese-twin grandfather clocks faced in genteel lime-stone. In recent years, the mansion has been turned into a museum, so anyone can go and see how Amsterdam's other half used to live—and cook. Remarkably, the kitchens have been left unchanged since the seven-teenth century. And what kitchens they are! If this was the McMansion of its day, these were most definitely trophy kitchens. The larger of the two has some fifteen running feet of marble counters, a marble floor, two wall ovens, a stovetop range, as well as a fireplace, and everywhere, tasteful blue and white delft tiles. The sink even has running water! Yet despite the kitchen's high-tech appurtenances, there is every indication that the Cromhouts ate in a distinctly old-fashioned style.

To get an idea of what was served in the next-door dining room, it's worth leafing through Peter Rose's translation of *De verstandige kock* (The Sensible Cook), a popular cookery manual that saw at least ten editions between 1668 and 1711. Peter will be the first to insist that most people ate rather well in seventeenth-century Holland. She rapidly turns the pages of the cookbook pointing to recipes featuring veal, venison, suck-ling pig, turkey, partridge, heron, herring, turbot, sturgeon, endive, as-paragus, and artichokes to prove her point about what you could get in Amsterdam in the 1600s. Not that this was the kind of food you'd find in the local beer hall. Like all cookbooks of its time, it was intended for the affluent, a point made obvious by the recipes' abundant use of spices. The recipes are reminiscent of Italian cooking of about a century earlier, with a predilection for sweet-and-sour flavorings that use verjuice to pro-vide the tang and plenty of sugar to sweeten the pot. Some combination of nutmeg, pepper, mace, cloves, and cinnamon appears in just about every meat preparation, though less often with fish and vegetables. Peter insists that the amount of spice was moderate, certainly compared to medieval standards. But if I'm right and medieval food was less spicy than com-monly thought, it's likely that Dutch food was actually *more* highly seasoned than its predecessors. What's more, having tasted that *nagelkaas,* I have no illusions about Netherlanders' appetite for spice. Admittedly, like most cookbooks of the time, it's seldom clear how much cloves or nutmeg the cook is supposed to add. Nevertheless, in the few recipes where quantities are given, they are prodigious. A recipe for *hase-saus* (hare sauce) uses a sweet-and-sour base of about a cup of verjuice combined with a dozen sugar cookies, an indeterminate quantity of "whole cloves, pieces of cin-namon, a few blades of mace," and a scant tablespoon of powdered cin-namon. To sweeten it further, the author instructs you to add a handful of sugar. In another recipe, for *venesoen-pastey* (a kind of meat pie), where quantities are specified, three pounds of beef are seasoned with almost two tablespoons of pepper, four of ginger, two and a half of nutmeg, and a half tablespoon of cloves before being baked in pastry. The fourteenth-century *Ménagier de Paris* could never compete with this!

Whether Jacob and his wife, Margaretha, ate like this every day or whether this sort of preparation was mainly meant for company is un-clear. The Dutch population as a whole certainly consumed way more spices than the average European, but then many more Netherlanders could afford the exotic aromatics. By the late sixteen hundreds, pepper and ginger could hardly be considered luxuries, though cloves, nutmeg, and mace, if anything, increased a little in price.* But then most people would buy the spices in small quantities, a half ounce package or even less. Paintings from the period occasionally feature little paper cornets (apparently, these were recycled from newspapers or almanacs) filled with a few pennies' worth of ground pepper.

You can learn a lot about the taste in food of Jacob Cromhout's gen-eration from the thousands of still lifes that were produced to decorate all those houses built to accommodate Amsterdam's booming population. The Dutch bourgeoisie was mad for pictures, all sorts of pictures: land-scapes, genre scenes, portraits, and still lifes. And food was a hugely pop-ular subject. The paintings glitter with imported Chinese porcelain, sparkling Rhenish glass, and even the occasional polished brass mortar for grinding spices. Art historians who specialize in these glory days of the still life argue endlessly about how true to life they really were. Were these moral lessons disguised as luscious food displays? Were they vehicles to

---

* After 1650, the East India Company set the wholesale price of cloves at 3.75 guilders per pound (494 grams, or about 1.1 pounds) and nutmeg at roughly 3 guilders—or about 50 per-cent higher than they were earlier in the century. Once Ceylon was theirs, they doubled the price of cinnamon to about 3 guilders as well. By comparison, you could buy almost 3 pounds of pepper and about 8 pounds of ginger for a single guilder late in the century—this at a time when modestly skilled craftsmen earned a little more than a guilder a day and a second-rate still-life painting would run to about 20.

In seventeenth-century Amsterdam, even middling craftsmen could afford a few grams of pepper, sold freshly ground and packaged in recycled almanacs.

show off an artist's virtuosity and therefore collected by connoisseurs of the finest brushstroke? No matter what the artists' intentions, the results are undeniably sensuous, even prurient. The hams are spread out just waiting to be sliced into translucent rosy slivers, the ripe fruit oozes tantalizing juices, the oysters glisten with their briny liquor, so realistic you can feel them slipping down your throat. You can't convince me that the pleasure of eating wasn't foremost in the mind of the painter or the patron. That is not to say that what you saw on the canvas was exactly what people were eating. The relationship was probably no greater then than it is now between the picture-perfect recipes in food magazines and what actually lands on our tables. But some relationship surely existed, just as it must have between the instructions in *De verstandige kock* and the dishes assembled on the Croumhouts' marble counters.

Looking at the pictures and reading the cookbook makes me a little suspicious of the opinions of Dutch food given by foreign visitors. How much of Abbé Pierre Sartre's descriptions can be attributed to his Gallic blinders when he writes, "Their meat-broth is nothing more than water full of salt or nutmeg, with sweetbreads and minced meat added, having not the slightest flavor of meat"? (Admittedly, he was writing in the mid-eighteenth century, a period of Dutch decline.) Perhaps we would do better to listen to Sir William Temple, who visited the lowlands in the early sixteen hundreds. Though the Englishman has a decidedly mixed opinion of the Dutch, he does show some grudging admiration for Dutch enthusiasm at the table. "To a feast they come readily, but being set once you must have patience," he warns, in contrast to the Frenchman. "They are longer eating meat then we preparing it. If it to be supper, you conclude timely when you get away at day-break." He is also taken with the Dutch skill in fish preparation. Perhaps it is his English background that makes him so generous in this regard. But he is in full agreement with an Iberian contemporary who was shocked at the Netherlanders' poor table manners. On a visit to The Hague, the Spanish ambassador came across a group of deputies to the States General ripping apart hunks of dark bread and gnawing cheese while waiting for the session to open. This was clearly a far cry from the highly formalized dining rituals of the Most Catholic King's court, but in a way, he was impressed at the informal ways of his enemies, declaring, "Such a people is invincible!"

The Dutch did eat plenty of cheese. The Germans called their neighbors "cheese-heads," but there was a hint of envy in the moniker. Holland not only had enough cheese to feed the nation, but it could send it abroad for hard cash.

The Dutch, almost uniquely in Europe, had plenty to eat, and this was across the population as a whole. Again, the paintings of the period open a window into the ordinary kitchens and taverns of the time. No one shows the middling classes at table and country folk eating, drinking (and falling down) better than the painter Jan Steen. His versions of keg parties are particularly true to life, no doubt because he knew the subject firsthand: he started life as a brewer. The Joe Six-Packs in his pictures do not sip Rhine wine from delicate glass tumblers and dine on spiced hare off of Italian majolica as they might have on the Herengracht. They guzzle beer and chomp down on fat slices of cheese and ham with hunks of dark bread. Wages were higher in seventeenth-century Holland than anywhere else in Europe, and the grain brought in from the Baltic was relatively cheap. Consequently, the staple black bread cost little enough that a skilled laborer could pick up a three-pound loaf for a few pennies and still have change left over to spend on vegetables, cheese, and herring.* It's one reason he could afford the imported spices, even if his family tasted the more expensive ones only once a year in the holiday gingerbread. The famine-prone peasants of southern Europe would have stood with gaping mouths in front of the paintings of plump children in Amsterdam orphanages receiving a weekly ration of meat or fish to supplement their everyday diet of bread, beans, and beer. As a result of this relative affluence, and unlike the rest of Europe, there were barely any food riots reported in the newly minted republic in the sixteen hundreds.

The market gardens surrounding Holland's cities kept the urban population well supplied with vegetables, and cows grew nice and fat on the green grass that grew in the incessant Dutch drizzle. However, Holland's quality of life could hardly be sustained on local supplies alone. "This country produces little wheat and not even rye because of the low ground and wateriness," noted an impressed Italian visitor in 1567, "yet enjoys so much plenty that it supplies other countries. . . . It does not make wine, and there is more wine and more of it is drunk than in any other part where it is made." All this is to say that every aspect of Dutch cooking was dependent on imports, whether of herring from the nearby North Sea, wine from the Rhineland, rye from the Polish plains, sugar from South America, or nutmeg from halfway across the world in the Moluccas. There is a Dutch expression, *Wat men van veerst haelt, dat smaecket soetst,* which means, "The things that you bring from farthest taste the sweetest" (or, more prosaically, the best). Since most of the land wasn't much good for anything but grazing dairy cattle, anyone with ambition had to look beyond the dikes and polders. Just like in Venice and Lisbon, the path to riches led overseas.

---

* An Amsterdam ship's carpenter earning some 30 *stuivers* (1½ *guilders*) a day might pay some 4½ *stuivers* for a three-pound loaf of bread, 2½ *stuivers* for a pound of Gouda, ½ *stuiver* for a "green" or new herring, and about the same for a half-ounce package of pepper.

As they say in the real estate business, location is everything, and the Low Countries occupied a plump spot. This is where wine and coal sent up the Rhine were repacked from river barges to seagoing ships, where the Portuguese delivered their oil and salt for the German market, where Genoan and Venetian galleys made their last stop before turning home. Early on, it was the southern Netherlands (today's Belgium) that got to cream the profits from the passing trade. In the Middle Ages, the great Flemish metropolis of Bruges was the place to be if you wanted to swap English wool for Persian silks and Swedish furs for pepper from Malabar. In later years, when the torch of the spice trade was wrenched from Venice, and Lisbon ruled the waves, the action moved to Antwerp and then finally to Amsterdam in the late fifteen hundreds as a result of the war with Spain. But real wealth, the kind of money that could build the mansions on the Herengracht and make it possible for craftsmen to eat like gentlemen, only came later, in the seventeenth century, when—as a result of war, luck, and a generous pinch of savvy—Amsterdam became the spice capital of the world.

A DAM ON THE AMSTEL

If, like most people, you arrive at the city's Centraal Station, take a moment to look north from platform 15 at the panorama just across the narrow neck of water. Not so long ago, everything that you see here—the high-rises and trees, the housing developments and children's playgrounds, the parks and factories—all used to be swamp and sea. In order for the city to exist, Amsterdamers have never stopped digging ditches and canals, and draining boggy soil. Even the Victorian railway station was built on pilings right in the middle of what used to be the city's great harbor. Seventeenth-century engravings show scores of ships anchored where the station now stands with a grand watery boulevard leading to the heart of the city at the Dam. No wonder the Dutch have a reputation for being tough and ornery. Can you blame them after all those centuries fighting the sea? Still, this watery cradle had its advantages. As one English visitor noted, "[They] all are seamen born and like frogs can live both on land and water." This would come in handy as they transformed Lisbon's Indian Ocean empire into a Dutch pond.

Compared to Lisbon, and even Venice, Amsterdam made rather a late arrival on the European stage. At a time when the cries of muezzin echoed through the alleys of the Alfama, and the Rialto rustled with gossip about the fork-wielding princess from Constantinople, the interior of what the Romans had called Batavia was a sparsely populated wetland crisscrossed by meandering rivers. Then, sometime in the twelfth century, a series of enormous floods turned the Netherlands into a giant water-filled bowl with an enormous bay, the Zuiderzee, at its center. At the southern edge of this inland sea, a small community dammed up the Amstel, a little river that connected to the mighty Rhine. Accordingly, people called the place Amstelredamme (Amstel Dam), later shortened to Amsterdam. The open area near the dam, today presided over by the Royal Palace and Madame Tussaud's, started its life as a market, which eventually turned into the city's main square. It is still called the Dam, even though the Amstel has long since been rechanneled and paved over.

Soon enough, the locals started to travel for business. We know this because some, at least, got into trouble along the way. Apparently, a ship from "Amstelland" was confiscated in the Baltic town of Lübeck as early as 1248. Those first traders brought back all sorts of goods—from leather and furs to grain and honey—but they would soon specialize in one critical commodity: beer. Especially German beer. Around 1365, an impressive twenty-five hundred tons, or about a third of Hamburg's total beer export, was shipped into Amsterdam each month. And despite the Dutch talent for drinking, this was considerably more than the city's three thousand inhabitants could consume. They sold what they could not imbibe.

During the fifteenth and sixteenth centuries, Amsterdam merchants branched out from beer to herring to grain. In need of ships to carry all these commodities, Scandinavian timber was imported, too, and sawed into planks for a booming shipping industry. (You can still make out the crossed arms of the last of the old city's wind-driven sawmills when you look east from the Centraal Station.) The little city grew by inscribing a series of semicircular canals in the surrounding bog, all centered on the Dam. All the same, a map from 1482 shows a town that would fit handily into one of Venice's smaller neighborhoods.

Even as late as the 1560s, most of the world didn't give much thought to Amsterdam—or, for that matter, any of the Dutch. Well, almost. There was one obsessive-compulsive personality who had become fixated with the Netherlands or, more to the point, with all the Hollanders who had signed up with the schismatic cults of the Reformation. In the early sixteenth century, the territories of what are Belgium, Luxembourg, and the Netherlands had come under Spanish rule, and the ultraorthodox Philip II had no intention of allowing heresy to breed in his backyard. And he had the resources of five continents to prove it. The Dutch, for their part, were none too fond of "the Most Catholic King" either. The absentee monarch not only insisted on imposing Catholic orthodoxy on the population of newly minted Lutherans, Sacramentarians, Anabaptists, and above all, Calvinists, but he tried to pay for it by taxing the same people he was trying to reconvert. Naturally, the stubborn Dutch, especially the prosperous (and largely Protestant) towns of the province of Holland, would have none of it. In 1568, Philip decided to solve the problem by sending in a small fragment of his enormous army. What began as a police action turned into a vicious war that wouldn't officially end for eighty years. The Spanish soldiers arrived like crazed crusaders, massacring whole towns and executing thousands. Yet while initially successful, their torch-and-burn strategy became literally bogged down in Flanders. Finally, the last Spanish incursion was crushed in 1574, when the citizens of Leiden broke open their dikes and drowned the Catholic army.

When the gun smoke had cleared and the dikes had been repaired, what emerged after 1587 were two de facto states. In the south, the so-called Spanish Netherlands (essentially, today's Belgium) retained an overwhelmingly Catholic population, while in the north, the United Provinces of the Netherlands (or more commonly, the "Dutch Republic") were a mix of Catholic and Protestant—though in the economically dominant provinces of Holland and Utrecht, the Calvinists ruled the roost.

The war was a stroke of supreme luck for Amsterdam, which, after 1575, had little personal experience of Philip's shock troops. The city would certainly not have become involved in the East India spice trade as early if it hadn't been for the Most Catholic Majesty's jihad. After all, before the Spanish annexation of their neighbor's empire in 1580, the Batavians had been free to sail down to Lisbon, where they would pick up all the spices they could carry. In those days, the spices were then distributed mostly through the southern Netherlands city of Antwerp. Why risk going all the way to India, even if the profits from dealing between Lisbon and Antwerp weren't quite as plump? But all this changed with the arrival of the Spanish Inquisition. The Dutch were cut out of the Lisbon market, and with the arrival of Philip's battalions, Antwerp's economy crashed and the city burned. The result was a huge windfall for Amsterdam as the bankers, merchants, painters, and doctors who had once flocked to Antwerp now fled north. In the booming city on the Amstel, they joined the crowds of recently arrived Protestant refugees from France and Germany, as well as Jews escaping autos-da-fé in Lisbon and Seville.

The ongoing war resulted in rivers of bad blood on both sides. Dutch captains felt completely justified in attacking any and all Spanish vessels, piling atrocity upon atrocity. In a typical move, when Dutch ships intercepted Spanish troop transports in the English Channel in 1605, the Dutch admiral, rather than take prisoners, had them all thrown overboard, tied back-to-back. All the same, while every one of Philip's ships was considered a legitimate target, the Dutch privateers seemed especially diligent in carrying out their patriotic duty by hijacking galleons loaded down with American bullion. Not that they would turn up their noses at a lesser prize. Portuguese *naus* laden with pepper and cinnamon became almost as enticing after 1580, when Portugal came under Spanish rule. Now all of Portugal's Indian spice empire was considered fair game—the entire Estado da Índia no more than one really big, fat prize for the privateer republic to seize from the iniquitous Papist tyrant. Amsterdam prospered as doubloons destined for Philip's army were instead used to pay tavern bills on the Dam and cargoes of pilfered pepper scented warehouses once reeking with herring.

Yet even before the first Dutch prow was moistened by an Indian Ocean wave, the ambitious city was prospering. As early as 1596, Amsterdam could boast that the volume of trade and shipping controlled by the United Provinces was far greater than that of England and France combined! Customs documents show that the number of Dutch ships entering the Zuiderzee in the last hundred years had gone up 400 percent, and a good number of those were docking where the Centraal Station's steeples now rise. So the motivations for getting into the spice trade had to be different here than they once were for the Venetians or the *Lisboetas*. In 1600, Amsterdam's prosperous merchants, who had mostly made their money on decidedly unglamorous commodities like timber and herring, certainly had no illusions that the spice trade could be the mother's milk of prosperity as it had been in Venice. No doubt the way Lisbon's treasury depended on the pepper *naus* would have struck these practical Hollanders as preposterous. The profit margins were certainly tempting. In the first half of the seventeenth century, the gross profit on grain was some 30 to 40 percent, while on spices, it would be more like 300 percent (admittedly, with higher expenses). Yet in the early days, at least, these hard-bitten venture capitalists were surely also drawn a little by the whiff of glamour that had long been associated with the Orient's smelly little berries, buds, and bark. And with the war, there was now a window of opportunity to muscle in on the enormous profits that the Portuguese were supposedly making. The trouble was, the Dutch financiers didn't really know much about the business.

But then, in 1592, young Linschoten arrived home to Enkhuizen, still flushed from his tropical tan. Although Jan Huyghen van Linschoten was only in his late twenties when he returned from his long sojourn in Goa, he probably knew more about the Portuguese spice empire than any other Hollander alive. He had certainly collected enough material for a bestseller, something that the town surgeon, the self-promoting Berent ten Broecke, quickly recognized when he insinuated himself as a coauthor. The resulting *Itinerario* was just what the investors needed: a how-to book on getting into the exotic spice trade. Linschoten blew the lid off the decrepit state of Portugal's far-off empire. The book was crammed with navigation charts, maps, sketches, and descriptions of the remote lands. It cataloged commodity prices in Cambay and spice prices in Malacca. Here were juicy descriptions not only of India but of Sumatra, Java, and the nutmeg isles to the east. When it came out in 1596, the *Itinerario* was snatched up not just in Amsterdam but also by would-be entrepreneurs all over Europe.

There was still the matter of money. How do you go about raising the venture capital for such a risky enterprise? When Dom Manuel sent Vasco da Gama off to Calicut, he didn't have to answer to any investors, but the merchants on the Dam would be risking their own shirts. At the time, their solution was revolutionary, though it would be familiar to anyone taking a new company public on today's New York Stock Exchange. After an initially lackluster attempt to form several regional business entities, they created a joint-stock corporation—the first ever, according to most historians—naming it the United Dutch East India Company.

Compared to the Portuguese—whose motives for getting into the spice trade intertwined dynastic, religious, and commercial ambition—and even compared to the Venetians, who saw fit to invoke God at every turn, the Dutch motivation was much more modern: it was about making as much money as possible. Though, even here, among capitalism's nursemaids, a powerful dose of religious fervor nourished the expansion east. After all, the Dutch East India Company was born out of a battle of religions, even if the conflict with the Estado da Índia increasingly looked more like a trade war. But whatever the underlying motivations, the Dutch did not send their ships round the Cape of Good Hope in the pursuit of a crusade, the Company had no vice president in charge of proselytization, there was no expense line for churches and missionaries. Their spices were unsullied by any association with Eden. In other words, they were running a business, selling commodities not so different from lumber and beer. They were the kind of businessmen we'd recognize today, largely unencumbered by the ancient romance of their stock-in-trade.

LUNCH AND THE SPICE TRADER

"We don't care what they do with them as long as we get a good price," Lavooij responds to my question about how the spices he imports are used, no doubt echoing the opinions of his colleagues four hundred years back. Frank Lavooij is president of Rotterdam-based NedSpice and one of Europe's largest spice dealers. "We don't mind if they smoke it, eat it, or throw it away," he continues, glancing at the commodity price numbers skidding across his computer screen. As an example, he mentions the tons of cloves that go up in smoke in the form of clove cigarettes. He is even more bemused with another important use for *kruidnagel* (literally, "spice nail" in Dutch). In South Asia, these little "nails" are used to fasten together the leaf used to wrap up pan, the mildly narcotic spice and betel nut packages chewed daily by hundreds of millions of Indians. Here, before popping the mixture into the mouth, the clove is just discarded. Indians have been importing cloves for this very purpose for hundreds of years. (It was the same type of narcotic mélange that the zamorin of Calicut chewed during his long interview with Vasco da Gama in 1498.)

If you want to learn about the spice trade today, you won't get far in Amsterdam, where you are more likely to come across the scent of cannabis in the street than the sweet smell of nutmeg or mace. Rotterdam is where real business is done; the harbor here has long since replaced Amsterdam as Holland's shipping powerhouse. And Frank Lavooij is the man to talk to.

The train from Amsterdam's Centraal Station meanders through the typical Dutch landscape of reclaimed land, neatly partitioned into radiant green quadrilaterals by ribbons of reflected sky. You know you've arrived in Rotterdam when windmills and steeples give way to high-rises and brand-new minarets. Once you've stepped out of the central station here, you might as well be in Minneapolis. Whether you look left or right, all you see are bland office towers. After being almost completely destroyed in the Second World War, Rotterdam was rapidly rebuilt, and that hurry to get on with business still permeates the air. Lavooij's office is a short walk from the station in one of these anonymous new blocks.

Yet here, at least, there is a whiff of why I've come: a faint but distinctive smell of pepper hovers over the polyester aroma of the newly installed carpeting in the NedSpice president's office. The smell of pepper comes from a mill that sits on Lavooij's desk. A nice touch, since the bulk of the company's trade is in pepper. Cloves, nutmeg, mace, cinnamon, and allspice make up most of the remainder. "If you're big in spices, you have to be big in pepper," he pronounces from behind the expanse of his desk.

Frank Lavooij is not someone most people would notice in a crowded room. He is of moderate height and modest build, looking younger than his CV would suggest. Yet this fifty-eight-year-old spice merchant is about the closest you can come today to one of the directors of the Dutch East India Company who ran the city of Amsterdam in its golden age. As well as the co-owner of NedSpice, he is president of Rotterdam's Chamber of Commerce. Later, when we are dropped off by his chauffeur at one of Rotterdam's power broker restaurants, the other diners rise like a pack of wolves at the arrival of the alpha male. Not that Lavooij comes across as especially predatory; on the contrary, he exudes self-confidence in a quiet, almost painfully courteous way. His spot at the head of this pack means he must play the politician as well as the businessman. He is cool, calculated, cosmopolitan, and a little humorless—though a hint of a grin does break through when I get him on the subject of the raw herring he would eat growing up in a small town in the southern Netherlands.

I was disappointed to learn that raw herring is not on the menu at the spice trader's lunch spot. The restaurant is as generic as the rest of Rotterdam, located in an upscale strip mall and serving (admittedly well-executed) French cuisine that might have garnered its stars anywhere. As I nibbled on my roast venison with wild mushroom foam, Lavooij once again reminded me how little the spice business has changed since Linschoten's time. Some of the details have been modified, of course. These days, the Malabar Coast no longer has a monopoly on the shriveled black berries that launched a thousand galleys, caravels, and *naus,* and even Java is no longer a player. Now the largest exporter of pepper in the world is Vietnam, followed at a distance by India, Indonesia, and Brazil. As a result, Lavooij's partner is continually shuttling between the Netherlands and Southeast Asia to keep in touch with the company's agents who are working to teach Vietnamese farmers how to grow this scruffy vine.

Most of the spices are still grown by small farmers in upland areas as a sideline, much as Thomas Thumpassery does in the hills above Quilon. Middlemen collect the product and send it to brokers in towns like Cochin. Today, however, instead of selling it to Gujarati merchants, the Estado da Índia, or the Dutch East India Company, they forward it to international spice-trading companies like NedSpice. The spices are then shipped to Holland, repackaged, and redistributed across Europe and the Americas. Perhaps the biggest change is that the transportation time has been cut from the six or seven months it used to take in the seventeenth century to some two weeks today—not a big deal, Lavooij points out, since the shelf life of many spices is measured in years. And, of course, nowadays, the ships arrive in Rotterdam rather than in Amsterdam or Lisbon.

Just like in the glory days of the Dutch East India Company, hardly any of the spices—no more than 5 percent, Lavooij estimates—stay in the

Netherlands once they've landed there.* The rest are sent to Germany, Britain, and the United States, mostly to disappear into processed food. Despite his protestations to the contrary, the president of NedSpice isn't entirely oblivious to the demand side of the business. The market for spices is steadily increasing year by year, which, in his opinion, can be directly attributed to people's eating more processed food. Cooks at home are certainly not loading up their spice racks with mace and cardamom. "The spices in our kitchen," the president of NedSpice says of Dutch cooking, "are black and white pepper, nutmeg, and cinnamon. But there aren't a lot of people who say, 'Oh, I must add some mace.' " Yet they'll be eating mace, turmeric, and cloves all the same. The spices are there in prepared food, the convenience food bought in Wal-Mart and Carrefour hypermarkets on both sides of the Atlantic. "We continue to see a steady, steady, steady increase in consumption, and the price doesn't seem to affect it," he notes of this subversive new golden age of spice. Given the way more and more consumers across the world are becoming dependent on convenience food, it would be hard to imagine the demand for pepper, say, collapsing or even sagging. Lavooij tells me this on the way back to the train station as a confident smile flits briefly across his deadpan face.

On the eve of the seventeenth century, Dutch businessmen couldn't summon up the spot prices at the Cochin pepper exchange at the click of a mouse like today's spice trader, nor could they present charts to demonstrate the growth in European fine-spice consumption at their stockholders' meetings. But they did have Linschoten, who told them you could buy more than seven pounds of nutmeg for a guilder in Malacca while they knew they could sell it in Amsterdam for more than a guilder a pound. The competition—the underresourced, poorly managed Estado da Índia—was ripe for picking. In cities across the Netherlands, the venture capitalists gathered to plan a hostile takeover.

FOLLOWING LINSCHOTEN

If you're anywhere near Nieuwemarkt square in central Amsterdam, the Oost-Indisch Huis is easy enough to find. Just follow the blond college stu-

* While this may be true of NedSpice's imports, Holland as a whole consumes about a third of its spice imports and exports the rest, though any numbers are highly suspect, since they don't take into account spices present in imported and exported processed food.

dents on their bicycles. They all seem to park their bikes—hundreds of
them completely obstructing the sidewalk—in front of the imposing edifice. Like so many old buildings in Amsterdam, there is something of a
gingerbread quality to the structure's four-story, block-long façade,
though here, you have to imagine sufficient gingerbread to feed a nation
of Hollanders. As the bicycles make clear, this is now part of the university, but when the building was first erected around 1660, it was the nerve
center of the East India Company in the days when Amsterdam was a
company town.

When the original offices were set up here in 1603, they were modest
enough. The Company made do by renting part of an arms depot from
the city. But with success came the need to expand. The headquarters
eventually took up an entire block facing Hoogstraat. In later, less prosperous years, it was deemed essential to have a grand façade to camou-
flage the oceans of red ink.

Back in 1600, the market for the more expensive spices seemed limit-
less. The demand for cloves, nutmeg, and mace, especially, had been
growing by leaps and bounds. According to one widely accepted estimate,
the consumption of these so-called fine spices may have gone up 400 percent in the course of the sixteenth century—admittedly, from a very low
starting point. Pepper sales, on the other hand, at least on a per capita
basis, remained sluggish. This makes sense in light of the economic situation of the times. Across most of Europe (Italy seems to be a bit of an exception here), the standard of living for the poor was slipping as wages
stagnated, but the cost of staples like bread was going through the roof.
Little wonder that the less advantaged would scrimp on life's little luxuries
and stop buying the pepper they could once afford. The rich, on the other
hand, were barely affected by this inflationary spiral, since they never devoted more than a small percentage of their income to the staples. They
spent most of their money on luxuries (books and servants come to mind),
which, in contrast to the essentials, were getting cheaper by the day. No
wonder more of them could afford to buy expensive Moluccan spices.

But the economic explanation only goes part of the way in explaining the resurgent fashion for well-seasoned food. Better to look at the influence of (increasingly affordable) cookbooks that were rolling off the
presses in Venice, London, and Antwerp. Admittedly, it was Italian cook-

books that set the standard, but there were lots of local publications in much the same vein. The earliest printed cookbook in the Dutch language, *Een notabel boecxken van cokeryen* (A Notable Little Book of Cookery), was already replete with recipes calling for not only inexpensive pepper and ginger but also for pricier spices such as cinnamon, cloves, nutmeg, and mace. Much like other cookbooks published in the Netherlands both before and during the war of independence, this one attests to the ongoing popularity of a well-spiced, sweet-and-sour cuisine.

While the demand was certainly there, it took the Dutch investors several years to figure out the supply part of the equation. The earliest Dutch forays to South Asia were a mixed bag of abysmal failures and some modest successes. Among the former, perhaps the most misguided were several attempts to reach India via the Arctic Ocean! In the wake of Linschoten's report, would-be spice traders organized some half dozen ad hoc companies all across the Netherlands. Not only Amsterdam but also Hoorn, Enkhuizen, Delft, and Rotterdam financed their own fleets and sent them east. In the resulting free-for-all, they had to devote at least as much energy to competing with one another as to fighting the Spanish monarch's galleons. The government in The Hague may have been run by businessmen, but that did not mean they had any ideological investment in free enterprise. The cutthroat competition among the East India traders was bad not only for profits but also for the war effort, so the Republic's leaders pressured the separate companies to join forces. The result was De Vereenigde Oost-Indische Compagnie ("the United East India Company"), or VOC, for short. Bringing these fierce competitors into a single organization wasn't easy. After months of messy negotiation, a rather awkward board structure was established in 1602 in which each of the eight smaller towns got one member while Amsterdam itself got eight. One more rotating seat was added, for a grand total of seventeen, or the *Heren XVII* (the seventeen lords), as they would now be known.* The ornately penned company charter with its massive government seal was unusual in other respects, too. Interestingly, it gave a preferred status to

---

* Financial historians point to the VOC as perhaps the first modern corporation. Needless to say, the resulting innovations in corporate structure are beyond the scope of this work, to say nothing of way beyond my ken.

smaller investors. (In this respect, it was a little like the ordinances in Venice, which required galley captains to take on cargoes of even small-time spice traders.) And the little guys rushed to invest their few *stuivers* in this sexy new start-up.

As any economic historian will be quick to tell you, irrational exuberance is hardly a modern phenomenon. The Dutch were just as susceptible to falling for an overhyped investment opportunity as any twenty-first-century day trader, perhaps even more so. Given the times, it's not hard to understand. Put yourself in the shoes of the average Amsterdam taverngoer circa 1600. Every day, new books are being published full of the wonders of worlds revealed by Columbus, Cabot, da Gama, and Magellan. Your brand-new nation has beaten off the armies of the greatest (or at least the largest) empire the world had ever known. Dutch sailors have sailed right up to Gibraltar and sunk a good portion of the Most Catholic King's fleet. Doesn't that make it abundantly clear whose side God is really on? Rumor on the street has it that a group of rich and respected merchants is organizing a grand venture that will wrest the Portuguese spice empire from the Spanish tyrant and that small investors are especially welcome. Is it any wonder that grocers, masons, and midwives lined up to pour their pennies into the new company?

Just to be clear, though, when the governing States General granted the VOC its charter, they had more in mind than organizing a get-rich-quick scheme for the man on the street. The country was at war, and accordingly, the East India Company was seen as a potentially strategic asset. The charter makes this clear. Even while it deals mostly with financial affairs, one particular clause makes it evident that this was to be a special sort of corporation. The article authorizes the newly created company to make treaties with princes and potentates in the government's name. Moreover, it allows the VOC directors to build forts and garrisons where they deem necessary and to appoint governors and judges to police these new possessions. In effect, the Dutch government created a state within a state, a paramilitary corporation designed to attack Spanish interests even while making a profit for the shareholders. In this way, it had a mixed mission, just like the Estado da Índia. But whereas the Portuguese organization often worked at cross-purposes when it came to the Christians and spices, with the VOC, there was no mistaking that profit came first. In this, the

Dutch were much more like the Venetians than the Portuguese; while the organizational structure would have been unfamiliar to the crusading doge Enrico Dandolo, I'm sure he would have fully understood the need to secure the trading empire by any means necessary. The goal of building an empire in East Asia may not have been contemplated by the signers of the Dutch charter, yet the fine print made it almost inevitable. It certainly did not bode well for the current residents of the far-off spice archipelago.

THE SPICE ARCHIPELAGO

On today's map, the tiny specks where nutmeg and cloves used to grow are lost amid the countless islands that make up Indonesia. The once-fabled Moluccas are a world away not only from Holland but from anywhere, some thousand miles south of Manila, a thousand miles north of Australia, and more than fifteen hundred miles east of the Indonesian capital at Jakarta. Some, like the clove-growing island of Ternate, rise to smoldering volcanic peaks, their rugged hillsides covered by shaggy jungle with palm trees thrust above like scruffy mops. The Banda group, once covered with tall and graceful nutmeg trees, is ringed with coral beaches that yield to transparent azure sea, surrounded by reefs unspoiled as a consequence of their isolation. The Europeans who were convinced that spices grew in paradise weren't so far off the mark. This particular Eden, though, has seen a lot of strife since the Portuguese and Dutch arrived. Today, if you've heard of the Spice Islands at all, it is because you happen to follow State Department warnings on civil unrest. Ternate and the surrounding islands were the site of ethnic and religious conflict in 1999 and 2000, a vicious bloodbath that resulted in more than a thousand people killed and more than ten thousand refugees.

The few foreigners who set foot on Banda today mostly come to dive in the crystalline waters. Ternate sees the occasional intrepid vulcanologist. But almost nobody comes here for the spices. Most of the world's cloves are now produced off the east coast of Africa on islands such as Madagascar and Zanzibar. Banda produces about one-tenth of the nutmeg it did a hundred years ago. Today, the nutmeg superpower is the Caribbean island of Grenada, where the spice has become so central to the economy that the country has even put a nutmeg on its flag. In the

meantime, the Indonesian islands have been submerged by the tides of history. Their fate was set back at VOC headquarters on Hoogstraat, some seven thousand miles away.

When the Dutch ships set out on their first sortie to the spiceries, the locals had been in the spice business here for at least a thousand years. Even the Portuguese arrival had not shaken things up in Southeast Asia as it had in the western Indian Ocean. Most of the spices grown in what is now Indonesia continued to be sold to Asian customers. Javanese and Gujarati traders sold pepper to the Chinese and the Persians; Chinese cassia and Ceylonese cinnamon filled junks and dhows; and the cloves, nutmeg, and mace that grew only on the isolated Moluccas were distributed by Muslim and Chinese merchants from Kyoto to Cairo. The modest leftovers made it to the kitchens and pharmacies of Europe.

While pepper was by far the most widely traded of all spices, pound for pound, the Moluccan spices were vastly more valuable: perhaps three to six times as expensive, depending on the place and time.* It was simply a matter of supply and demand. Whereas pepper and ginger grew across thousands of acres in South India and Java, cloves (*Syzygium aromaticum*) were limited to a line of minor volcanic protuberances straddling the equator in the Molucca Sea. If you put together Ternate and its neighbors—Tidore, Makian, Motir, and Bacan—they wouldn't be much bigger than Martha's Vineyard and Nantucket combined. Nutmeg and mace (*Myristica fragrans*) were more restricted yet, growing on the Banda group of islands, a collection of even smaller flecks of igneous debris some four hundred miles south of Ternate.

Over the centuries, the Bandanese had increasingly come to depend on nutmeg for their livelihood. Much like soybean farmers in Iowa, they sold off their solitary cash crop in order to buy their bread and butter—or, in this case, rice and sago. (The starchy interior of the sago palm is a local staple.) At times, they sailed their junks as far as Java to deliver their perfumed crop and pick up groceries.

Nutmegs grow much like lemons or plums on trees that, given the room, rise in handsome symmetrical cones of lustrous green foliage. When ripe, the apricot-sized globes turn the color of pale flesh, then split and fall. The fallen fruit is undeniably luscious. As the nutmeg ripens, its tan flesh spreads open into a deep slit, revealing the brilliant carmine filaments of the mace and, deeper yet within, the jet-black shell of the nutmeg itself. As is still evident from the name given to mace by several European languages (in French, it is *fleur de muscade;* in German, *Muskatblüte*), medieval Europeans mistakenly thought that mace was the flower of the nutmeg tree. (Technically, the membrane covering the nutmeg shell is called the aril.) The mistake, made by Marco Polo and others, is a natural one. As you would expect of a flower, when dried, mace is more aromatic than nutmeg and fades to a lovely pink color.

By the sixteen hundreds, Europeans could read plenty of more or less

---

* To give just a random sampling of numbers: in the early twelve hundreds, the Genoese sold cloves and nutmeg to their customers for something like four times the price of pepper; in Alexandria in 1347, ten kilos of pepper could be had for 7½ ducats, while cloves were more than 22; and according to Linschoten, even in relatively nearby Malacca, pepper cost about half the price of cloves and a third the price of mace. Here, though, nutmeg was actually cheaper!

Wood-block prints, such as this one from an herbal by the sixteenth-century Florentine Pier Andrea Mattioli, made plants like nutmeg much less exotic to the European public.

factual descriptions of this legendary evergreen. The Spanish colonial historian Argensola left us a particularly evocative image when he wrote about the spice in 1609 (the translation is from 1708):

> They are like the European Pear-Trees, and their Fruit resembles Pairs [*sic*], or rather in Roundness the Melocotones [peaches]. When the Nutmegs blosom, they spread a cordial Fragrancy; by degrees they lose their Native Green, which is original in all Vegetables; and then succeeds a Blew, intermix'd with Grey, Cherry-Colour, and a pale Gold Colour, as we see in the Rainbow, tho' not in that regular Division, but in Spots like the Jaspar Stone. Infinite Numbers of Parrots, and other Birds of various Plumage, most delightful to behold, come to sit upon the Branches, attracted by the sweet Odour. The Nuts, when dry, cast off the Shell it grows cover'd with, and is the Mace, within which is a white Kernel, not so sharp in Taste as the Nuts. . . . Of this Mace, which is hot and dry in the second Degree, and within the third, the Bandese make a most precious Oil to cure all Distempers in the Nerves, and Aches, caus'd by cold. . . . With [the nuts] they cure, or correct stinking Breath, clear the Eyes, comfort the Stomach, Liver, and Spleen, and digest Meat. They are a Remedy against many other Distempers, and serve to add outward Lustre to the Face.

Whereas some confused mace with a bloom, cloves are, in fact, flowers—or, more accurately, the buds of a bushy tropical tree. The shoots grow in clusters, in a bouquet of some thirty yellow blossoms, each little bud looking like a tubby, lemon yellow clove. Surrounded by fleshy foliage, they are reminiscent of rhododendrons in bloom—except these trees may reach some fifty feet tall. The entire plant is intensely aromatic; not just the flowers but also the leaves have the unmistakable, slightly sickly smell of cloves. After a tropical downpour, the smell of a clove plantation is almost unbearable. The sixteenth-century Portuguese botanist da Orta reports smelling clove-laden ships from miles away:

> The scent of the clove is said to be the most fragrant in the world. I experienced this coming from Cochin to Goa, with the wind

from the shore, and at night it was calm when we were a league from the land. The scent was so strong and so delicious that I thought there must be forests of flowers. On enquiry I found that we were near a ship coming from Maluco [the Moluccas] with cloves.

The dried buds fetched the best price, but there was also a market for clove stems. While noticeably less aromatic, they were a lot less expensive—at times as cheap as pepper in the Mediterranean market.

While just about every spice has been used for its medical properties (real or imagined), both nutmeg and cloves have demonstrable pharmacological effects. Both the buds and leaves of cloves contain eugenol, which can be used as an effective local anesthetic, a fact long appreciated by dentists (and their patients). The little dried buds used to be made into a preserve with vinegar or with sugar for export to India. In South Asia, they were used for perfuming the breath, for chewing with betel, as well as for their anesthetic properties.

Nutmeg has more psychedelic effects. Taken in small doses, it can act as a sedative. When I had lunch with Frank Lavooij, he recommended taking nutmeg in a glass of warm milk to put you to sleep, though it is just as well he is a trader rather than a pharmacist—the quantity he suggested would have sent me tripping.* A chemical in nutmeg called myristicin is believed to account for the spice's hallucinogenic effects. Though I can't vouch for it from personal experience, the spice's psychotropic effects are apparently a widely shared secret. Both American prison inmates and hippies grooving on Goa's beaches have gotten high on nutmeg. In Zanzibar local women will chew nutmeg in lieu of smoking the local marijuana. The Spanish missionary Frei Sebastien Manrique describes how in Bengal in the early 1600s, junkies would mix opium with nutmeg, mace, and other aromatics to supercharge their fix. Apparently, the response to

---

* According to Paul Gahlinger, the author of *Illegal Drugs*, "Eating twenty grams of ground nutmeg can produce very severe physical and psychological effects varying with the person." Prolonged nausea is replaced by silly feelings and giggling, and then a feeling of euphoria accompanied by hallucinations. Motor functions may be confused and speech incoherent. He goes on to say, "the after-effects are usually quite unpleasant: aching bones, sore muscles, painful eyes, runny nose, tiredness, depression and headaches."

nutmeg intoxication is extremely varied: some individuals experience a profound distortion of time and space, while others have visual hallucinations. The first recorded hallucinogenic effect was noted by the Flemish physician Lobelius in 1576, when he described a pregnant English lady who "became deliriously inebriated after eating 10–12 nutmegs," apparently while trying to induce an abortion. For readers looking for a cheap high, it should be noted that tripping on nutmeg can have all sorts of nasty side effects, such as vomiting, headaches, and prolonged disorientation.

Back in Europe, people had known about the Spice Islands with their drug plantations at least since Marco Polo's day. They even had a rough idea of their location. The peripatetic Venetian had his facts more or less right when he wrote, "[The sea] lies towards the east and according to the testimony of experienced pilots and seamen who sail upon it and are well acquainted with the truth it contains 7,448 islands, most of them inhabited. And I assure you that in all these islands there is no tree that does not give off a powerful and agreeable fragrance and serve some useful purpose." His numbers were a little off; the actual count is more than 25,000. But he never made it that far. The first Europeans to arrive were Portuguese.

What they found was a world very different from India. Here, there were no great kingdoms or empires but rather hundreds, if not thousands, of minor principalities and a handful of great port cities that had grown rich off the spice trade. Malacca, Macassar, and Achin were comparable to cities like Genoa and Antwerp in size and importance, though the volume of spices that passed through their gates could only be compared to the great entrepôts like Venice or Alexandria.

Despite bullying their way into the neighborhood in the early 1500s, the Portuguese had little influence here. Sure, they grabbed a few strategic spots—mainly, the city of Malacca, which, like today's Singapore, had a stranglehold on the principal route between East and South Asia. And the conquistadores did put up a fort on Ternate, where they attempted (unsuccessfully) to control the clove trade. But a hundred years later, when the first Dutch ships nosed round the Cape of Good Hope, the Southeast Asian spice trade was, to all intents and purposes, the same as it had always been. A gaggle of sultans, princes, and local chiefs controlled the sale and production of spices while the usual suspects redistributed them across the region. Even most Portuguese vessels were manned almost entirely by local Malay sailors. The Estado da Índia had become just another player among many. But a profound change was in the offing, for neither the Portuguese nor the wealthiest of the sultans were a match for the cut-throat business practices of the Dutch.

THE COMPANY DROPS ANCHOR

Today, the forty-eighth sultan of Ternate still presides over his two-hundred-year-old palace on the principal clove island. He is attended by courtiers who strain their necks to keep their heads below his in the name of tradition. His faithful address him by the divine title *Jo'o*, or "Lord." And whenever the smoldering peak of Gammalama threatens to erupt, the semidivine dignitary rides out on a dugout canoe in order to calm the island's volcano by a ritual circumnavigation. Not that he has any political power under Indonesia's constitution. This is a pity, at least according to the current sultan, Dr. Mudaffar Sjah (who holds a PhD from the University of Indonesia). In an interview given to the *South China Morning Post* on the royal back porch, he suggests that the current religious conflict would go away if people just returned to the old ways, to the traditions of the past. Between sips of lychee juice, the Muslim VIP muses about the golden era when his ancestors had real power, when they were the rulers of the spice archipelago. The would-be monarch has his detractors, though, the ones who remember the sultan's long tenure in the corrupt Suharto regime. Local villagers accuse him of fomenting the sectarian bloodshed. And they are quick to remind you of the centuries when the sultans of Ternate collaborated with the Dutch colonial regime. True enough, yet after their experience with the Portuguese, could Mudaffar's forefathers have imagined that the Dutch could be worse?

The first locals to come face-to-face with the Europeans lived several hundred miles south of the sultan's capital. In 1511, Admiral Afonso de Albuquerque had just barely restocked his fleet after conquering Malacca when he sent out three ships to search for the fabled isles. This mini-armada, under the command of Captain António de Abreu, presumably hired (or shanghaied) Malay pilots to guide their two-thousand-mile sail past Java, Bali, and Timor, for they found the tiny Banda Islands without any trouble. They were apparently well received by the inhabitants, who were familiar enough with foreign visitors, even if these bushy-bearded Europeans were a little out of the ordinary. They were happy to sell the Portuguese nutmeg, mace, and even some imported cloves for what the Europeans considered a bargain price. Back in Lisbon, they figured, they would make a 1,000 percent profit. Interestingly, one of the sailors on the expedition was Fernão de Magalhães (better known to the world as Magellan). It was his personal experience in Banda that later helped him convince the Spanish king to finance his trip round the world.

The next hundred years or so were less amicable, at least on the clove islands to the north. In 1522, the Portuguese built a fort at Ternate, spitting distance from the sultan's palace. They then proceeded to depose or kill one ruler after another, poison the heirs, and remove whole royal families to the Estado da Índia's stronghold in distant Malacca. Finally, the assassination of the ruling sultan in 1574 proved to be one murder too many for the locals. They rose up the following year and expelled the foreigners from their island. Not surprisingly, when the Dutch arrived in 1599 promising help against the Portuguese, the Moluccans jumped at the opportunity of an alliance.

The Dutch had a knack for getting people to cooperate; it was a system that would be familiar to any mafioso working the garbage-collection business in Lower Manhattan. Ships bristling with guns anchored a stone's throw from the headmen's villages (or royal palaces) and offered "protection" in exchange for the right to buy up all the local spice crop at prices set by the Company. A typical example was the agreement signed by several Banda *orang kaya* (local headmen) invited on board the armed merchant ship *Gelderland* on May 23, 1602. No doubt the chiefs were given a selective tour of the ship and taken down the narrow staircase onto the gun deck for a thorough examination of some two dozen polished cast-iron cannon aimed at their fragile homes. They may even have been treated to a demonstration of their lethal effect. Surely they grasped this better than the sheet of parchment scrawled with legal jargon that the pink-faced interlopers thrust at them. They certainly couldn't have understood the terms of the Dutch-language contract, which specified that, in exchange for protection against the Portuguese and English, the Bandanese granted the Dutch an irrevocable monopoly on nutmeg. Under the circumstances, few of the headmen refused. But it's hardly remarkable that the islanders also tried to evade the contracts. After all, had the locals taken the agreement too much to heart, they would have starved. By this era, the nutmeg islands were totally dependent on imported food, yet the Hollanders had no interest in transporting bulky and perishable commodities such as sago and rice. Instead, they brought Indian calico, which they insisted the islanders exchange at fixed prices. Of course, as far as the legal counsel of the VOC was concerned, these agreements were all aboveboard and perfectly lawful—if the natives had nothing to eat, that was their own affair—so when the locals did not live up to the letter of the documents, the Dutch felt completely justified sending in their enforcers.

This worked smoothly in Southeast Asia, where the Estado da Índia was thin on the ground. There, the Dutch were easily able to fend off a Portuguese invasion of Banda in 1600, and a year later, the company's ships sank a Portuguese fleet in a full-scale naval battle in the Bay of Bantam, which assured access to Javanese pepper. In 1605, the VOC nabbed the Portuguese fort of Amboina, strategically sited between the clove islands and the nutmeg archipelago. India was another matter. The original plan had been to evict the Portuguese from the entire subcontinent, but the decrepit empire had more kick in it than the Dutch had counted on. After several unsuccessful attacks on Golden Goa, the VOC satisfied itself with a temporary treaty of alliance with the rulers of Calicut, who were still fuming about Vasco da Gama and his lot.

Back in Amsterdam, news of the VOC's successes and failures sent the Company's share prices on a roller-coaster ride. The rapid ascent of the initial stock offering turned into a free fall when news trickled back that the clove island of Tidore had been recaptured by the Spanish and that the Moluccas might be a lost cause. The situation in Holland was actually made worse by the fact that arriving VOC ships continued to unload bales of pepper on every wharf. Not only the Netherlands but all of Europe was awash with Dutch, Portuguese, and now even English pepper. (The English East India Company was chartered in 1600.) In Amsterdam alone, according to Buzanval (the French ambassador as well as a VOC shareholder), warehouses were packed to the roofs with pepper worth more than a million guilders that went begging for customers. In a short time, shares that once seemed like they would zoom into the stratosphere were being dumped at 60 percent of their face value. In the Oost-Indisch

Huis boardroom, it was plain to see that the Company could not depend on pepper alone to keep its shareholders happy. The *Heren XVII* decided to rework their business plan, to focus their attention on the islands ruled by the sultans of Ternate.

After my long, civilized lunch with the genteel Frank Lavooij, I could only wonder how much the world of business has changed. Just how many of today's mouse-wielding financiers would have the stomach or the audacity for what VOC employees were expected to carry out? When I hear Lavooij discuss his company's well-regarded policies, according to which he encourages farmers to produce organically and builds processing plants in third-world countries (all because it is more profitable, he readily admits), I think back to the well-regarded practices of 1600, pondering what decisions Lavooij might be making were he sitting in the chamber with the Seventeen. When you look into the eyes of the many portraits of the East India Company's functionaries, it's hard to conceive of them condoning slave trading and genocide in the name of their shareholders.

Well, that's not quite right: there's one face that is all too telling.

THE COMPANY MAN

Of all the original towns that made up the "chambers" of the United Company, none is as delightful as Hoorn. Unlike Amsterdam, this small city has never had its second life, so nobody found it necessary to tear down street after street of pert seventeenth-century town houses to put up something more up-to-date after the town's harbor silted up in the eighteenth century.

It was an unusually sunny afternoon when I left Amsterdam's Centraal Station for the forty-minute trip to Hoorn so that I could look into the eyes of the town's most notorious son. The pale winter sun turned the polders a particularly luminous green; wooly clumps of sheep plodded contentedly between the sky blue canals. As I left Hoorn's railway station behind, it became immediately evident how important the East India Company used to be here. You see it in the VOC insignia that peek out from under eaves, in the impressive old Company warehouses that tower five stories above the town's principal canal, in a street named Peper Straat, but perhaps most poignantly in the faces of former company officials who peer from the walls of the local history museum.

The quirky Westfries Museum presides over Roode Steen, a postcard-perfect rhomboid of a medieval square a few steps from the old harbor. The museum is fronted by a stepped façade plastered with a busy display of insignia, giving it all the appearance of an overwrought sports trophy—in an endearing, Renaissance sort of way. Inside, it is all crooked passageways and leaning stairs filled with dusty portraits of plump and jolly militiamen (the town had to pass an ordinance to limit the duration of parties thrown by these seventeenth-century weekend warriors to no more than three days, a museum guide tells me) and cluttered with souvenirs from Holland's glory years.

Up the creaky stairs, pride of place is given to a high, timbered room devoted to the East India Company. Here, the musty stench of ancient stuff is made even thicker by the slightly sickly smell of cloves mingling with nutmeg and mace. The curators had the clever idea of installing rough burlap sacks of sweet spices to remind you of what put their city on the map. It's a clever conceit, especially when you read that each sack would have been worth the price of a house in seventeenth-century Hoorn— a rather nice house at that. The hall's walls are lined with group portraits of men who look as if they didn't party much with the militiamen downstairs. These are the businessmen who ran the East India Company. Up on the left is the fleshy figure of the VOC officer Cornelis de Groot, his image the cliché of the capitalist fat cat with his pencil-thin mustache, double chins, and bland smile. Nearby stands the Hoorn chamber director and some-time mayor, Francois Van Brederhoff, looking as if he were late for a meeting. Others lounge and lean, surveying the room. There's one person in the room who doesn't seem as if he much liked having his portrait painted. But that would have been typical of the man whom many consider the greatest villain (and some, a towering hero) of the Dutch spice trade.

Jan Pieterszoon Coen sat for his portrait after he became the Company's chief operating officer in the Far East. His crew-cut, chiseled, leathery head pokes out of a fashionably frilly collar like an ill-tempered tortoise dressed for the prom. He looks across the room at a group portrait of luxuriantly bewigged and chubby-cheeked VOC functionaries arranged around a long table draped with a splendid carmine Turkish rug. It may be irritation at the painter's slowness that shows in Coen's hard eyes, but I can't help but imagine scorn when I follow his gaze.

Jan Pieterszoon Coen sat for at least two portraits. This one belongs to the Rijksmuseum.

What did these young and comfortable upstarts know of Coen's distant world filled with armed, recalcitrant natives unwilling to submit to his business plan? To these well-fed gentlemen, the festering jungles and pirate-filled bays were no more than marks and scratches on globes and maps. What did it matter to them how Coen dealt with the assets and liabilities in the Far East as long as the investors were happy? Did they not, after all, have a fiduciary responsibility to their shareholders? Jan Coen has been systematically vilified by modern Dutch historians, but as far as he was concerned, he was simply carrying out the Company's policies to their genocidally logical conclusion even as the boardroom barons claimed plausible deniability. As he looks across at these boys of privilege, you can almost hear him say (as he did in letter after irritated letter to headquarters), You may not have liked my methods, but where would you be now without me ?

Coen began his company career after serving a seven-year accounting apprenticeship in Rome, where he had studied the latest in Italian finance. He came home in 1605, just around the time the first spice-loaded VOC ship returned to Hoorn with a cargo worth more than a million guilders (equivalent to something like two hundred million dollars today). That shipment alone gave the shareholders a 75 percent return on their investment! The same year, VOC shares were trading at 200 percent of their face value on the Amsterdam exchange. No wonder all the ports in Holland were feverish with excitement. Though it's hard to conceive of the Coen of the Westfries portrait being swept up in any sort of frenzy, he clearly saw the opportunities in the spice trade that an overgrown village like Hoorn could never offer. With this in mind, the twenty-year-old managed to get himself a job on the lowest rung of the VOC corporate ladder, as submerchant, at a monthly salary of thirty-five guilders plus room and board. His bosses recognized his talent and quickly promoted him. By the age of thirty-one, he had the top job in the Far East. Leave it to the Dutch to pick an accountant to build their empire.

A SAILOR'S LIFE

In Amsterdam, the naval museum has at least as many models of the old ships that traveled the spice route round the Cape of Good Hope as Lisbon's fine collection of miniature galleons and *naus*, but at least in one respect, the Amsterdamers can lord it over the *Lisboetas:* they have a life-size reproduction of an East Indiaman. The ship, appropriately enough named the *Amsterdam,* lies at anchor by the waterfront, several canals east of the Centraal Station, just about where the seventeenth-century VOC shipyards used to be. Naval historians will scoff that it's a copy, and of an eighteenth-century ship at that, but that would make it only a little more luxurious than earlier models. This is decidedly no cruise ship. The quarters assigned to merchants like Coen wouldn't pass muster as a walk-in closet, and the ship's galley would qualify as such only in a New York studio apartment. The downstairs deck is about half the size of a basketball court, which seems spacious enough until you realize it had to accommodate more than three hundred rowdy and bored sailors.

The men who boarded ships like the one carrying Jan Coen to the East Indies in 1607 would have been a motley and unruly bunch. But at least they were free men—unlike the slaves and convicts who populated the *Carreira da Índia*'s later crews. The Dutch seamen were assembled by professional recruiters—known as *zielverkopers*, or "soul merchants"—who trolled the taverns and back alleys of Holland's slums. One favorite ploy was to advance wages to the impecunious recruits, who typically drank the money at the nearest bar. Now they were not only broke but in debt. They had no choice but to go east. Some never got out of arrears to the Company and remained free men in name only. Later, when the alehouses proved inadequate, the VOC regularly turned to the governors of orphanages and workhouses to supply additional souls to man the Company's ships. Like the Portuguese, Dutch sailors died by the hundreds from accidents, violence, and disease, with the result that the soul merchants were never out of work.

The discipline aboard Dutch ships was perhaps even more brutal than on other European merchant ships of the time. Maybe people were more hardened after the atrocities of the Spanish war, or perhaps commanders were just desperate to keep their brawling, drunken, malnourished, and often sick crew from murdering one another. The official rule books allowed captains to punish any seaman who injured another by pinning him to the mast with a knife through his hand until he tore himself free. Anyone who killed another was to be bound to the dead victim and thrown overboard. You have to wonder, though, just how often a skipper would resort to punishments that would leave him with even fewer sailors to run the ship.

Yet, in spite of the crowded conditions, the population of a ship like the *Amsterdam* was far smaller than that of the virtual floating cities that set out from Lisbon. For one thing, the early Dutch vessels carried neither settlers, priests, nor colonial functionaries with their attendant slaves and servants. From the standpoint of quantity, the average sailor was probably better fed than his Portuguese counterpart, at least once the Dutch had figured out what would make it through the equatorial heat. (In the first voyage to the Indies and back, half the crew died.) The officers did have the occasional culinary perk, but they were hardly living it up like the *Carreira da Índia*'s elite. If the *Amsterdam*'s kitchen is in any way representative, all the cook had to work with to serve some 333 bodies was a modest grill and a built-in cooking basin just big enough to submerge one big turkey. Any sort of baking was out of the question, so *scheepsbeschuit*, or hardtack (the tough, crackerlike bread universal to all sailing nations), was the only bread for officers and crew alike after the first few days out. (To make it palatable, it was often soaked with beer and sweetened with treacle.)

Food preservation methods were just as limited as they had been in Vasco da Gama's day. Moreover, to the great consternation of the Dutch crew, beer would not last more than a month or two in the tropical heat. The men were stuck with fetid water washed down with a little wine, which held up better. And not even enough water at that. Shipboard diaries report that sailors had to subsist on something like a quart of water a day, a minuscule quantity when you consider the sweaty work, salty food, and sultry climate. In the first few weeks, they occasionally got to taste a little fresh meat to relieve the monotony. Official VOC provisioning lists allow for several live pigs on board as well as several dozen hens to provide fresh eggs for the sick. But the shelf life of the livestock on board wasn't much better than the beer. Once the fresh meat had been consumed, the crew was stuck with a diet of boiled salted beef, boiled salty bacon, boiled gruel, and boiled peas. The officers did have it a little better, at least in one intriguing respect. Whereas the only seasoning included on an official VOC provisioning list for the sailors was mustard and horseradish, the officers had a substantial allowance of both domestic and Asian spices to season their gruel—something on the order of three ounces a week.* This may be the best indication yet of just how much spice middle-class Netherlanders really ate around 1700.

One source of Dutch protein that was denied to Portuguese seamen on the pepper *naus* was, of course, cheese. The weekly three-quarters of a

---

* Admittedly, more than half of the spice consumed was domestically produced aniseed and cumin (the officers' mess even offered cumin cheese), but the rest—about a pound of pepper, ginger, cloves, nutmeg, cinnamon, and mace for each officer for the duration of the trip— were exotic imports.

pound of cheese each India-bound sailor received may alone explain why the Hollanders were considerably taller than the Portuguese and better fed than their competitors. Still, by the time they rounded the cape, the ships' supply of fuel—most likely, dried peat or German coal on the outbound voyage—would often have run out, so, unable to cook, the dehydrated sailors were stuck with little more than worm-infested biscuit to gnaw with their Gouda.

Is it any wonder that the half-starved, alcohol-deprived sailors disembarking at Cochin headed straight for the public houses, where they drank themselves insensate? As the partying ordinances in Hoorn make clear, Calvinist society did not condone indulgent behavior—or at least, not too much of it. Admittedly, even back home, Dutch sailors were notorious for their drinking, fighting, and whoring, but in India, half a world away from nosy neighbors and purse-lipped ministers, the seamen could indulge in every vice without a look back. (Though, if the small number of mixed-race offspring produced by the Dutch in the Far East is any indication, their consummate skill with the tankard may have made them less successful in other indulgences—at least, when compared to the Portuguese.) Knowing full well what fueled a Dutch sailor, Linschoten had reassured his readers that a distilled liquor called arrack existed in plenty in the Indies; he particularly recommends the arrack from Malaysia. In India and Indonesia, arrack was made by distilling the fermented nectar of the palmyra palm (though fermented sugarcane and rice were also used), resulting in a relatively neutral-tasting white firewater.* A Portuguese visitor to India in 1587 commented that that "araca" is very strong but improves with age, and that raisins were thrown into it to take off its roughness and sweeten it. A commercial version of this same liquor is sold today in little corner shops all over Goa, where it is called *feni*. Goans usually drink it straight, though, for the tourists, they mix it with lime soda. There is also a homemade version, which regularly kills people.

The arrack naturally led to every indiscretion you could think of, and not by common sailors alone. At the Dutch "factory" in Jakarta, the se-

---

* Palmyra palm nectar ferments naturally in the blossoms, yielding a mildly alcoholic beverage called toddy to anyone who makes the effort to tap the flowers. The same sap is also boiled down to make palm jaggery, or sugar.

nior Company official made no friends by repeatedly sexually harassing the wives of high-ranking Javanese. This was apparently not an isolated incident. An anonymous journal from a few years later reads like a kinky novel. According to our reporter, the entire senior staff of the same fort behaved in a most un-Calvinist way, with the *dominie* (pastor) jumping right in. It apparently all began with Spanish wine (rather than the local tipple) when four Indonesian/Portuguese mulatas were invited to the officers' mess to partake of the evening meal. But more was to come:

> After the sub-merchants and assistants had left, Raey, the Captain, Dominie Hermans, the Lieutenant, and the Cornet [another officer] remained with the women. They were gay and happy and drank Spanish wine and dallied with those women, singing: *Tabe, tabe, Signora moeda—bawa bantal tikar—betta mau rassa!* [Greetings, young signora—do bring your sleeping mat and pillow!] What the Dominie had preached during the day was already forgotten; all were too busy with those luscious women . . . The pleasures lasted until one or two in the morning when everyone went to his bunk and three women slept upstairs . . . The Cornet took [one of the women] home and had his fun with her in her house.

No wonder Coen would later harangue the *Heren XVII* to send a number of "solid Protestant clergymen, not such stupid, uncouth idiots as you have sent heretofore." All the same, this rowdy, unruly atmosphere dominated the Dutch trading posts throughout most of the early years of the VOC. "It is human beings Your Honors have here, not angels!" Coen repeatedly pointed out to his superiors.

As Coen ascended the Company's ranks, this sober Calvinist found all the undisciplined behavior not merely distasteful but a drag on the bottom line. He wanted God-fearing families to come establish some sort of core of decency. "Even if they come naked as a jaybird we can still use them," he wrote to Amsterdam. He was particularly in favor of sending young women to the Indies, which would have the twofold advantage of emptying the orphanages back home and providing wives to Dutchmen overseas. How morally uplifting these "company maidens" would prove to be is highly debatable, but they were to be a feature of the East India trade for centuries. Unlike the Portuguese, the Dutch never made much of an effort to convert anyone to Christianity. As a result, marriages between Dutchmen and locals were rare. In another letter, Coen harps on the fact that the local Muslims will not allow their women to marry Christians, and what's more, they "kill their children or abort them so that the mother won't bear heathens."

"A Thorough Grasp of Commerce"

"This Coen is a person with a thorough grasp of commerce as well as statecraft," wrote the outgoing governor of the Dutch East Indies in 1613 about the newly appointed president and "bookkeeper-general" of the Company's Indonesian offices. "He is honest, well-balanced, and does not waste any time. I am certain that there has never been anyone here, nor will there be, who surpasses him in efficiency, as Your Lordships will be able to judge from his letters."

We can learn a great deal about Hoorn's best-known son from his profuse letters. (He issued so many reams of correspondence that the ships returning to Holland around the first of every year became known as "book ships.") Impatience and conceitedness are the leitmotif of his correspondence. "I am almost weary, my voice weakens and the pen falters, to have to repeat that while in some cases you show great courage, there is always something in which you fall short." Then again and again: "I swear to you by the Almighty that the General Company has no greater enemies than the ignorance and shortsightedness, pardon my words, which seems to prevail among Your Lordships and outvotes the intelligent."

While he may have been impertinent, Coen delivered, and the directors were quick to promote him up the company ranks. Between 1607 and 1613, he went from humble clerk to chief merchant in charge of two ships to bookkeeper-general (essentially, the chief financial officer). When he got this last promotion, his assignment was to compile a comprehensive financial report of all the activities of the VOC from Cochin to Nagasaki, a job that he fulfilled with such alacrity that headquarters immediately promoted him to the number two position in the field, director-general. Though he did not get the top post of governor-general for another five years, this effectively put the twenty-seven-year-old Coen in charge of the East India Company's operations across Asia. All he lacked was the title and the salary—points on which he harped with great regularity in his missives back to Hoogstraat.

As far as Coen was concerned, the company's efficiency was not impeded merely by the degeneracy of its workforce and the doltishness of the leadership in Amsterdam but by the uncooperative producers of the very spices that were the whole point of the enterprise. In all probability, Coen had personally witnessed just how disobliging the natives could be. It is almost certain that he was part of a 1609 fleet under Admiral Verhoef sent to build a fort on the Bandanese island of Neira to make sure the natives understood just how seriously the Dutch took their contracts. Needless to say, the Bandanese had not been consulted about the building project and showed their displeasure by massacring the admiral and some thirty members of his staff. The last time Coen saw his commander's head, it was likely skewered on the end of a Bandanese battle lance. Of course, the Dutch took their revenge, and the fort was built after all. Subsequently, at least some of the local chieftains, the *orang kaya*, agreed (once again) to Dutch demands for a mace and nutmeg monopoly throughout the archipelago. The island of Neira itself was seized outright in the name of the Company and the States General "to be kept by us forever," making it the Netherlands' first official East Indian colony. It seems that Coen learned two things from this encounter: that you could not trust the "perfidious Moors," as he tended to call the natives, and that a little bloodletting yielded results. At the time, he was in no position to do anything about it, but years later as governor-general, he took these lessons to their chillingly logical conclusion.

He got the top job in 1618. Now he had the authority to carry out the Company's mission as only he saw fit. His first move was to transfer his base of operations from Bantam, where the ruling sultan wouldn't play by Dutch rules, to Jakarta. When the locals there objected, he had their town burned to the ground. On the ashes of Jakarta's mosque and marketplace, Coen built a brand-new city named Batavia. (Coen originally wanted to call it Nieuw Hoorn after his hometown, but headquarters wouldn't go for it.) The inspiration for Batavia was supposedly the Estado da Índia's capital at Goa, though the VOC base could hardly compare to the gilded

"Rome of the East." The company town looked like it had sprouted from some polder in Holland. Narrow houses topped with stepped gables sat at the edge of straight canals while windmills towered above the city walls. The locals called this tropical Hoorn "Kota Djankong," the city of Jan Coen; people in Amsterdam and The Hague referred to it as an "honorable prison." It must have been a pretty lively prison, though, the streets a menagerie of local Javanese and VOC employees, overseas Chinese settlers and Indian merchants, voluntary migrants from Europe and slaves forcibly transported from Madagascar—all drawn here by the smell of money emitted by ships loaded with sweet spice.

Once the obstinate Javanese had been put in their place, the governor-general turned to the Moluccas. As years had stretched to decades and the stubborn Lusitanians refused to make themselves scarce, the directors of the Dutch East India Company had regretfully come to the conclusion that a pepper monopoly wasn't in the cards. But the case of nutmeg and cloves was a different matter. Now the trouble was the English, who had begun to butt into the spice trade, even setting up a trading post in the Bandas. Needless to say, Coen was not going to let those sorts of details get in his way. In spite of specific instructions not to use force, the impatient governor-general sent in his troops. They not only sent the English packing but in the process massacred or expelled the entire population of the Bandanese island of Ai. A happy consequence of this (for the VOC, at least) was that the Dutch could now impose a new, 20 percent lower price for nutmeg on the producers. But that was a mere Band-Aid applied to a festering sore, as far as the governor-general was concerned.

It would appear that Coen had the glimmerings of a final solution to the supply problem at least as early as 1618. In a letter of that year, he notes that Laurens Reael, the company's rep in Banda, had suggested that the VOC pay a higher rate for nutmeg so that the locals would not be tempted to sell it to others. "But I say NO!" thundered the governor-general. "Do not give in or the whole business will go to the devil. It were better that all the Bandanese leave their islands; then we could plant Dutch colonies there." Not everyone was quite as single-mindedly devoted to the Company's bottom line as Jan Coen. The same Reael who recommended paying more for nutmeg had the temerity to suggest that strict enforcement of the monopoly would result in the wholesale destitution of the natives. "We are so much concerned with profits," he wrote, "that we do not allow anyone else to make a penny." In a similar vein, a Dutch admiral on the scene complained that by eliminating local traders, the Company had driven the Moluccans to the brink of starvation. "It can be done, but with what right?" was his comment. Others spoke up for a more equitable solution in the East Indies. But how could the bean counters on Hoogstraat object to Coen's tactics when they were so effective in shoring up the VOC's share prices?

Coen waited until 1621 to strike. His flotilla dropped anchor in the crystalline waters off Lonthor (Banda Besar), the largest island in the archipelago, in early March. On board were close to two thousand men, including slaves and some one hundred Japanese mercenaries. As the dawn of March 21 dabbed the crowns of the nutmeg trees pink, Coen's troops tumbled onto the coral beaches and clambered up the island's dark volcanic cliffs. The sweating, armored soldiers marched through the scented forest of the interior and up narrow footpaths into the sticky jungle as the inhabitants scattered to escape the invaders. Where the Company's steel and bullets failed, Dutch silver managed to do the trick. In one case, a bribed Bandanese defector guided the attackers to a strategic victory for the handsome sum of 250 reals.* Other, less amenable natives plunged from cliffs into the roiling breakers rather than surrender. By the end of the day, as the red-dyed sun dipped behind the smoldering peak of the Gugung Api volcano, Jan Coen could tick off item number one on his strategic plan: the island was effectively his.

Item number two fell in his lap quickly enough when a delegation of *orang kaya* arrived on Coen's ship to sue for peace. The governor-general demanded that the natives level all their fortifications, give up their weapons, hand over their sons as hostages, and, from now on, pay a tribute of 10 percent of the nutmeg harvest. The rest had to be sold exclusively to the VOC at prices fixed by the Company. Hardly in a position to argue, the chiefs submitted—though, not surprisingly, there was little

---

* This was roughly equivalent to Coen's monthly salary at the time.

good faith on either side of the bargain. By his own admission, Coen neither expected nor wanted the Bandanese to honor the commitments; he
was merely waiting for an excuse to finish what he had started.

By now, the Bandanese had fled to the hills, leaving mounds of fleshy
nutmegs to rot as they fell to the ground. After failing to entice the inhabitants out of the hills, Coen could now justify his endgame. He sent soldiers to torch what remained of the abandoned villages and to hunt down
the inhabitants on every one of the Banda Islands. Anyone who could be
captured was herded onto troop transports and shipped off to Batavia,
where they were sold as slaves—the ones that made it, that is. In at least
one consignment of 287 men, 356 women, and 240 children, 176 died on
the way. Others, trapped in hilltop crevices with no access to food, died by
the thousands—of exposure, starvation, and disease. Then, finally, just to
make sure that no one could come back to interfere with his agenda,
Coen blockaded the islands to cut off any escape. The accountant's geno-
cidal program was highly successful. It appears that no more than about
1,000 Bandanese out of an original population of about 15,000 survived.

Ever meticulous, Coen gave his actions a legal underpinning by holding a trial of some two score prisoners before his final assault. The men,
after being subjected to torture (a routine tool of seventeenth-century jurisprudence), confessed that they had broken the terms of the peace
treaty and conspired against the life of the governor-general. Yet even
some of the Dutch were appalled at the ensuing injustice. "The condemned victims being brought within the enclosure, six Japanese soldiers
were also ordered inside, and with their sharp swords they beheaded and
quartered the eight chief *orang kaya* and then beheaded and quartered the
thirty-six others," wrote a naval lieutenant who witnessed the sight. "All
that happened was so dreadful as to leave us stunned. The heads and
quarters of those who had been executed were impaled upon bamboos
and so displayed. Thus did it happen: God knows who is right. All of us,
as professing Christians, were filled with dismay at the way this affair was
brought to a conclusion, and we took no pleasure in such dealings."

So far, the plan had proceeded like clockwork, the governor-general
could inform headquarters on his return to Batavia. Back in the cool and
clammy chambers of the Oost-Indisch Huis, however, the Seventeen

were a little taken aback by Coen's bloody methods. Still, they sent back the expected letter of commendation, even if it was a little diluted by pious reservations about his tactics: "We had wished that it could have been accomplished by more moderate means." Two years later, though, just to make sure there were no hard feelings, they awarded Coen a compensation package worth close to forty-five thousand guilders, three thousand of which was specifically assigned for the conquest of the spice archipelago.

The Banda genocide did not solve all of the Company's problems. The Dutch faced the same situation the Spanish had experienced when they wiped out the indigenous population of their Caribbean conquests: there was nobody to work the plantations. They also came up with the same solution, importing African slaves and Asian coolies to do the work. There was also the perennial issue of smuggling. Despite the Company's ruthless enforcement of its monopoly, nutmeg continued to leak onto the world market, though in a much more limited fashion now that the Bandanese had been extirpated.

When it came to cloves, the East India Company had a more intractable problem. Unlike nutmeg and mace, which were limited to the minute Bandas, clove trees grew all over the Moluccas, and the trade in cloves was way beyond the limited policing powers of the corporation. Smugglers could easily get double the Company's fixed price if they could slip by the guns of the enforcers. But here, too, the Netherlanders showed their business acumen. If they couldn't control the clove plantations, they would simply burn them down. In 1625, some sixty-five thousand trees— and the lives, villages, and livelihoods of thousands—were destroyed on Ceram's Hoamoal Peninsula alone. Agents went in with axes and torches to wipe out clove plantations elsewhere on Ceram, on Tidore, and on Ternate. (The sultan was paid off with "extirpation moneys" to keep mum.)

The contraband trade thrived partly because there were harbors willing to take it in. So the Company went after the Portuguese, with whom, incidentally, they were no longer at war; Malacca fell in 1641, Ceylon in 1658, and finally even Cochin in 1663. In Indonesia, the VOC seized the independent ports of Aceh, Macassar, and Bantam. It took a good part of the seventeenth century, but by the late 1660s, the Dutch could claim a virtual monopoly on nutmeg, mace, cloves, and cinnamon. And their price by century's end reflected it. In Amsterdam, all these spices (except nutmeg) were selling for easily double what they had been in 1600.

Not that Jan Pieterszoon Coen would live to see the empire built upon his bloodstained foundation. Life expectancies were brief in the East India trade no matter what your rank. The governor-general died in Batavia on September 21, 1629, at the age of forty-two, reportedly from a sudden seizure of "dysentery" (probably cholera). The following day, he was buried with great pomp and ceremony, at company expense. Apparently, when word got back to Hoogstraat that they had picked up the bill, the Seventeen were incensed that they had been charged. Yet no doubt their anger was short-lived, as they saw profits rolling in.

One of the effects of the Dutch entry into the spice trade was that the price of the spices in which they did not gain a monopoly, such as pepper and ginger, plummeted, while the price of the "fine spices" of the Moluccas as well as Ceylonese cinnamon rose. So now pepper and ginger, which had never been exceptionally expensive, became commonplace condiments, while the others became rarer as the VOC strangled the supply at its source to guarantee a high price. In the seventeenth century, cinnamon was still very popular among the cognoscenti, but the "it" spice, especially in France and England, was increasingly nutmeg.

The sixteenth- and early seventeenth-century explosion in the demand for the rarer spices can at least partly be attributed to their use as nutraceuticals. Asian aromatics—and in particular, the "fine spices"— had been used to cure ailments of all kinds at least since the days when Romans used to send their merchants to Cochin. But the printing revolution of the sixteenth century created a whole new market for diet books trumpeting the use of spices as a dietary supplement to balance and "correct" other foods. Any doctor worth his salt had to know the many uses of pepper and, more important, cloves, cinnamon, and nutmeg in his practice. The directors of the Dutch East India Company had only to walk out the front door of company headquarters and glance up the Kloveniersburgwal Canal to Amsterdam's spice market on the Nieuwemarkt to see perfumed bales dispatched to apothecaries across Europe. What they didn't see, or understand, was that the current diet advice was headed the way of the grapefruit diet.

PRESCRIBING SPICE

After all I had read about the Nieuwemarkt, I suppose I had expected the square to be lined with picturesque Dutch façades and have a whiff of nutmeg in the air as I wandered by one foggy Tuesday morning. Instead, the broad plaza is framed by a jumble of plain shops and modern office buildings. The square would be almost homely were it not for the pointy-towered, cinnamon-colored fortress that squats at its center. When this fortified gate was built in 1488 to protect the up-and-coming hamlet of Amsterdam, it was planted with its feet in the canal that encircled the city like a moat. Then, when the city burst its walls in the early sixteen hundreds, the authorities constructed this *nieuwe markt* ("new market") by paving over a section of the canal. The new market specialized in the aromatic treasure brought from the East, and the tower became a weighing station for the spices that canal boats brought down from the harbor.

The perfume of that time has dissipated over the centuries, but not entirely. At the edge of the Nieuwemarkt, you can still detect a hint of spice in the air in an old house that leans gently toward the Kloveniersburgwal Canal, as if tired out by standing here so long. The sign identifies the building as the Apotheek Jacob Hooy, which claims to be the city's oldest pharmacy, founded in 1743. The interior sure looks it. Ancient yellowed drawers are inscribed in florid Latin script—*Piper nigrum, Piper alum*—to indicate their contents of black and white pepper. Chocolate brown barrels line the shelves like the brown cheeses at the Kaaskamer, though these, unlike the spiced cheeses, are just for show. All the same, you know you're in the twenty-first century quickly enough when you see the display of herbal pastilles on the counter promoting stress reduction.

Yet despite the shelves of organic bug repellent and world music CDs, the store is still primarily an apothecary, and the pharmacist's job is still to consult with his customers on just which herbal cocktail will best combat their flatulence or common cold. Ginger and mace are certainly still for sale here, but the attendant tells me that spices are now used mostly in Ayurvedic medicine, not the traditional European medicine that is Jacob Hooy's stock-in-trade. The Dutch are much more eclectic than Americans in their approach to healing. So-called "natural" remedies exist side by side with more "conventional" allopathic practices, while homeopathy is also commonplace. Ayurvedic medicine, however, is relegated to a fringe of medical connoisseurs. This is somewhat surprising, since a system much like it dominated European medical practice for more than a thousand years. It was in this, the so-called Galenic system, that spices used to hold pride of place. When the pharmacy first opened its doors, the chamomile and mint sold at Jacob Hooy would have been considered good enough for chambermaids and fishwives, but for the more cultured classes, only the likes of expensive nutmeg and cloves would do.

In 1600, the Galenic system was the conventional medicine of the day and, after more than a millennium of elaboration, consisted of a vast and esoteric body of knowledge. It had all started with the writings of a second-century Greek physician named Galen, who began his career employed in the ER of a gladiator school in Asia Minor and worked his way up to attending to Caesars. By the early Middle Ages, his writings had been preserved mostly in Arabic compilations, which were, in turn, translated into Latin. In the Renaissance, the Galenic school got a new shot in the arm when classics scholars unearthed Galenic writings in the original Greek. Leading the way was the Venetian university town of Padua, with its links to Greece (recall that Greek exiles flooded into Venice after the fall of Constantinople), but other centers of learning, including the University of Leuven, in the southern Netherlands, were part of the trend.

Ironically, it was university-trained academics, not practicing physicians such as Galen, who now compiled the medical manuals. No wonder that the attraction of the Galenic system, particularly in its later incarnations, was more metaphysical than practical. (This may, in part, explain the appeal of esoteric spices brought from mystical lands.) Because the scheme was not dependent on empirical data that might cloud its clarity, the medical theoreticians could build a model of transparent symmetry and logic.

The system that underlay Galenic theory could be compared to the workings of a compass, where anything can be mapped according to its four points. North, south, east, and west correspond to four elements (water, fire, air, and earth); which, in turn, match up to four bodily humors (phlegm, bile, blood, and black bile); which are associated with the four seasons; which reflect the four ages of man, the four periods of the day, the four colors, the four flavors, even the four Evangelists . . . Anyway, you get the idea. By definition, any and all phenomena could be plugged into this paradigm. So, a fish would naturally be cold and wet because of its watery habitat, a spice hot and dry because of its biting flavor and torrid growing conditions. As far as people went, the temperament of any given individual was determined by his or her particular mixture of humors. We occasionally still use these terms when we describe a person as phlegmatic, bilious, or sanguine, though psychiatrists nowadays generally don't treat depression by prescribing mace to purge their patients of black bile.

In the old days, when a physician was called in, his first job was to diagnose his patient's temperament so he could calibrate the diet. Most experts believed that everyone's humors were a little out of whack and needed correction, which, in all but the most extreme cases, could be done by fiddling with the nutritional regimen. So someone with a phlegmatic (that is, cold and moist) "distemperature" could be corrected by prescribing a hot and dry diet that might include an abundance of heating nutrients such as cinnamon or mustard. The spices would increase the person's "choleric" humors, his temperament would return to balance, and all would be well. Incidentally, the concept of "diet" was seen rather broadly. Depending on the authority, it might include not only food and drink but also air quality, exercise, sexual activity, emotional state, and lots of other factors believed to affect nutrition. For example, our phlegmatic patient could also crank up the choleric humors in the body by standing in a hot and dry wind, exercising vigorously, or even getting really angry. The charm of the system was that you could explain anything to anyone. Once all the inputs were considered, a well-read doctor could tell you just what to eat before going for a walk on a rainy spring day, or the dire consequences of indulging in sex too early on a humid summer morning.

The tricky part of the diagnosis was to first determine a person's temperament, since everyone was made up of a cocktail of all of the humors, and a clear-cut case of, say, a completely sanguine personality was rare. Sex, age, lifestyle, and climate were all factored into the analysis, as was profession. (Poets and prophets are notoriously melancholy, as we all know.) The physician often resorted to even more nebulous criteria, such as personality, body type, and physiognomy. You could tell a lot from a person's complexion: sanguine people, having an abundance of blood, were supposed to have ruddy skin, while phlegmatics looked pale and watery.

This was all very well for the purposes of prescribing diet (in the broadest sense), but to make a diagnosis of an actual illness based on a person's profession and complexion was harder still. In the absence of blood tests and X-rays, medieval doctors depended to some degree on external indicators such as a high fever or an abnormal pulse as a sign of disease. Urine analysis was also a favorite diagnostic technique. By examining, smelling, and even tasting a patient's urine, much could apparently be learned and the appropriate measures applied. Bleeding was always a big favorite. (It's why medieval doctors were often called "leeches.") This was a quick, efficient way to relieve the many illnesses caused by an excess of blood. As you might imagine, the success rate of this sort of medical practice was rather uneven, and consequently, wiser physicians stuck to Hippocrates's injunction, "First do no harm," limiting their advice to diet tips or at least reasonably harmless potions.

Of course, the Renaissance doctor's authority, much as it does today, depended on keeping the system as arcane and jargon-filled as possible. For this, physicians required fat Latin volumes filled with humoral system analyses of Talmudic complexity. Publishers were happy to oblige. However, more popular interpretations of Galenic theory were a big hit as well. Platina's bestselling *De honesta voluptate,* for example, was intended to be as much a dietary guide as a cookbook and provided all sorts of advice on judicious humor balancing. Even Linschoten's *Itinerario* was packed full of advice on the dietary uses of the Eastern commodities. Along with data on the cost of cinnamon and the mating habits of Portuguese *fidalgos,* Linschoten's collaborator (a graduate of the prestigious medical school in Padua, no less) adds, "Cinnamon warms, opens, and tones up the intestines." He writes, "It is good for catarrh, making it move down from the head to the lower parts. It cures dropsy as well as defects and obstructions in the kidneys. Oil of cinnamon strengthens all organs: heart, stomach, liver, etc." Nutmeg is just as much a wonder drug, according to the good doctor: "[Nutmegs] fortify the brain and sharpen the memory; they warm the stomach and expel winds. They give a clean breath, force the urine, stop diarrhea, and cure upset stomachs."

Writings on diet circulated widely in manuscript before printing came around, but those laboriously copied volumes of bound parchment had only been available to a tiny elite. As with Bibles and cookbooks, the revolutionary impact of Gutenberg's invention brought this highly specialized subject to the attention of a much wider public. Much as it does today, the market for dietary self-help books seemed insatiable. From the 1470s to 1650, a flood of dietary literature rolled off the presses across Europe. As with so many other subjects, Venetian publishers led the way. By the mid-1520s, even editions of Galen in the original Greek were printed by the Aldine Press in Venice. With Venice's decline, the presses in Amsterdam and other northern cities took up the cause.

In Amsterdam, Margaretha Cromhout, the wealthy timber merchant's wife, could now instruct her cook on the fine points of balancing the phlegmatic and the bilious humors much the way diet-obsessed Americans calculate their grams of fat and carbohydrates. Others of a less exalted status followed suit. In Protestant Europe, the reading public was not limited to the wealthiest classes, even though they probably had more time to worry about their diets than seamstresses and shoemakers. One of the unintended but profound aftereffects of the Reformation was an enormous increase in literacy, since everyone was now supposed to read the Scriptures. The middling classes could purchase cheap pamphlets and almanacs much like the flimsy little diet books you find today in supermarkets. The fact that the perennially popular "book of secrets" by the sixteenth-century Dutch surgeon (and cookbook writer) Carolus Battus was expressly intended for the "common folk" underlines just how broad-based the reading public was in the Netherlands.

As in the case of Platina, the line between cookbooks and health manuals was as blurred as it is today, and the advice seemed similarly confusing and contradictory. Who couldn't use the advice of experts in negotiating all the complexities of this arcane dietary system? And didn't everyone need a little fine-tuning of their humoral makeup? Yet how could a layman even begin to gauge the delicate balance among nutriments? Chicken might be too sanguine for spring because of its airy temperament, pepper too fiery for someone with a sanguine makeup, turnips too dry and cold for an old man with a young wife. The diet guides had all the solutions, even if the specifics varied from author to author. They explained in great detail, for example, how you could correct fish's watery (phlegmatic) nature by roasting it or serving it with an appropriate sauce. The term often used is to *temper* a dish or a sauce with an appropriate seasoning to make it digestible. (The Portuguese still use the verb *temperar* for "season.") For this, spices were seen as particularly effective. The following advice is typical:

> Sauces should be made according to the nature of the season, for in summer sauces are composed of relatively cool ingredients, whereas in cold weather they are made of warm ingredients. Consequently in summer the proper ingredients are verjuice, vinegar, citrus and pomegranate juices, with sugar and rose water. . . . In cold weather the proper ingredients are mustard, ginger, pepper, cinnamon, cloves, garlic, sage, mint, parsley, wine, meat broths and vinegar that is so weak it approaches the nature of wine. Between times, when neither too warm or too cold, you make sauces of tempered warmth and cold.

In light of the need to continually correct a recipe according to all these factors, it's hardly surprising that medieval and Renaissance cookery guides were so imprecise when it came to quantities. Just how much ginger went into the ubiquitous carmeline sauce often depended on the intended consumer. That is not to say that cooks didn't also spice food for reasons of taste or that people didn't eat what they liked in defiance of every dietitian's advice, just as they do today. Platina, for one, is continually adding comments to Martino's recipes that make you wonder at first how anyone could eat them. Typical are the notes that follow instructions on how to make *torta ex riso,* a kind of rice pudding. First, the Vatican scholar recommends the dish for being nourishing. Then, in the same sentence, he adds, "It delays for a long time in the stomach, dulls the eyes, creates stones, and induces blockages." Perhaps the diners experienced that same guilty titillation we get from forbidden foods like Häagen-Dazs and triple-crème cheeses. How else to explain the medieval popularity of melons despite their being roundly decried by every professional?

In general, fine-tuning your diet was sufficient to get you on the straight and narrow, but in the case of illness or other physiological dysfunction, the healing professions turned to what might be loosely described as drugs. While common people depended on the kinds of herbs sold today by Jacob Hooy, the wealthy preferred more exotic remedies. Typically, these included all sorts of precious ingredients, spices being only the most digestible. An early Italian nostrum for "soothing the heart" includes gold, silver, pearls, emeralds, sapphires, and other precious stones, along with cinnamon, cloves, aloeswood, saffron, cubebs, cardamom, amber, coriander, camphor, and musk. The ingredients were to be finely ground, mixed with sugar, and taken in wine.* Once again, the demand for these cure-alls escalated after the printing revolution. One of these "books of secrets," titled the *Secreti del reverendo donno Alessio Piemontes*, was first published in Venice in 1555. Shortly thereafter it appeared in Latin, French, English, Dutch, and German translations. By 1575, fifty editions had been printed, promising to deliver the recipe for a fountain of youth. An English edition opens with a prescription "to conserve a manne's youthe, and to hold backe old age." The secret lies in a "miraculous" distilled cocktail of Asian spices, saffron, sugar, citrus, minerals, and alcohol, which was to be stirred into veal, chicken, or pigeon broth or diluted with white wine.

Both physicians and cooks frequently turned to spices to fix humoral imbalances because they were considered a particularly concentrated corrective. Accordingly, a relatively small amount of hot and dry pepper could make dangerously cold and moist fish safe to eat. Given the quantity of fish eaten in pre-Reformation Europe, it is not surprising that a suf-

---

* In Portugal, at least, badger powders had their day as a cure for the plague. In a letter written in 1430 to King Duarte, his doctor gave specific instructions on concocting one of these nostrums. First, you had to get a badger drunk on wine filtered through camphor and blended with a compound of gold, seed pearls, and coral. You then decapitated the animal, drained it of its blood, and removed the heart and liver. The blood was mixed with 2 ounces of very fine cinnamon, 1 ounce of *geuaana* (Guinea/melegueta pepper?), ½ ounce of verbena, ¼ ounce of ginger or saffron, ⅛ ounce of fine clove, 1/32 ounce of myrrh, 1/16 ounce of aloes, and 1/64 ounce of fine "unicorn horn," and this mixture was dried out under a "slow sun" or in the "heat of a fire." Into this, you would stir 2 ounces of the poor badger's pulverized heart, liver, and even teeth. To serve, the mélange was dissolved in wine or in water seasoned with vinegar. Once the remedy was consumed—"the best possible thing against the pestilence"— the patient had to lie down, cover up warmly, and perspire for some six hours, without sleeping, eating, or drinking. He could then drink and eat, but only water and bread soaked in cold water. If the pain of the swellings persisted, it was permissible to bleed him in the aching leg or arm.

ficient supply of pepper was needed to maintain public health—at least, by those who could afford it. For more careful adjustments, spices could be combined to reach just the right balance. Thus black pepper, not surprisingly, was considered hotter than cinnamon. By combining the two, a more nuanced effect could be achieved.

There were, of course, more cheaply available correctives, such as garlic and even salt, but it was generally accepted that people of a "finer" composition needed more refined seasoning. This was explained by the self-evident fact that the humoral makeup of a peasant was necessarily different from that of a merchant or scholar. Numerous writers warned of the pains and illnesses that came about from eating foods inappropriate to a person's social position. The ruling classes could suffer just as much from eating thick peasant soups as common folk from ingesting more refined foods. Suffice it to say that oat bran never would have made it into upper-class medieval diet books.

Not that spiced food was deemed appropriate for everyone, even if class and cost were not at issue. Women, for example, were often warned off spices because of their supposedly delicate nature. With obvious disapproval, the sixteenth-century surgeon William Bulleyn describes how some women used pepper to "dry up" their complexion to make it seem more fashionably pale: "Although pepper be good to them that use it well, yet unto artificiall women that have more beastliness then beauty and cannot be content with their natural complexions, but would fayne be fayre: they eate peper, dried corne [grain] and drinke vinegar . . . to dry up their bloude." Another seemingly contradictory explanation about why women should avoid hot spices was for just the opposite reason: that they stimulated blood flow that might lead to sexual arousal. If the number of recipes purporting to cure performance problems is any indication, men, on the other hand, seemed to need all the help they could get in this regard. According to contemporary theory, spices, with their concentrated heating ability, were just the potions to get the job done. Cloves "augment miraculously the force of venus," as one writer puts it. The way the mechanism was supposed to work is that heating foods would agitate and engorge the penis, while an increase in the circulation of blood would aid in the production and eventual delivery of the sperm. Applying the same reasoning, cold foods should have the same effect as a cold shower, so accordingly, bachelors and priests were supposed to eat plenty of lettuce. Even in the Middle Ages, real men did not eat salad. Interestingly, today spices are still widely used in men's colognes, aftershaves, and so on, whereas the preference for women's scents tends toward the floral.

Dry and heating foods were not seen merely as a performance enhancer in the bedroom, they were also supposed to increase mental acuity. It was common knowledge that sanguine and phlegmatic people were slow-witted and forgetful; thus, a dry constitution would seem to guarantee intelligence. Here again, it was upper-class men, who were presumably the only ones making the big decisions and thinking deep thoughts, who were more likely to benefit.

Does this mean that rich people ate spices only because they thought they were good for them? This theory has been popular of late among food historians as a way of explaining the late medieval penchant for imported spices. And while there is probably something to it, the spice-balancing explanation has probably been overplayed. Certainly, if the reaction of today's public to nutritional pronouncements is any indication, adherence to humoral principles was at best mixed. What's more, a plethora of sixteenth-century literary parodies from Shakespeare to Rabelais seems to indicate that physicians, dietitians, and the diets themselves were often a subject of ridicule.

It's worth noting that humoral medicine wasn't the only game in town. Much like we turn to herbal medicine and yoga when more conventional medicine fails, people in medieval Europe turned to prayer, miracles, and magic when the humoral system couldn't deliver the goods. Not surprisingly, this happened a lot. In any case, the line between healer and magician was often fuzzy. In 1403, five "sorcerers" were allowed to attempt to cure Charles VI of France. Unluckily for them, the king's idea of a malpractice award was to burn the quacks at the stake. Other healers were accused of employing sorcery, astrology, and an assortment of other unorthodox medical techniques, though that didn't stop them from having a successful practice.

During the Renaissance, spices had their place in everyday medicine, but they also had more esoteric uses. In the sixteenth century, alchemy was all the rage. Alchemists operated on a more metaphysical plane than ordinary doctors and nutritionists, but their arcane insights often trickled down into general dietary theory. These protochemists are often carica-tured as obsessed with turning base metals into gold, but many were more preoccupied with discovering a prescription for eternal life, while others had even more transcendent goals. One influential school, led by the Flor-entine physician and humanist Ficino and his protégé Paracelsus, came up with a notion of hyperawareness that they called the "spiritus," which could be achieved through a very particular alignment of the humors. Through this "spiritus," the melancholic individual (refined melancholia was naturally the prerequisite for genius) would be able to perceive the world without having to resort to more ordinary senses. In other words, transcendent genius could be achieved if you carefully calibrated the in-take of your micronutrients. Of course, the highly concentrated humors in spices made them perfect for the job. Paracelsus, for one, was fond of a kind of metaphysical aromatherapy in which his spice-scented concoc-tions were meant to be inhaled rather than consumed. In one recipe in-tended to kick-start this "spiritus," a potion of potable gold was perfumed with cardamom, cinnamon, mace, and cloves, along with flower and ani-mal gland extracts.

While the obscure concerns of Paracelsus were hardly of interest to the man in the street, many of the ideas filtered down to the popular press. Who wouldn't want to find out the secret formula of a long and healthy life, especially in an era in which pestilence and disease were all too commonplace and a fifty-year-old person was considered a doddering relic?

Yet even as the details of the venerable humoral system became avail-able to the widest public ever, Galen's theories increasingly came under attack from rival camps.

SPICES LOSE FAVOR

In one of Rembrandt's more famous paintings, a group of lace-collared men huddles around a limp body entirely naked except for a skimpy loin-cloth. They are all bathed in a ghostly light that seems to emanate from the white cadaver at their center. One of the men, the only one with a plain collar and a hat, pries apart the dead man's left arm with a pair of for-ceps, exposing the meat, muscle, and sinew beneath the skin. The picture, painted in 1632, is known as *The Anatomy Lesson of Dr. Tulp* and depicts a scene that took place in the old spice-weighing tower in Nieuwemarkt. By this point, the building not only served to regulate the traffic in nutraceuticals like cinnamon and nutmeg but was also used by the Amsterdam Guild of Surgeons for their annual public dissection. Dissection had been made legal only a few years earlier, and there was still a level of prurient titillation to the rare occasions when the public was invited. The rule was that only the cadavers of convicted criminals could be pried open for inspection. This one had just been hanged for armed robbery. As the tangled innards of the thief's arm dangle from the end of the doctor's instrument, the famed surgeon Nicolaes Tulp looks out, presumably to the assembled audience in the operating theater. Apparently, he was as skilled at wooing an audience as wielding a scalpel. He later held the position of city treasurer eight times and of burgomaster (mayor) four times.

Surgeons did not used to be this highly esteemed. In medieval Europe, the messy business of surgery was often a sideline practiced by barbers and dentists, lowly professions compared to the learned ranks of physicians, who kept their clothes clean and handed out carefully penned prescriptions. People turned to surgeons only as a last resort. The Catholic Church had long had an issue with dissecting corpses, with the result that most surgeons had to learn on still-living patients—obviously with variable success. Yet once Holland had declared itself for the Protestant side, the taboo against cutting open cadavers was slowly relaxed, and doctors could finally study the subcutaneous world.

In the Middle Ages, the inside of the human body had been as much a terra incognita as the far-off Indies, and the first explorers of hearts and spleens made discoveries that were often just as surprising as those made by da Gama and Columbus. What they found often contradicted what they'd read in the erudite textbooks of Galen's apostles. But perhaps more important, it was the empirical approach of Tulp and his colleagues that made the Galenic model—that exquisitely constructed house of cards built of deductive reason—wobble at its foundations. Over and over in seventeenth-century texts, you read the revolutionary refrain that since the ancients had lived in another time and place, they could hardly be regarded as the source of all knowledge. The humoral system was not yet thrown out the window, but it was precariously balanced on the ledge, with competing systems making its hold on medical orthodoxy ever more tentative. What happened then is just what happens today when medical opinion begins to shift: the public got confused. As far as spices went, who knew where they were now supposed to fit in the people's diet?

Whereas spices' overseas origin had once been a selling point, now it became controversial—at least, in some quarters. The Portuguese and Castilian voyages in search of Christians and spices had come home with reports of hundreds, if not thousands, of plants nobody in Europe had ever heard of and plenty of specimens, too. Dietitians and naturalists had the prodigious task of sorting them all out so they could be plugged into the humoral system. Many of the new plants were viewed with suspicion. (Famously, tomatoes and potatoes were long considered toxic.) Arguments simmered about whether imported plants and medicines were well suited to Europeans. According to the xenophobic camp, when God created the world, he had provided all that was necessary for each group of people in their own backyard—thus, local medicines like chamomile and henbane were better for curing local ills than exotic cloves and nutmeg. Conveniently, this happened to align with the opinions of those Calvinist preachers who regarded the likes of cinnamon and cloves not as missives from paradise but as the harvest of a pagan and hedonistic soil. As such, they were sure to beguile men away from a decent, God-fearing life, a life that could come only from a diet of homegrown turnips and spice-free cheese.

While the religious climate in the Netherlands may have become more tolerant toward slicing into cadavers, Protestants and Papists alike became ever more puritanical when it came to the pleasures of living flesh. Eating well (however that was defined) was increasingly seen as the problem rather than the solution, as it had been earlier. The diet books make this change in medical opinion abundantly clear. Ken Albala, an American food historian who has studied the early nutrition guides, points to a shift from fifteenth-century books—which are generally tolerant and, at times, even promote the pleasures of the table (Platina's best-selling *De honesta voluptate et valetudine* means "On Honest Pleasure and Good Health," after all)—to a more preachy and uptight approach that has no use for fine cooking. In 1530, Luis Lobera de Ávila, a Spanish dietitian, could still advise his readers to "eat all that is most delectable and delicious for it is also the most nourishing." By the seventeenth century, you are more likely to read opinions such as those of Leonard Lessius, the author of a popular lifestyle guide, who ranted against "lickorish cooking" and "curious dressing of meats."

The change in medical fashion was no doubt accelerated by the technology of printing itself. The arrival of mechanical printing didn't merely mean a cheaper, quicker alternative to hand-lettered manuscripts. It bore about as much relationship to the earlier technology as Google does to a card catalog. Printing fundamentally changed the way people learned about the world. Without (relatively) cheap Bibles, the Reformation is unthinkable; without copies of cookbooks rolling off the presses by the hundreds of thousands, the coming Europe-wide revolution in fine dining would likely have been no more than a localized uprising.* Because of its volume, the business of printing books always needs new products, new ideas. By its very nature, it cannot recycle the same information over and over—as was the case in the days of few and precious manuscripts. After all, just how many reprints of Galen can your customers buy?

It's more than likely that the same mechanism we see in today's diet-book racket got its start in the Renaissance. Then, as now, publishers were always on the lookout for someone with a bright idea that would resonate with the public. If the book sold, other authors imitated it. As consumers tired of the same old thing, a new (or repackaged) idea came along, and everybody jumped on the new bandwagon. This may explain, at least in part, why, long before anyone could imagine an Atkins diet, nutrition trends came and went for no reason other than a shift in fashion. Naturally, the changes came faster and faster as more publishers increased production and as more people could read and afford to buy books.

By the middle years of the seventeenth century, it seems that readers were fed up with diet books, and the market for these self-help works dried up. It may be that all the competing medical systems of the time just made the public throw up its hands and give up on the experts. Maybe people were sick of being nagged about what they should eat and just

---

* While it is impossible to quantify the number of cooking and dietary books that were printed between 1550 and 1700, historians have estimated that perhaps four hundred million books were printed overall. Even if we conservatively assume that food books made up a paltry 0.1 percent of the books produced (today, it's more like 10 percent), we're still talking four hundred thousand books, and the number was surely higher.

stopped listening. Or perhaps it was merely that another cycle of the publishing business had come full circle.

All this religious, scientific, and intellectual ferment was going on as Europe was embroiled in yet another round of her murderous wars. Philip's crusade against the Dutch was only one among many. In the center of Europe, what had begun as a campaign against Czech Protestants in 1618 spun out of control, drawing in every major power in Europe. The Thirty Years' War, as it would come to be known, careened across the center of the continent like an insatiable tornado. In its wake, cities lay devastated, fertile plains burned to ashes, whole economies collapsed. When it wiped out the Republic's customers in central Europe, it was the war, not the Portuguese or Dutch, that delivered the coup de grâce to Venice's ailing spice trade. But everywhere in Europe, the political system was realigned. Christendom had entered the seventeenth century dominated by one militantly Catholic superpower, Spain. By the time the bloodbath was over, the states that emerged—most notably, France and Austria—were much more interested in keeping their borders intact than in crusading against Protestants or Moors. Europe's lines of demarcation hardened along nationalist lines. Countries increasingly came to be defined by language and cuisine as much as by creed.

The wars of religion had implications for scientists, cooks, and publishers as they had for politicians and priests. In Catholic Italy, the proudly independent medical faculty in Padua was brought to heel by the pope's Jesuit watchdogs. As a result, it quickly lost its primacy to more progressive Protestant European schools, such as the Dutch university of Leiden. Notoriously, Galileo was forced from Padua after repeated run-ins with the Inquisition. Many alchemists and astrologers went underground, lest they be accused of practicing necromancy—a serious charge that could get you sent to the stake. Then, in concert with the religious zealotry, witch trials swept the continent during the later years of the Reformation. This wave of persecution peaked in what some historians have called a "witch-hunting craze" of the hundred years between 1550 and 1650. (The Salem witch trials were a distant echo of this Europe-wide phenomenon.) Not surprisingly, physicians who knew what was good for them tried to distance themselves as much as possible from any of the occult arts that had once been part of their medical kit.

So what did all this tumult mean for the consumption of spices in Europe? In the short term, not much. Outside of France, late-seventeenth-century recipe collections seem just as enthusiastic about cooking with spices as they had a hundred years before. Just look at the penchant for spice in *De verstandige kock*. Nutmeg and cloves also still show up regularly in physicians' medical kits. But increasingly, national cuisines started to diverge. And in France, which had now overtaken Italy as Europe's style-setter, the fashion in spicing was changing. In Versailles, well-spiced cuisine lost its cachet. Elsewhere in Europe, fashionistas took note. None of this happened overnight or everywhere, but the seeds of what we might call modern European cooking (and consequently, American cooking, too), with its emphasis on local seasonings, were planted just as the Dutch East India Company was raking in its greatest profits from the blood-stained nutmeg groves.

THE GOLDEN AGE LOSES ITS LUSTER

Despite Jan Coen's mostly terrible reputation today, there is no shortage of streets and other landmarks named after him across the Netherlands. In Amsterdam, he has lent his name to a major tunnel and a harbor nearby. Coenhaven (the harbor) is a short bicycle ride from the Centraal Station. The route takes you past the old wood harbor where the timber for the East Indiamen arrived. These days, the old jetties are lined with crusty barges converted into houseboats, festooned with planters and children's swing sets that glow magenta against the leaden sky. When you look ahead, giant cranes hover above container ships, like enormous praying mantises readying for combat. Coenhaven is like any other modern harbor, with rows of low, sprawling warehouses painted with gray and more gray. But sniff the air. The usual salt and diesel harbor smell mingles here with the darker, loamier scent of cocoa. Amsterdam long yielded preeminence to the superior modern harbor at Rotterdam, but it nonetheless manages to lead the world in cocoa imports. Still, Coen's harbor with its scattering of cargo ships is no more than a shadow of the old port packed with hundreds of ships, in the radiant days when Amsterdam's spice imports made her the envy of the world.

In the beginning, the VOC business model worked sufficiently well to make a lot of seventeenth-century Amsterdamers rich enough to build

fancy houses and fill them with exquisite paintings, but it had a funda-
mental built-in flaw. It did not take into account that spices are not the
same kind of trade good as herring and beer, that the demand for luxuries like pepper and nutmeg was not based on price but rather on more
ineffable, even metaphysical, attributes; fashion is fickle. Once the Dutch
had figured out how to take over the supply side of the equation, they assumed that demand would just keep on growing. The trouble was that
spices, once they had been turned into an ordinary commodity and lost
their symbolic resonance, had only a marginal place in the modern,
postmedieval world.

In the seventeenth century, the chocolate that scents Coenhaven's
briny breeze, as well as tea and coffee, came to be the new darlings of the
in-crowd. The new tropical imports were sometimes even hyped in the
same words as the old Asian seasoning. In much the way that some spices
had earlier been prescribed to increase mental agility, the stimulating effects of tea and coffee in particular were recommended to the movers and
shakers of the new rational age. They certainly had none of the fusty and
sensuous associations of the Oriental scents or the soporific effects of
spiced wine and beer. Heavily spiced beverages, in particular, lost market
share to the modern stimulants. Admittedly, chocolate (the drink) had a
reputation that was a little more ambiguous than the other brews, perhaps because it had arrived in Europe by way of the decaying Madrid
court, but as Amsterdam came to dominate the cacao business, it, too, became a staple in any modish drawing room. The VOC got into the coffee
and tea business as well, but it was never able to control the market as it
had for the fine spices. As the demand for the East Asian condiments
sagged, the shine began to wear off Amsterdam's golden age.

There were many factors that led to Amsterdam's slow slide from
her perch atop the world. In much the same way that the city's initial ascent was not wholly dependent on the East India trade (compared to Lisbon, say), her tumble down had many causes. But the drop-off in the
spice business was symptomatic of problems all around. Unlike Venice,
which managed to reinvent herself as an amusement park, giving the city
its long half-life, or Lisbon, which rose again in the eighteenth century on
an updraft of Brazilian gold dust, Amsterdam mostly lapsed into obscu-
rity and relative poverty by the mid-1700s. The ambitious expansion

plan for the ring of canals that built the Herengracht for the booming seventeenth-century city was left uncompleted and only partially populated until the industrial age.

Given the fact that Amsterdam had made its fortune during the years of conflict with Spain, the trouble began with a short-lived fashion for signing peace treaties. The first bit of bad news came in 1648, when word circulated on the Dam that an end had been declared to the Spanish war. To make things worse, the Thirty Years' War in central Europe had finally ground to its weary conclusion that same year. Three years later, the English stopped slaughtering one another in their Civil War. Now, all of a sudden, Europe's great powers could pause to turn their greedy heads upon the riches of the minute republic.

Spain was out of the picture for good, but now England was feeling her oats. In a series of wars between 1652 and 1678, the new naval superpower gnawed off chunks of the Dutch empire from Malaysia to Manhattan. In mainland Europe, the French invaded the Netherlands itself. Wars against Louis XIV's armies were bad enough, but what really hurt the economy of the Hollanders was when one Dutch business after another was expelled from the Sun King's realm in the name of French protectionism.

All over Europe, absolutist monarchs and their ministers were entranced with the economics of mercantilism, subsidizing exports and cutting off imports. The French founded their own East India Company so that they wouldn't have to buy spices imported by foreigners. They set up a little colony at Pondicherry, on India's southeast coast, to supply their pepper ships and even tried to seduce the ruler of Ceylon away from the embrace of the Dutch. But as one Frenchman pointed out, "No lover is as jealous of his mistress as the Dutch are of their trade in Spices," and the maneuver ended in failure. Virtually all of Europe's pepper continued coming through Amsterdam and London, and the Netherlands alone controlled all the cinnamon, nutmeg, mace, and cloves that reached Europe's shores. And yet, while it does not appear that Dutch spices were particularly singled out for sanctions by the Versailles government, it does seem awfully coincidental that heavily spiced cooking loses favor among the elite in France, and only in France, during just this period. You have to ask, how seemly would it have been to serve food highly seasoned with the foreigners' spices to the king and his mercantilist ministers? Still, mercantilism can at best offer only a fragment of the explanation for the French revolution in cooking of the sixteen hundreds.

It's hardly surprising that Europeans would give up medieval cookery just as they were abandoning feudalism, counterpoint, egg tempera, and a Ptolemaic universe. But why was France the hotbed of this innovation? The court of Louis XIV was hardly known for its revolutionary spirit. Renaissance France had no Galileo or Monteverdi, no Spinoza or Rembrandt. But it had La Varenne.

A glance at François Pierre La Varenne's seminal 1651 cookbook, *Le cuisiner françois,* reveals how much things had changed in France.* Gone are the generous helpings of sugar and exotic spice of the Italian Renaissance masters, replaced by local herbs and mushrooms. Though this nouvelle cuisine was definitely more delicate (or blander, depending on your point of view), the French chef still includes nutmeg or cloves in plenty of his recipes, though he does so in stingy quantities. A typical recipe will call for "two or three" cloves and a grating of nutmeg. Pepper and ginger are mostly absent, and cinnamon has been quarantined in the dessert chapters.

There are a number of reasons why the seventeenth-century culinary revolution sprouted in French soil (even while it was pollinated by Europe-wide trends). To a greater degree than elsewhere, the old and once-powerful French aristocracy was increasingly dependent on the whim of the king. As early as 1586, a Spanish commentator (admittedly, not the most impartial source) mentions that in France, the courtiers and grandees are such slaves to royal fashion that they will ape the king even if he has a taste for foods that are "vile and common, which even the poorest wretches would not consent to eat." (Was he referring to truffles and mushrooms?) To some degree, feasting in the new absolutist monarchies now had a fresh purpose. Whereas, in the olden days, lavish feasts were put on to impress a noble's underlings, they now headlined an aristocrat's talents as a sycophant. Ostentation took on a slightly revised

---

* The book's immense influence was seen not only in France, where it went through some thirty editions in seventy-five years, but also in reprints and translations in Holland (1653), England (1653), and even Italy (1690).

form. One thing is sure, though: French aristocrats certainly did not stop using spices because they were now cheap. The fine spices were at least twice as expensive at the end of La Varenne's seventeenth-century revolution as they had been at its beginning. But it is true that with the establishment of a worldwide colonial system that produced bulk commodities instead of aromatic missives from paradise, spices lost much of their cachet.

Yet just how quickly the new style penetrated beyond the kitchens of Francophile gourmets is impossible to pin down with any precision. Looking at cookbooks, you would deduce that the upper classes of eighteenth-century England, Italy, and Spain were taking their cues from the French, and probably by the nineteenth century, so were the Portuguese and central Europeans. But when you look at the import numbers, you realize that the decline in spice use must have been very gradual. There was certainly no sudden drop in spice imports in the age of Louis XIV, for even as La Varenne was revising his radical manifesto, other cookbooks of the old-fashioned, well-spiced persuasion kept being published. What did happen, however, was that the astonishing increase in spice use that had taken place in the sixteenth and seventeenth centuries slowed and then halted, even while the population surged. Even today, French butchers still flavor their pâtés with a mixture called *quattre épices*, which includes pepper, cloves, ginger, and nutmeg, and English hams are still studded with cloves. But that is now the exception. Outside of Holland, the spices that used to be stewed with capons and sprinkled on roast sturgeon are now typically used only in sweets. While it is true that the Europe-wide appetite for spices certainly abated after the seventeenth century, that is perhaps the less dramatic transformation. The big change is that Europeans invented sugar-based desserts.

In the Middle Ages, sugar was simply another spice, used in increasingly greater quantities in meat pies and roasts. There were certainly "sweetmeats," which we might call dessert, but they were mostly served right along with the meat, fish, and vegetable dishes. There was no distinction to speak of between "savory" and "sweet" courses. An Italian Renaissance pigeon pie might include as much sugar as a typical American apple pie today. As the Portuguese set up their overseas sugar colonies in the fourteen hundreds and the other Europeans jumped aboard a hundred years later, sugar became something everyone could afford. At the same time, a barrier was gradually erected between sweet and salty. As La Varenne's book so clearly illustrates, cinnamon, so often partnered with sugar in meat-based Renaissance recipes, was now segregated to the sweet side of the wall, penned in with ginger. At least for a while, cloves, nutmeg, and pepper were allowed to roam free among soups and ragouts, though their quantities were severely circumscribed. This exclusionary fashion was uneven across Europe (witness the idiosyncrasies of Dutch cooking, for example) and across the culinary repertoire, but the trend is the same everywhere throughout Christendom. People continued to use the imported aromatics, but since many were now restricted to desserts while others were just plain restricted, there was less and less demand.

This would explain, at least in part, why the market for VOC spices stagnated, even as Europe's population surged. As best we can tell from the numbers, the European demand for pepper had been increasing by modest increments in the fifteenth and sixteenth centuries. Then, when the price war among the Dutch, English, and Portuguese sent the price tumbling, demand doubled within a few decades. But that was it. Even as Europe's population surged in the eighteen hundreds, the hunger for pepper crashed into a rock-solid ceiling.* Just why that occurred may be connected to the continually declining standard of living that regular folk—the ones who had long consumed most of the pepper—experienced up until the Industrial Revolution. The other spices followed much the same boom-and-bust trajectory, though for a different reason. Here, the Dutch may have strangled their own golden goose. In order to maintain high prices, they controlled just how much cinnamon, cloves, nutmeg, and mace made it to their European customers. Their profit margin may have been higher, but the overall amount of fine spices available to Eu-

---

* Roughly speaking, pepper imports were a scant 1.2 million kilos in 1500, when Europe held some eighty million people; about 1.5 million in 1600, when the population had risen to one hundred million; and perhaps as much as 7 million in the 1670s, when the population was roughly the same. But this volume of pepper could not be sold, no matter how low the price went. In 1688, the *Heren XVII* estimated that the European demand was only 3.5 million kilograms. Fifty years later, European imports had dropped to just that number and stayed there until the early nineteenth century. Clove imports peaked in the 1620s at about 350,000 kilos, a number they would not recover until the mid-twentieth century.

rope's cooks was artificially restricted. There was actually less spice on the market in 1700 than there had been half a century earlier. When torching spice plantations in Asia didn't do the trick, the *Heren XVII* burned their stock in Amsterdam. Close to 2 million pounds of stored (and admittedly stale) nutmeg and mace were burned in the 1730s alone—and this at a time when annual sales were in the 250,000-pound range! Consequently, even those who wanted to cook in the old-fashioned style had no choice but to use less of the Moluccan spices.

When it came to pepper, the VOC couldn't control the supply. As a result, in the waning decades of Amsterdam's golden age, the European market was awash with more Dutch (and English, French, and even Danish) imported pepper than could be sold. All the while, the English East India Company kept right on the VOC's heels, increasing its pepper cargoes year after year. The VOC's declining profits, however, could not be blamed just on the pesky English. There is some question whether the Vereenigde Oost-Indische Compagnie ever made money, even in the early years when the appetite for spices seemed insatiable. Whatever the fine print of the balance sheet, it seems the Company had a good run for the first ninety years or so of its existence. Perhaps more dividends were paid than might have been justified by the profits, but those payments kept the Amsterdam economy humming, even if the VOC needed to borrow more and more money to keep itself solvent.

In the early days, the directors had tried to save cash by handing out dividends in the form of actual spices. In 1610, shareholders were left holding a bag of peppercorns and mace instead of hard currency (only about 7.5 percent was paid in cash). Altogether, some 40 percent of the declared value of all VOC dividends in the first fifty years took the form of cloves, mace, and pepper. For some of the larger investors who were in the spice-trading business anyway, this was no hardship, but the cobblers and barkeeps who owned no more than a share or two were about as happy as the stockholders of Heinz would be if they got their dividends in the form of pickles. Those who didn't want to dump all their investment into the stewpot had to peddle their odiferous dividends at fire-sale prices. Eventually, there was such a backlash from investors that, after 1644, the VOC was stuck with paying in cash. As a consequence, by 1692, the company was four million guilders in debt. The problem was that the cost of maintaining a private empire in order to support the spice monopoly was absorbing all but a tiny fraction of the gross profit.

Then there was the issue of the workforce. The VOC had always suffered from incompetent and greedy employees, but there were enough trustworthy people at the top to keep the rest at least moderately honest. Now corruption within the company's ranks increasingly siphoned profits away from Hoogstraat. There had been plenty of fraud in the Estado da Índia, too, but not every employee of the Portuguese crown was in India just for the money. Most were, of course, but a large minority had come for fame or for salvation, too. The Dutch, on the other hand, were there for lucre alone, and, at the low wages paid by the VOC, no one was likely to get rich quick from just his salary. Whatever charges have been leveled at Jan Coen, no one ever accused him of graft. In the next century, though, corruption reached into the highest levels. When Governor-General Van Hoorn resigned from his East India post in 1709, his fortune was estimated at ten million guilders. The kickbacks and profits raked in from the illicit trading of spices became an open secret. In parts of India, the Company's officials pooled the spoils and redistributed them in proportion to the salary each received, to assure each employee an appropriate share of the embezzled cash. In the early eighteenth century, annual losses mounted from two to four and even six million guilders. Before long, the Company was technically bankrupt.

If the VOC had been merely an ordinary joint-stock corporation, it would surely have gone under. But the Dutch East India Company was much more than that: it was effectively a state within a state. And like many governments do today, it was able to continue functioning simply by borrowing more cash. It could get away with it in the eighteenth century because, in spite of its relative decline, Amsterdam was still the prime capital market in the world. Investors from all over Europe kept propping up the Company, and the VOC continued to pay out dividends year after year, even if its imposing shipyards and perfumed warehouses had little more substance than crumbly gingerbread. This might have worked even longer than it did if the Company's mainstay—the clove and nutmeg monopoly—hadn't been broken. But finally, around 1750, the French East India Company succeeded in breaking the Dutch lock on fine spices. One of its employees, Pierre Poivre (appropriately, "pepper" in French), stole nutmeg and clove seedlings, which he then successfully propagated on the French Indian Ocean colonies of Mauritius and Réunion. Finally, after years of sagging profits and government bailouts, the VOC was liquidated in 1799, and the Dutch government took over the East Indies. In the Banda Islands, Dutch planters continued to rule over their nutmeg plantations until 1950, when, despite armed Dutch opposition, Indonesia gained its independence. Almost all of the ethnically Dutch population left or was expelled. Batavia became Jakarta once more.

As it had during the religious wars of the sixteenth century, Holland's cities had to deal with and assimilate a flood of immigrants and refugees. And that was just the start. Over the last fifty years, the Netherlands has morphed into a multicultural society, with all the variety, tensions, and new flavors that such transformations bring.

NASI GORENG

When I asked the president of NedSpice about what Netherlanders eat at home, Frank Lavooij listed the traditional staples: *erwtensoep* (pea soup), *stamppot* (sausage and potatoes mashed with kale), and *nasi goreng* (Indonesian fried rice). "My wife is just as comfortable making *nasi goreng* as *pankoeken* (Dutch pancakes)," he assured me. *Nasi goreng* is as much a fixture of the Netherlands as Queen Beatrix.

The degree to which the Dutch colonial experience has infiltrated everyday food becomes immediately evident if you visit any Amsterdam supermarket. Take the Albert Hein market just off the Dam, for example. The Albert Hein devotes as much space to Indonesian and other Asian products as an American market would to breakfast cereals. Not that most Dutch cooks would ever consider making the Indonesian food so popular now from scratch. No, they go to their local supermarket for the appropriate spice and seasoning mix, adding meat, chicken, or whatever the package instructs. In aisle 1, you have at least seven types of mixes for *nasi goreng.* Some call for almost no expertise, while others you actually have to cook. Shelf-stable *saté stokjes* (skewered chicken in peanut sauce) need only have a brief encounter with the microwave, while others require you to buy fresh chicken and chop vegetables before adding the packaged seasoning. To make the meal complete, shelves are crowded with bags of *kroepoek,* puffy Indonesian cassava and shrimp chips. (These taste—not altogether unpleasantly—of puffed grease with a counter-point of fish flavor and, occasionally, hot pepper.) All told, these kinds of products number in the hundreds. While some come from niche Asian food specialists, most are manufactured by multinationals such as Heinz, McCormick, and Knorr.

Even when not cooking specifically Indonesian food, Hollanders turn to ready-made spice mixes. In aisle 2, dozens of these Dutch masalas come ready-mixed. There is *vleeskruiden* for beef (coriander, black pepper, chili, ginger, marjoram, and thyme) and *kipkruiden* for chicken (paprika, white and black pepper, nutmeg, coriander, mace, curry powder, cardamom, and oregano) as well as seasoning mixes for oysters, mussels, chili con carne, spaghetti, gyros, and, naturally, *nasi goreng.* The display holds some twenty-seven spice mixtures in all!

Immigrants arrive in Holland every day now, bringing seasonings from the four corners of the world. The new mix of race and creed is not always harmonious, and the Dutch, despite their fabled tolerance, have become less welcoming to dark-skinned migrants than they used to be. People's everyday food choices, however, are being increasingly influenced by the corner stand selling *döner kebabs* or skewers of *satay.*

Just like the Crusaders of yore, the Dutch are coming home after their frequent vacations abroad with a taste for more pungent flavors. "I remember going to Spain for the first time in 1961 and bringing our own food," Lavooij recounts with an ironic half smile, explaining how the Dutch vacationers worried they might have to eat food cooked with olive oil and garlic. "Now it's almost the opposite," he adds. Nowadays Amsterdamers, just like well-off Londoners and Angelinos, take for granted that dinner might be Thai one night and Italian the next. Much as in the United States, these flavors in particular—the vaguely Italian combination of garlic, olive oil, and herbs on the one hand and an Asian sweet and spicy approach on the other—have captured foodies' imaginations. You'll find these tastes as ubiquitous among the affluent classes of the developed world as the mixture of cinnamon and sugar once was in the Renaissance.

The Dutch were introduced to fusion cooking earlier than most when they were forced out of newly independent Indonesia in the 1950s. Not that dishes from the East Indies were entirely a novelty in the mother country. A Dutch manuscript from 1790 includes recipes for *achar* (a spicy condiment) and other Indonesian dishes. Throughout the colonial period, there was always a trickle of people coming back with tastes acquired in the Spice Islands, but this was nothing compared to the flood of the 1950s. That was when some three hundred thousand refugees arrived in Holland with what little they could carry. Crammed into their luggage, along with all the resentments and nostalgia, they had packed a menu for an elaborate meal they called the *rijsttafel*.

The *rijsttafel* is a peculiar invention of colonial cuisine in which dishes from Bali, Java, Sumatra, and other Indonesian islands are combined into an enormous buffet. The idea is loosely based on the kind of elaborate banquet you might be served at an Indonesian wedding, though in prosperous colonial households, it became a much more everyday affair. The cooks were often ethnic Chinese, which affected not only the flavors but also the ingredients. In particular, they added lots of pork to what was originally a Muslim feast. Meats of all kinds, whether skewered as *satay* or cooked in a spicy stew like *babi ricah*, became the focus of the meal.

There are dozens of places to eat *rijsttafel* in today's Amsterdam, from neighborhood take-out joints that give you a choice of some two dozen dishes arrayed in steam tables to white-tablecloth restaurants where the waiters smile and gently guide you through the smorgasbord. I chose, one night, to splurge at a restaurant called Puri Mas. The restaurant is just inside the Singelgracht, the last canal that was incised around the city in the sixteen hundreds, down a honky-tonk street where you have to dodge restaurant hawkers pushing everything from pad Thai to spaghetti Bolognese. It is a couple of bridges away from the Rijksmuseum, so not surprisingly, it is packed with tourists recovering from too much Rembrandt. Yet a kind of genteel atmosphere fills the room, mingling with aromas of fish sauce and spice. You can choose a modest *rijsttafel* for a succession of thirteen small plates, but better to opt for *Rijsttafel Royaal*, with a deluge of sixteen dishes. Plate after plate after plate arrives. The table is set with *kroepoek*, cassava shrimp chips, along with a little bowl of the chili- and ginger-spiced *sambal* sauce that is as common as mayonnaise in every Amsterdamer's refrigerator. Egg rolls and batter-fried shrimp come with little turnovers exuding a sweet and savory aroma of coriander, black pepper, cumin, and turmeric. There is an assortment of *satays*, chicken, pork, and lamb on skewers, hot with chilies, sweet with sugar, and sour with tamarind. Then come little plates of stew: pork scented with chilies and ginger; chicken with chilies and coriander; lamb in a dense masala of cardamom, cumin, turmeric, fennel, cinnamon, cloves, and pepper. There are a few vegetables and then the obligatory coda, *nasi goreng.* This *nasi goreng* has a few flecks of chicken amid the fried rice with just a suspicion of spice.

If you stop for a moment to analyze the avalanche of flavors, you realize that the dominant tastes are of sweet and of sour, along with a judicious sprinkle of exotic spice—the same kind of flavor combination (setting aside the chili) you might have found in medieval Venice or sixteenth-century Amsterdam. No wonder that the seventeenth-century Dutch who arrived in Indonesia took to this style of cooking: it had a lot in common with what they ate at home.

We seem to have come full circle. Today, the spiced cooking of the Renaissance seems no more exotic than the Puri Mas's *rijsttafel.* Certainly, the old way of cooking is much more comprehensible than it was even fifty years ago, when French historians rolled their eyes in horror at that earlier era's "orgy of spice." Now there is no more mysterious East, Prester John, or miraculous spices as precious as gold. The cuisines of every corner of the earth are as familiar as jet travel—or a visit to a shopping mall food court. Americans import more spices per capita than the medieval ruling class ever did, and many Europeans are not far behind. Flavors that were once exotic imports—the very scents of paradise—are now common, everyday, and ubiquitous. The Dutch are perhaps more responsible for this than anyone. Under their watch, spices became an ordinary—if not quite cheap—commodity, as common as herring or lumber or beer.

Epilogue

•

BALTIMORE AND CALICUT

THE SPICE CHAMBER

If there is an heir today to the Estado da Índia and the Dutch East India Company, it would have to be McCormick & Company. So, hoping to catch a glimpse of today's dominant spice multinational, I called up its headquarters in Baltimore. Easier said than done. When I requested a tour of the plant, the press officer turned me down flat. "We don't do tours," she snapped. When I asked for an interview, she grilled me about just what it was I wanted to know and then promised to get back to me. She never did. I felt like a Dutch spy trying to break into the offices of the Portuguese viceroy. What dark secrets could be sequestered in the bowels of the world's largest spice company?

But I persisted. Six months and several rounds of bureaucratic gymnastics later, I pulled into the McCormick parking lot. The company headquarters is in a large, fortresslike building isolated in a sylvan corporate park just north of Baltimore. McCormick gave up its previous facilities in the inner city in the early 1980s to move closer to the processing plant and away from the then-derelict waterfront. Luckily, it salvaged some of the old headquarters. Behind the receptionist hangs one of the original Depression-era murals rescued from downtown, depicting East and West Indians gathering black pepper and vanilla—still the company's top sellers. (McCormick is the world's largest buyer of vanilla.) Much to my surprise, the receptionist asks for neither fingerprints nor a retina scan before I enter. She is downright friendly as she pages James

Visitors to McCormick headquarters are greeted with a vintage painting of pepper picked and dried much the same as in Roman times.

Lynn, my inside source at the corporation. As Jim shakes my hand and guides me inside, the secrets seem to dissipate, though not the peculiarities—this is Baltimore, after all.

McCormick not only transplanted some of the old pictures, it lifted an entire mock Elizabethan hamlet from the old offices and shoehorned it here into the new suburban location. As you step through the generic corporate lobby past the bank of elevators, you are suddenly confronted by a street of timbered cottages and leaded glass windows. (The village had been built to promote tea, which was an important McCormick product in the 1930s.) To your left is "Ye Olde McCormick Tea House," where visitors used to be offered tea by a wench in period costume at the old harborfront main office. Company guests could also visit the next-door "Tea Museum" to examine tea memorabilia and educate themselves in a six-foot-high book entitled "Ye Story of Tea." The wench, unfortunately, fell victim to corporate downsizing a long time ago, though Jim does sit me at a rustic oaken table and offer me tea. Jim Lynn works in corporate communications, but on the side, he is an amateur authority on the company's history.

Like Heinz, Kellogg's, Hershey's, and so many other grand American brands, McCormick was founded in the waning years of the nineteenth century. Jim describes a tough and feisty Willoughby M. McCormick, who got his start selling flavored syrups out of a basement in Baltimore. He survived the great Baltimore fire, the Great War, the Great Depression— all the while enlarging his portfolio, adding spices, tea, mayonnaise, and even insecticides. And he gave tours of the factory. (Today's reluctance to host visitors is simply corporate caution, Jim assures me.) When it came to spices, McCormick satisfied its needs by buying on the New York Commodities Exchange, then processing and packaging the imported spices.

Up until the Second World War, the spice export business was still mostly in Dutch and English hands.

Under W. M. McCormick's successors, the American company went public and gradually assembled an international potpourri of spice companies from Shanghai to San Salvador. Investors can read all about it in the company's annual report, where they'll also find out that McCormick's profits are soaring, mainly because world spice consumption keeps going up and up.

If McCormick headquarters holds a secret, it is on the fourth floor. This is where the carpeted hallways of the lower floors give way to barren institutional corridors lined with anonymous doors. Jim leads me to one of these doors, slides a key into the lock, and flips the light switch. As the fluorescent lights flicker to life, the little room bursts into a riot of words and colors. Hundreds, thousands of neatly arrayed packages from little one-shot servings of Moroccan chicken seasoning in hot pink tetrahedrons to giant food-service packs of Key West Style Seasonings labeled in tropical turquoise are arranged in row after row after row. A shelf of chili-flavored mayonnaise from the Central American division is squeezed next to a display case for Stange, the Japanese division. ("Taste the magician" is the only part of that package that I can read.) Here, in McCormick's secret spice chamber, is a snapshot of the world spice market today and where spicing around the globe is going. Today's company has divisions in Australia, Belgium, Canada, Central America, China, Finland, France, Great Britain, India, Japan, Mexico, the Netherlands, Switzerland, and Turkey as well as the United States, and many of those national brands are exported elsewhere. The company that started selling vanilla syrup to Baltimore soda fountains is now the epitome of globalization, sourcing its vanilla in Uganda and Vietnam to flavor chocolate bars in Switzerland and Argentina. But then the spice business has always been a worldwide affair even before the Castilians and the Portuguese set in motion the first great push for a global trade network.

Yet the way the world eats is changing, and these changes may be even greater than they were after the "Cabralian" exchange that redistributed New World peppers and peanuts along with Old World black pepper and sugarcane across the continents. One of the things made graphically clear in McCormick's spice chamber is that people don't cook anymore. They assemble. "Yes, we have all our gourmet jars of spice," Jim assures me, "but much of what we put our attention to are blends— seasoning blends and grilling sauces—because people can come home and *chuhk, chuhk, chuhk* [he makes the noise of shaking sauce out of a bottle]." For every package of nutmeg and paprika on the shelf, there are dozens of ready-made mixes of multiple spices: to make teriyaki beef (the United States), chili con carne (the Netherlands), Moroccan *tajines* (France), or Balti chicken (the United Kingdom). Even in India, where the fashion for spices never faded, women today are as likely to rip open a polyethylene envelope of commercially processed masala as to pull out the mortar and pestle. For good or ill, the decisions about what your food will taste like are made at corporate headquarters.

And even that is only part of the picture. Jim Lynn explains how McCormick has increasingly moved into the food-service branch of the industry, so that now half its business involves products that never even reach the consumer's cupboard, or at least not directly. That secret seasoning boasted of by a certain southern chicken chain—"They don't like us to mention the name," Jim says with a grin—is a McCormick spice mix; that special sauce at the hamburger chain with the arches is concocted in Baltimore. McCormick flavors everything from chips to beer. Processed food is where the future lies. The tastes in that food are often cooked up in McCormick's "Technical Innovation Center." Even food processors don't want to come up with their own seasoning. "A food manufacturer doesn't want a truckload of ginger; they want a containerload of a ready-made flavoring mixture," the corporate communicator informs me. Which is why he keeps emphasizing that McCormick now wants to be seen as a "flavor company" rather than a spice company. You can be sure its flavor decisions do no harm to its spice business.

As Frank Lavooij, the Dutch spice trader, happily informed me, people are eating more spice, and they aren't even aware of it. There is an apocryphal story about a research project in which dogs are given increasing quantities of chilies in their food. Eventually, they find chili-free food so bland that they refuse to eat it. The dog study apparently never took place, but we are undergoing a similar experiment. More and more of us are eating processed food that is increasingly spicier.

If the Dutch had figured out how to influence demand as well as control supply, Europeans and their New World colonies might never have given up the spice habit to begin with. But the kind of vertical integration that McCormick has accomplished was inconceivable in seventeenth-century Amsterdam. The *Heren XVII* could only wring their hands as the fashion for the exotic aromatics waned and per capita spice use sagged in the seventeen hundreds. The appetite for pepper, which the VOC had calculated at about seven million pounds in 1688, remained more or less stuck at that figure until the eve of the French Revolution, even as Europe's population finally surged. Eventually, in the late nineteenth century, the overall demand for spices grew as living standards rose. Just about everyone could now afford to use cloves and cinnamon. But it was a pinch here and a pinch there. Victorians recoiled in horrified fascination at the earlier orgy of spice.

In the West, this abstemious approach has begun to change only in the last fifty years. Between 1961 and 1994, the volume of spices imported into the United States increased close to 400 percent and doubled again in the next decade. The average contemporary American eats more pepper than any medieval aristocrat, on top of all the other spices once traded on the Rialto and the Nieuwemarkt. But today, *Piper nigrum* is no longer the king. Dried capsicums have long since overtaken the berries from Malabar as America's favorite spice.

The reasons that lie behind the transformation in the American taste for spice are much the same as in the Netherlands—or anywhere in the developed world, for that matter. Immigrants bring the taste for chili and ginger from Latin America and Asia while at the same time overseas travelers (professional chefs among them) return with an appetite for the more complex flavors they've tried. However, companies such as McCormick do not merely capitalize on these trends; they shape them and, when it suits their purposes, transform them. Thus, foreign flavors that might be too pungent are mellowed for the domestic market. (You can rest assured that McCormick's "Balti curry spices" wouldn't knock anybody's socks off in Baltistan.) But you can't really fault Baltimore for that. If the seasonings remained in their original, "authentic" concentration, they would never reach a broad-based audience. Nevertheless, just like the apocryphal dogs, the public is experiencing more and more spicy heat without really noticing it.

A global company such as McCormick also takes advantage of trends that appear in one market by introducing them in another. When single-use packaging (packets of a few grams of spice in much the same spirit as the little cones of pepper sold in old Amsterdam) became popular in the United Kingdom, similar packages followed in the United States and France.

Globalization has not only affected how people eat around the world; it has also changed what farmers grow and where they grow it. To some extent, this was true when Malabar pepper was transplanted from India into Indonesia in the early Middle Ages and ginger was brought to the Caribbean by the Portuguese. But now spices come from all sorts of unlikely spots. Guatemala is the world's largest cardamom exporter, even though the locals barely know what to do with the stuff—virtually all of it is exported to the Middle East. Most of the world's vanilla—an orchid of Mexican origin—comes from Madagascar and Indonesia, but there are other, relatively new sources. Today, McCormick obtains a lot of its vanilla from Uganda. Because of ever-increasing demand, even the Indian Spices Board is encouraging pepper farmers in Malabar to grow the long, skinny pods. The new kid on the block is Vietnam, which, in ancient times, used to import black pepper from Malabar and is now the world's premier pepper producer, undercutting everyone else's prices. (Indonesia and Brazil come next; India is a distant fourth.) These days, Indian farmers worry about cheap pepper exports from Indochina much as American textile workers bemoan imports from South Asia. But even in India, people realize that the spice trade is changing, and perhaps more than elsewhere, they are trying to prepare for a karmic rebirth.

WEAPONS AND NUTRACEUTICALS

The first hint of how seriously spices are taken in India was driven home when I boarded a domestic flight to Calicut. Before I passed through security, the sign warned, "Passengers are requested not to carry pickles, chilly powder, masala powders"—as well as the usual forbidden arsenal of lighters, sharp objects, and nail clippers—in their hand luggage. ("Pickles," in this case, refers to highly spiced condiments such as mango pickle.) In India, scientists have studied how spices can be used as weapons, food preservatives, colorants, drugs, and nutraceuticals. Naturally, there are also efforts to improve the strains of spices grown for better flavor and hardiness.

As a result of this ongoing research, the Indian government is especially wary of "biopiracy," something I learned when I tried to get permission to visit the main research facility in the spice-producing state of Kerala. Luckily, I had been hardened by my McCormick experience. So, a half year's correspondence later, I arrived at the Calicut airport clutching a handful of letters, duly stamped, dated, numbered, and signed by the undersecretary to the Government of India, Ministry of Agriculture, Department of Agricultural Research and Education. A large white taxi sent by the Indian Institute of Spices Research (IISR) awaited my arrival.

The institute is located on the outskirts of Calicut, just a little inland from where da Gama's men first made their landing. To get there, you must brave the usual suicidal Indian car trip—dodging motorcycles, auto rickshaws, oblivious pedestrians, stray dogs, and speeding buses that seem to use the median divider primarily as a centering device. The research campus can be seen from a distance, rising like a castle on a hill. To enter, I have to pass muster with the guard, who seems disoriented to find a foreigner having been granted access to the holy of holies. Then the road winds up the hill, tightly sealed in by a barbed-wire-topped wall. At the highest point, I am deposited before the immaculate buildings surrounded by meticulously manicured grounds. There is no time for greetings or introductions before I am whisked into the sparkling new visitors center, presumably to avoid any temptation to do or see anything not strictly authorized.

The visitors center is a temple to spice. The local farmers who are allowed access come here to look at photos, receive instructional pamphlets, and get advice. The guardians of the temple, the barefoot scientists, now cluster around me to offer their hands, a cup of *chai*, a plate of biscuits, and a bowl of cashews. They are perplexed by my presence but also my interest. Just like the guard, they can't quite understand how I found out the magic word to open the gate to their ivory tower. I am apparently the first non-Indian to have been afforded this honor.

The assembled cast represents the full range of the institute's research program. There is the careful biochemist in her emerald sari—still nervous about my presence. The wild-eyed and brilliant botanist stalks the room like a caged panther. I am introduced to the dignified botanical economist, the eager field botanist, and the silent young chemist. One by one, they gradually relax as they realize that I have not come to ransack their biological treasure chest. And as they let down their guard, their passions slowly unravel: the biochemist insists on reeling off numbers to explain the advantages of organic agriculture; the brilliant botanist riffs on the overuse of the planet's resources; the field botanist tries to convince me that our civilization would waste less if only we imitated the swamis who live on water and sunlight alone. Then, green coconuts are served as we cluster around the touch-screen computer module, where a slick interactive promo shows off the institute's successes.

The work they do here is the kind done at any agricultural research facility. They study root rot, explore issues of yield, and try to improve the quality of the cultivars. The biochemist launches into a highly technical description of the compounds that give pepper its unique taste. (To a biochemist, the flavors that sparkle on the palate are reduced to fractions and formulas.) An oil called piperine gives pepper its heat, while other trace oils give aroma. Typically, if one is high, the other tends to be a little lower, meaning that the hottest pepper is often not the most flavorful. The IISR maintains a germplasm bank of pepper, turmeric, and cardamom as well as other spices, and field-workers continue to collect wild varieties to add to the collection. The botanist with the guru's unruly gray hair tells me that they have more than 200 cultivars of pepper here, but then he shakes his quizzical head and offers me a half smile, "But the Brazilians claim to have almost 180." So much for keeping the secret at home. But then, even the Dutch policy of systematic murder couldn't maintain Holland's spice monopoly.

It turns out that the scientists are as frustrated by the government's paranoia as I was. Like researchers everywhere, they are eager to share their findings, but they are not allowed to present papers at overseas conferences. What seems to excite them the most these days is sustainable agriculture.

"In a natural undisturbed system, in the forest state," the irrepressible field botanist breaks in, "pepper plants exist that are a hundred years old. But when you disturb the natural system, by tilling and adding manure, the life will deteriorate. Under cultivation, the plant will have a productive life of [merely] seven to fifteen years."

"The disease problem is worse than it was a generation ago," the brilliant botanist silences the others to explain. "Nobody has specifically studied the causes. It could be climate change, the introduction of exogenous agents, or some other factor. One thing is for sure: once the people start applying chemical fertilizers, the local microorganism population—that used to sustain all the plantations in olden days—will decline. So when you use organic fertilizers, there is a very good response, not only with black pepper but all the crops."

Of course, organic is not popular just with the scientists; consumers in the developed world want it, too. Even McCormick has an organic line now. When I talk to the people in the middle, though—the farmers and the exporters—they're resistant. Nonetheless, there are a few who see the future in growing spices organically, as they have for hundreds of years.

The past may hold a prescription for the future in other respects as well. Medical researchers in India and elsewhere have been trying to isolate the properties that make spices so potent in Ayurvedic medicine. Like the old Galenic system, the traditional Indian practice of Ayurveda is based on a scheme of bodily humors that are naturally affected by what you eat. To Ayurveda practitioners, spices are as much drugs as flavorings. The scientists at the IISR are happy to shift from discussions of spectrum analysis and genetic engineering to trading opinions on traditional healing practices. The brilliant botanist turns out to be a font of information on the local medical uses of spices.

"Nutmeg is a natural remedy, here, for sleeplessness." He begins his monologue in an insistent staccato rhythm. "But you need just a small amount. We rub a little on babies' lips to make them sleep, but just a little grain." Myristicin, the active ingredient in nutmeg, has shown some potential as a weapon against cancer and liver disease, at least in animals. But there's the thorny problem of its hallucinogenic effects. "The hippies, you know, in olden times, they would take one glass of liquor and dissolve the nutmeg in it." The botanist tells the story and chortles. He adds, "Don't try it. It is toxic!"

"Pepper, too, is used in Ayurveda medicine," the spice guru continues.

"There are enzymes in pepper that have antibiotic properties." Mostly, though, scientists have focused on piperine's effectiveness as a "potency multiplier." Pepper is often added to Ayurvedic prescriptions to increase their effectiveness. It seems to do the same thing with more conventional medicines. In one study, researchers found that they could decrease the dose of a tuberculosis medicine by more than half with no loss in effectiveness; in another, chemotherapy for lung cancer seemed to work better when supplemented with piperine. An American has even patented Bioperine, a piperine extract, as a "bioavailability enhancer."

"All the spices have medical qualities," the others add their chorus of agreement. Ginger and cardamom are used to calm nausea. The capsaicin from chili peppers is widely used in arthritis creams. Galangal seems to kill cancerous cells while leaving the healthy ones alive, at least in the laboratory. In a study by the U.S. Agricultural Research Service, less than a half teaspoon a day of cinnamon reduced the blood sugar levels of sixty volunteers in Pakistan with type 2 diabetes who participated. Even their levels of LDL cholesterol (the bad one) dropped.

These days, though, the medical wunderkind of the spice world is turmeric. Curcumin, the active agent in turmeric, is a potent antioxidant and the subject of medical research at major universities around the world. The spice may protect against leukemia; it has been observed to inhibit the growth of cancerous cells in the lungs of mice with breast cancer; it seems to prevent the formation of diabetic cataracts; it pushes melanoma cells to self-destruct and may be useful in combating malaria, treating cystic fibrosis, fighting Alzheimer's, and reducing chemotherapy-induced fatigue. "Nature's gift to antioxidants," the botanical economist chimes in, chuckling. And it makes a fine "natural" colorant, too.

And what of spices as weapons? Capsaicin is widely used in pepper sprays such as Mace (no connection to the Moluccan spice) both as a self-defense aid and, by the police, for crowd control. In the United States, a high-potency spray is marketed as a bear repellent, and in Africa, fences are smeared with a cocktail of grease and capsaicin to keep elephants at bay. Scientists at India's Defense Research Laboratory have publicly identified the Tezpur as the subcontinent's hottest chili, though just what they plan to do with it is, I'm sure, top secret. (It's almost two hundred times as hot as a jalapeño.) Suffice it to say, it should probably be banned from hand luggage everywhere.

The scientists at the Indian Institute of Spices Research have more quotidian concerns. At the end of our delightfully informative interview, I wish them good luck in their battle against root rot and their search for the tastiest pepper, turmeric, and ginger. I pay the ten dollars that the Ministry of Agriculture requested for my admission to the spice temple and climb into the waiting taxi. I wave goodbye to the security guard at the front gate as the car swerves onto the main road to Calicut.

It had been a long trip from St. Albans to the pepper coast of Malabar, through a world of flavors and centuries of pungent smells. I recalled Luca's telling me—how many bottles of Prosecco had we drunk?—that the world changes but people don't. Spices were trendy for much the same reason in 1500 as they are now. Once again, people are looking to spices for the elixir of life or a ticket to paradise. And the future bodes well for people who study spices as well as for those who come up with new ways for us to consume them. As they have done for at least two thousand years, the people in the middle will take their share, paying the farmers as little as possible and charging us as much as they can get away with. As I looked out the window of the speeding taxi at the pepper woods flashing by behind fences painted with cell phone ads, it occurred to me that like those long-ago Venetians, *Lisboetas,* and Amsterdamers, we are living in a new golden age of spice.

ℒist of 𝒪llustrations and ℳaps

᳁᷒᳁

Bibliography

"The Account of the Great Household of Humphrey, First Duke of Bucking-ham." In *The Camden Miscellany XXVIII*, Camden 4th series, vol. 29, 1–57. London: Camden Society, 1984.

Achaya, K. T. *A Historical Dictionary of Indian Food*. Delhi and New York: Oxford University Press, 1998.

Adamson, Melitta Weiss, ed. *Regional Cuisines of Medieval Europe: A Book of Essays*. New York: Routledge, 2002.

Albala, Ken. *Eating Right in the Renaissance*. Berkeley: University of California Press, 2002.

————. "The Place of Spain in European Nutritional Theory of the 16th Century." Presented at the Cultural and Historical Aspects of Food symposium, Oregon State University, Apr. 9–11, 1999. http://food.oregonstate.edu/ref/culture/albala.html.

Allmand, Christopher, ed. *The New Cambridge Medieval History: Volume 7, c. 1415–c. 1500*. Cambridge, U.K., and New York: Cambridge University Press, 1998.

Andrews, Jean. *Peppers: The Domesticated Capsicums*. Austin: University of Texas Press, 1984.

————. *The Pepper Trail: History & Recipes from around the World*. Rev. ed. Denton: University of North Texas Press, 1999.

Anonimo Toscano. "Libro della cocina." In *Arte della cucina*, vol. 1, edited by Emilio Faccioli, 21–57. Milan: 1966. Digital version, http://staff.uni-marburg.de/~gloning/an-tosc.htm.

Anonimo Veneziano. *Libro di cucina del secolo XIV*. Edited by Ludovico Frati. Leghorn: 1899. Digital version, Thomas Gloning, 2000; v.1. http://staff-www.uni-marburg.de/%7Egloning/frati.htm.

————. *Libro di cucina del secolo XIV*. Edited by Ludovico Frati. Leghorn: 1899. Translated by Louise Smithson, 2002. http://www.geocities.com/helewyse/libro.html.

Ariès, Philippe, and Georges Duby, eds. *A History of Private Life*. Cambridge, Mass.: Harvard University Press, 1989.

Ashtor, Eliyahu. *Studies on the Levantine Trade in the Middle Ages*. London: Variorum Reprints, 1978.

———. "The Volume of Mediaeval Spice Trade." *Journal of European Economic History* 9 (1980): 753–63.

Barnes, Donna R., and Peter G. Rose. *Matters of Taste: Food and Drink in Seventeenth-Century Dutch Art and Life*. Albany, N.Y.: Albany Institute of History & Art; Syracuse, N.Y.: Syracuse University Press, 2002.

Battus, Carolus. *Eenen seer schoonen ende excellenten Cocboeck*. Dordrecht, Netherlands: Jan Canin, 1593. Transcribed and partially translated by Marleen Willebrands. Digital version, http://www.kookhistorie.com.

Benporat, Claudio. *Cucina italiana del quattrocento*. Florence: L. S. Olschki, 1996.

Blakely, Allison. *Blacks in the Dutch World*. Bloomington: Indiana University Press, 1993.

Boxer, C. R. *Four Centuries of Portuguese Expansion, 1415–1825: A Succinct Survey*. Berkeley: University of California Press, 1969.

———. *The Portuguese Seaborne Empire, 1415–1825*. London: Hutchinson, 1969.

"Breast Cancer: Curcumin Halts Spread of Breast Cancer in Mice." *Cancer Weekly*, Nov. 8, 2005, 23.

Bruijn, J. R., F. S. Gaastra, and I. Schöffer. *Dutch-Asiatic Shipping in the 17th and 18th Centuries*. The Hague: Martinus Nijhoff, 1987.

Buck, Paul. *Lisbon: A Cultural and Literary Companion*. New York: Interlink Books, 2002.

Camões, Luís de. *The Lusíads*. Translated by Landeg White. Oxford, U.K., and New York: Oxford University Press, 1997.

Cantor, Norman F. *The Civilization of the Middle Ages: A Completely Revised and Expanded Edition of "Medieval History: The Life and Death of a Civilization."* New York: HarperCollins, 1993.

Capatti, Alberto, and Massimo Montanari. *Italian Cuisine: A Cultural History*. Translated by Aine O'Healy. New York: Columbia University Press, 2003.

Castro, Filipe Vieira de. *The Pepper Wreck: A Portuguese Indiaman at the Mouth of the Tagus River*. College Station: Texas A&M University Press, 2005.

Chaudhury, Sushil, and Michel Morineau, eds. *Merchants, Companies, and Trade: Europe and Asia in the Early Modern Era*. Cambridge, U.K., and New York: Cambridge University Press, 1999.

"Chemotherapy Fatigue: Supplement Reduced Chemotherapy Induced Fatigue." *Cancer Weekly*, May 6, 2003, 68.

Cipolla, Carlo. *Before the Industrial Revolution: European Society and Economy, 1000–1700*. New York: Norton, 1976.

Città di Venezia. *Dinamica demografica.* Città di Venezia, Servizio Statistica e Ricerca, Popolazione, 2006. http://www.comune.venezia.it/statistica/ Statistiche/Popolazione/Dinamica_ Demografica/dinamica_demografica .asp

Clari, Robert de. *The Conquest of Constantinople.* Translated by Edgar Holmes McNeal. New York: Columbia University Press, 1936.

"Complementary and Alternative Medicine: Cinnamon Spices Up Insulin Sensitivity." *Health & Medicine Week,* Dec. 15, 2003, 188.

Conrad, Lawrence I., Michael Neve, Vivian Nutton, Roy Porter, and Andrew Wear. *The Western Medical Tradition.* Cambridge, U.K.: Cambridge University Press, 1995.

"Cystic Fibrosis: Scientists Test If Curry Ingredient Might Fight CF." *Genetics & Environmental Law Weekly,* May 15, 2004, 14.

Dalby, Andrew. *Dangerous Tastes.* Berkeley and Los Angeles: University of California Press, 2000.

———. *Flavours of Byzantium.* Totnes, U.K.: Prospect Books, 2003.

de Moor, Geertruida. "Wages and Prices from the Convent Leeuwenhorst, 1410–1570." International Institute of Social History, Prices and Wages. http://www.iisg.nl/hpw/data.html.

Desdier, S. *The City and Republick of Venice.* London: Printed for Char. Brome . . . , 1699. Early English Books Online. http://wwwlib.umi.com/ eebo/image/102922.

Deursen, Arie Theodorus van. *Plain Lives in a Golden Age: Popular Culture, Religion, and Society in Seventeenth-Century Holland.* Translated by Maarten Ultee. Cambridge, U.K., and New York: Cambridge University Press, 1991.

Duncan, T. Bentley. *Atlantic Islands: Madeira, the Azores, and the Cape Verdes in Seventeenth-Century Commerce and Navigation.* Chicago: University of Chicago Press, 1972.

Eisenstein, Elizabeth L. *The Printing Revolution in Early Modern Europe.* Cambridge, U.K., and New York: Cambridge University Press, 1993.

Ellen, R. F. *On the Edge of the Banda Zone: Past and Present in the Social Organization of a Moluccan Trading Network.* Honolulu: University of Hawaii Press, 2003.

Favier, Jean. *Gold & Spices: The Rise of Commerce in the Middle Ages.* Translated by Caroline Higgitt. New York: Holmes & Meier, 1998.

Febvre, Lucien, and Henri-Jean Martin. *The Coming of the Book: The Impact of Printing, 1450–1800.* Translated by David Gerard. London: N.L.B., 1976.

Feil, D. K. "How Venetians Think about Carnival and History." *Australian Journal of Anthropology* 9, no. 2 (1998): 141–62.

Feret, Barbara L. *Gastronomical and Culinary Literature: A Survey and Analysis of Historically Oriented Collections in the U.S.A.* Metuchen, N.J.: Scarecrow Press, 1979.

Fernández-Armesto, Felipe, ed. *The European Opportunity.* Aldershot, U.K., and Brookfield, Vt.: Variorum, 1995.

Food and Agriculture Organization of the United Nations (FAO). "Crops Primary Equivalent." *Food Supply,* in Faostat, Agriculture. http://faostat.fao.org.

Fuchs, Leonhart. *The New Herbal of 1543: New Kreüterbuch.* Cologne, Germany, and New York: Taschen, 2001.

Georgopoulou, Maria. "Late Medieval Crete and Venice: An Appropriation of Byzantine Heritage." *Art Bulletin* 77 (Sept. 1995).

Glamman, Kristof. *Dutch-Asiatic Trade, 1620–1740.* Copenhagen: Nijhoff, 1958.

Global Price and Income History Group. *Data File List.* University of California at Davis. http://gpih.ucdavis.edu/Datafilelist.htm.

Godinho, Vitorino de Magalhaes. *L'Économie de l'empire portugais aux XVe et XVIe siècles.* Paris: S.E.V.P.E.N., 1969.

Hanna, Willard Anderson. *Indonesian Banda: Colonialism and Its Aftermath in the Nutmeg Islands.* Philadelphia: Institute for the Study of Human Issues, 1978.

Hooker, Mark T. *The History of Holland.* Westport, Conn.: Greenwood Press, 1999.

Huizinga, Johan. *The Autumn of the Middle Ages.* Translated by Rodney J. Payton and Ulrich Mammitzsch. Chicago: University of Chicago Press, 1996.

———. *Dutch Civilisation in the Seventeenth Century.* Translated by Arnold J. Pomerans. London: Collins, 1968.

"Indian National Institute of Nutrition: Findings in Cataracts Provide New Insights." *Lab Business Week,* Sept. 4, 2005, 112.

Jansen, Guido, ed. *Jan Steen: Painter and Storyteller.* Washington, D.C.: National Gallery of Art, 1996.

The Journal of Friar Odoric. In *Principal Navigations, Voyages, Traffiques and Discoveries of the English Nation,* collected by Richard Hakluyt, edited by Edmund Goldsmid. Adelaide, Australia: eBooks@Adelaide, 2004. Digital version, http://etext.library.adelaide.edu.au/h/hakluyt/voyages/odoric/complete.html.

Kaplan, Marion. *The Portuguese: The Land and Its People.* London and New York: Penguin, 1991.

Katzer, Gernot. "Gernot Katzer's Spice Pages." http://www.uni-graz.at/~katzer/engl/index.html.

Kittel, Ellen E., and Thomas F. Madden, eds. *Medieval and Renaissance Venice.* Urbana and Chicago: University of Illinois Press, 1999.

Lane, Frederic Chapin. *Venice: Maritime Republic.* Baltimore: Johns Hopkins University Press, 1999.

Larner, John. *Marco Polo and the Discovery of the World.* New Haven, Conn., and London: Yale University Press, 1999.

Laurioux, Bruno. "Spices in the Medieval Diet: A New Approach." *Food and Foodways* 1 (1985): 43–76.

Linschoten, Jan Huyghen van. *The Voyage of John Huyghen van Linschoten to the East Indies: From the Old English Translation of 1598; The First Book, Containing His Description of the East, in Two Volumes.* London: printed for the Hakluyt Society, 1885.

"Loyola University: Early Diet May Play Key Role in Protecting against Childhood Leukemia." *Hospital Business Week,* Oct. 3, 2004, 30.

"Lung Cancer: Oral Supplementation of Piperine Altered Phase II Enzymes and Reduced DNA Damage." *Clinical Oncology Week,* Apr. 25, 2005, 186.

Luzzatto, Gino. "Il costo della vita a Venezia nel trecento." In *Storia dell'economia italiana,* ed. Carlo Cipolla, 409–24. Turin: Edizioni Scientifiche Einaudi, 1959.

Madden, Thomas F. *Enrico Dandolo and the Rise of Venice.* Baltimore: Johns Hopkins University Press, 2003.

Magalhães, Joaquim Antero Romero. *The Portuguese in the 16th Century World: Areas and Products.* Lisbon: Comissão Nacional para as Comemorações dos Descobrimentos Portugueses, 1998.

Mak, Geert. *Amsterdam.* Translated by Philipp Blom. Cambridge, Mass.: Harvard University Press, 2000.

Maria of Portugal, Infanta. *O "Livro de cozinha" da Infanta D. Maria de Portugal.* Coimbra, Portugal: Por Ordem da Universidade, 1967.

Marques, António Henrique R. de Oliveira. *Daily Life in Portugal in the Late Middle Ages.* Translated by S. S. Wyatt. Madison: University of Wisconsin Press, 1971.

Martin, John, and Dennis Romano, eds. *Venice Reconsidered: The History and Civilization of an Italian City-State, 1297–1797.* Baltimore: Johns Hopkins University Press, 2000.

Martino, Maestro. "Libro de arte coquinaria." In *Arte della cucina,* vol. 1, edited by Emilio Faccioli, 115–204. Milan: 1966. Digital version, Valeria Romanelli, 2004. http://staff-www.uni-marburg.de/~gloning/martino2.htm.

Masselman, George. *The Cradle of Colonialism.* New Haven, Conn.: Yale University Press, 1963.

Mathur, Ritesh, R. S. Dangi, S. C. Dass, and R. C. Malhotra. "The Hottest Chilli Variety in India." *Current Science* 79, no. 3 (Aug. 10, 2000): 287–88.

McCall, Chris. "Traditional Ruler Has Answer for Malukus' Ills—More Tradition." *South China Morning Post*, Mar. 18, 2002.

McCormick & Co. *Modern Marco Polo-ing.* Baltimore: McCormick & Co., 1939.

McEvedy, Colin, and Richard Jones. *Atlas of World Population History.* New York: Facts on File, 1978.

McNeill, William Hardy. *Venice: The Hinge of Europe.* Chicago: University of Chicago Press, 1974.

"Melanoma: Curcumin Blocks Growth of Melanoma in Lab Test." *Cancer Weekly,* Aug. 9, 2005, 198.

Le Ménagier de Paris. Translated by Janet Hinson. http://www.davidfriedman .com/Medieval/Cookbooks/Menagier/Menagier_Contents.html.

Le Ménagier de Paris: Traité de morale et d'économie domestique composé vers 1393 par un bourgeois parisien. Edited by Jérome Pichon. Paris: Crapelet, 1846. Digital version, Bibliothéque Nationale de France, http://visualiseur.bnf.fr/ Visualiseur?Destination=Gallica&O=NUMM-83111.

Messisbugo, Cristoforo da. *Banchetti composizioni di vivande e apparecchio generale.* Edited by Fernando Bandini. Venice: Neri Pozza Editore, 1960.

Milham, Mary Ella. "Martino and His *De re coquinaria.*" In *Medieval Food and Drink,* edited by Mary-Jo Arn. Binghamton, N.Y.: Center for Medieval and Early Renaissance Studies, 1995.

Montanari, Massimo. *The Culture of Food.* Translated by Carl Ipsen. Oxford, U.K., and Cambridge, Mass.: Blackwell, 1994.

Morgan, Jan. *From Holland with Love.* Amsterdam: Ideeboek, 1979.

Mueller, Reinhold C. *The Venetian Money Market: Banks, Panics and the Public Debt, 1200–1500.* Baltimore: Johns Hopkins University Press, 1997.

Nicol, Donald M. *Byzantium and Venice: A Study in Diplomatic and Cultural Relations.* Cambridge, U.K., and New York: Cambridge University Press, 1988.

Otterloo, Anneke van, and Cathy Salzman. "The Taste of the Netherlands and the Boundaries of the Nation State." Mededelingenblad en Verzamelde Opstellen. *Periodiek voor voedingsgeschiedenis, steekgastronomie en toerisme* 13, nos. 2–3 (Dec. 1995): 7–15.

Oxford Symposium on Food and Cookery, 1992 Proceedings. *Spicing Up the Palate: Studies of Flavourings, Ancient and Modern.* London: Prospect Books, 1993.

Pagrach-Chandra, Gaitri. *Windmills in My Oven: A Book of Dutch Baking.* Blackawton, Totnes, U.K.: Prospect Books, 2002.

Parker, Geoffrey, and Charles Wilson, eds. *An Introduction to the Sources of European Economic History, 1500–1800.* Ithaca, N.Y.: Cornell University Press, 1977.

Pearson, M. N., ed. *Spices in the Indian Ocean World.* Aldershot, U.K., and Brookfield, Vt.: Variorum, 1996.

Peterson, T. Sarah. *Acquired Taste: The French Origins of Modern Cooking.* Ithaca, N.Y.: Cornell University Press, 1994.

Platina. *Platina, On Right Pleasure and Good Health: A Critical Edition and Translation of "De honesta voluptate et valetudine."* Translated and edited by Mary Ella Milham. Tempe, Ariz: Medieval and Renaissance Texts and Studies, 1998.

Polo, Marco, and Rustichello of Pisa. *The Travels of Marco Polo.* Translated by Henry Yule. Edited by Henri Cordier. 1920. Project Gutenberg. Digital version, http://www.gutenberg.org/etext/10636.

Posthumus, N. W. *Nederlandsche Prijsgeschiedenis.* Leiden, Netherlands: 1943. Medieval and Early Modern Data Bank, Prices (Posthumus), http://sccweb.scc-net.rutgers.edu/memdb/databasesSpecificFiles/SearchForm/SearchForm_Metzpr.asp?provenance=databaseList.

Pounds, Norman John Greville. *Hearth & Home: A History of Material Culture.* Bloomington: Indiana University Press, 1993.

Priuli, Girolamo. *I Diarii (ca. 1494–1521).* Edited by Arturo Sagre. Città di Castello, Italy: Tipi della casa editrice S. Lapi, 1912.

Ramamurthi, Divya. "Curcumin May Be Used with Drugs to Fight Malaria." *Hindu,* Mar. 9, 2005.

Revkin, Andrew C. "Hot Idea Repels Crop-Munching, Crunching Elephants." *New York Times,* June 20, 2000.

Robbert, Louise Buenger. "Money and Prices in Thirteenth-Century Venice." *Journal of Medieval History* 20 (1994): 373–90.

Rodrigues, Domingos. *Arte de cozinha.* Lisbon: Imprensa Nacional–Casa da Moeda, 1987.

Rogers, James E. Thorold. *A History of Agriculture and Prices in England: From the Year after the Oxford Parliament (1259) to the Commencement of the Continental War (1793).* Vols. 1–3. Oxford, U.K.: Clarendon Press, 1866–1902.

Rose, Peter G., ed. *The Sensible Cook: Dutch Foodways in the Old and the New World.* Translated by Peter G. Rose. Syracuse, N.Y.: Syracuse University Press, 1989.

Saraiva, José H. *Portugal: A Companion History.* Manchester, U.K.: Carcanet, 1997.

Schama, Simon. *The Embarrassment of Riches: An Interpretation of Dutch Culture in the Golden Age.* New York: Knopf, 1987.

Shoshan, Boaz. *Popular Culture in Medieval Cairo.* Cambridge, U.K.: Cambridge University Press, 1993.

Subrahmanyam, Sanjay. *The Career and Legend of Vasco da Gama.* Cambridge, U.K., and New York: Cambridge University Press, 1997.

Sunderarajan, P. "Turmeric: A Potential Weapon against Alzheimer's." *Hindu*, Apr. 25, 2005.

Taillevent. *Le Viandier de Taillevent*. Translated by James Prescott. Eugene, Ore.: Alfarhaugr Publishing Society, 1989. Digital version, http://www .telusplanet.net/public/prescotj/data/viandier/viandier1.html.

Temple, William. *Observations upon the United Provinces of the Netherlands*. London: A. Maxwell for Sa. Gellibrand, 1673.

Tenenti, Alberto. *Piracy and the Decline of Venice, 1580–1615*. Translated by Janet Pullan and Brian Pullan. London: Longmans, 1967.

"Thai Food with Galangal Touted as Cancer Cure." Global News Wire–Asia Africa Intelligence Wire, Feb. 8, 2005.

Tracy, James D. *The Political Economy of Merchant Empires*. Cambridge, U.K., and New York: Cambridge University Press, 1991.

———, ed. *The Rise of Merchant Empires: Long-Distance Trade in the Early Modern World, 1350–1750*. Cambridge, U.K., and New York: Cambridge University Press, 1990.

Turner, Jack. *Spice: The History of a Temptation*. New York: Knopf, 2004.

Twain, Mark. *The Innocents Abroad*. New York and Oxford, U.K.: Oxford University Press, 1996.

"Type 2 Diabetes: Cinnamon Molecule with Insulin-like Properties for Type 2 Diabetes Noted." *Obesity, Fitness & Wellness Week*, Feb. 12, 2005, 1511.

U.C. Davis Department of Geology. "The Importance of Salt." http://teamwork .ucdavis.edu/~gel115/salt.html.

"University of Madras, Tamil Nadu; Oral Supplementation of Piperine Altered Phase II Enzymes and Reduced DNA Damage." *Nursing Home & Elder Business Week*, May 1, 2005, 134.

Usamah ibn Munqidh. *An Arab-Syrian Gentleman and Warrior in the Period of the Crusades: Memoirs of Usamah ibn Munqidh*. Translated by Philip K. Hitti. Princeton, N.J.: Princeton University Press, 1987.

Varthema, Lodovico de. *The Travels of Ludovico di Varthema in Egypt, Syria, Arabia Deserta and Arabia Felix, in Persia, India, and Ethiopia, A.D. 1503 to 1508*. Translated by John Winter Jones. London: Hakluyt Society, 1863.

Villehardouin, Geoffrey de. *Memoirs or Chronicle of the Fourth Crusade and the Conquest of Constantinople*. Translated by Frank T. Marzials. London: J. M. Dent, 1908. Medieval Sourcebook. http://www.fordham.edu/halsall/ basis/villehardouin.html.

Vries, Jan de, and Ad van der Woude. *The First Modern Economy: Success, Failure, and Perseverance of the Dutch Economy, 1500–1815*. Cambridge, U.K., and New York: Cambridge University Press, 1997.

Weiss, E. A. *Spice Crops*. Oxon, U.K., and New York: CABI Publishing, 2002.

Winius, George D., ed. *Portugal, the Pathfinder: Journeys from the Medieval toward the Modern World, 1300–ca. 1600.* Madison, Wis.: Hispanic Seminary of Medieval Studies, 1995.

Zumthor, Paul. *Daily Life in Rembrandt's Holland.* Translated by Simon Watson Taylor. London: Weidenfeld and Nicolson, 1962.

Index

A

Abreu, António de, 219
Acosta, José de, 171
Afonso V, King of Portugal, 125, 150
Afonso Henriques, King of Portugal, 123
Africa, Africans, 66, 149–50, 184, 189,
    212, 265, 268
  Brazilian sugar trade and, 182
  chili peppers of, 167–68, 171–72,
    174–75
  and finances of spices, 116–17, 159
  Gama's expeditions and, 130–31
  Indian spice trade and, 76, 144
  Portugal and, 61, 112–18, 120–21,
    125–26, 138, 142, 144, 156–57
  religious convictions and, 149, 156–57
  transfer of New World food to, 22,
    166–67
Albala, Ken, 248
Albert Hein supermarkets, 193, 259
Albuquerque, Afonso de, 136, 162, 219
alchemy, 6, 245–46, 250
Alexander VI, Pope, 150
Alexius IV, Emperor of the Byzantine
    Empire, 63–64
allspice, 6, 77, 127
aloeswood, 19, 43, 243
Amboina, 159, 179, 221
ambrosino, 79–80
Amsterdam, 125, 176, 221–22, 257–58
  and consequences of spice trade, 22
  demise of, 251–53, 257
  and demise of Portugal, 180–81
  dining in, 195–200
  Dutch East India Company and, 192,
    208–9, 225, 236

and finances of spices, 20–22, 197,
    204–5, 208, 221, 236, 257
  Jakarta operations and, 232
  mansions in, 194–98, 200
  and medicinal properties of spices,
    236–38, 241
  merchants of, 121, 181, 190, 193–94,
    200–204, 206–8, 210, 225, 231,
    251–53, 257, 267–68, 273
  paintings and, 196–98, 252
  pastries of, 189–90, 192–93, 196, 209
  rise of, 200–205
  Sinterklaas in, 189–90
  spice-flavored cheese of, 193–95
  surgeons in, 247
  see also Netherlands, Dutch
Anatomy Lesson of Dr. Tulp, The
    (Rembrandt), 246–47
aniseed, 192–93, 227*n*
Anonimo Veneziano, 78–81, 90
Antichi, I, 30–31, 69, 88, 99, 103, 106
Antwerp, 200, 209, 218
  black pepper and, 173, 178
  chili peppers and, 170
  Portugal and, 123, 178, 180
  printing revolution and, 96
  and rise of Amsterdam, 202–3
Apicius, 96
Aporvela, 112–14, 116, 120, 175
Arabs, Arabia, 41, 43, 70, 102, 134, 159
  ancient spice trade and, 16–17
  celebrity chefs and, 90
  Crusades and, 54–56, 59–60
  and finances of spices, 21
  Gama's expeditions and, 131

spice cakes, 191–94
Spice Islands, 212–22
  ancient spice trade and, 16–17
  black pepper of, 75, 213–14
  cape route to, 129, 140
  Columbus and, 126–27
  and consequences of spice trade, 22
  Dutch and, 66, 191, 207, 212–13,
    218–22, 228–31, 235, 261
  European familiarity with, 218
  and finances of spices, 15
  nutmeg and, 134, 191, 212–17,
    220–21
  Portugal and, 137, 159, 212–13,
    216–21
  and search for paradise, 11–12, 14
  see also Indonesia
spikenard, 42, 53, 80–81
Steen, Jan, 198
sugar, 4, 32, 86, 141, 175, 217, 228,
    242–43
  Brazilian trade in, 182
  Byzantium and, 42–43
  celebrity chefs and, 90, 93
  and changes in attitudes toward diet
    and nutrition, 254–56
  cinnamon and, 163–64
  Crusades and, 54–55, 57
  Dutch and, 189–91, 195–96, 199, 260,
    262
  Portugal and, 116, 118–19, 124, 132,
    143, 183–84, 191, 255–56
  and taste of food in past, 78, 80, 83
Sultan, 3–5
sweet peppers, 167, 170
Syria:
  Crusades and, 54, 56–57
  Indian spice trade and, 76
  Venice and, 46–47, 65, 136

T
Tacitus, 41
Taillevent (Guillaume Tirel), 81
Tapa Room, 24
tea, 252
Temple, Sir William, 198
Ternate:
  Dutch trade and, 219, 222

  Portuguese trade and, 218–20
  spices of, 212, 214
Tezpur, 272–73
Thirty Years' War, 103, 250, 253
Thumpassery, Thomas, 73–75, 172–73,
    207
Tidore, 179, 221
Tordesillas, treaty of, 126–27, 150
Torre de Belém, 176–77, 181–83
trade, trade routes, 16–23, 40–54
  ancient, 16–20
  chili peppers and, 167–68, 170–74
  consequences of, 22–23
  Crusades and, 53–54, 57, 59–60,
    63–64
  demise of, 248, 251–52, 254–56, 267
  of Dutch, vii, 16, 22, 70, 121, 140,
    153, 178–81, 190–91, 193–94,
    199–208, 210–13, 216–36, 251–54,
    256–63, 265–68, 270, 273
  of England, 70, 140, 159, 221, 232,
    253, 256–57, 265–66, 268
  of France, 253–54, 257–59, 266
  of India, 16–17, 41–42, 49, 70–72,
    75–76, 95, 103, 114, 117, 121–23,
    131–46, 150, 160–68, 171–72,
    178–82, 203–8, 214, 232, 265–66,
    268–70
  of Islamites, 17, 22, 160–62
  party towns and, 98
  plague and, 92
  of Portugal, vii, 16, 22–23, 111–27,
    129, 132–51, 153–54, 156, 159,
    162–63, 166–68, 170–72, 174–82,
    194, 199–200, 202–5, 207, 211–13,
    216–21, 225–28, 230–32, 235, 248,
    252, 255–56, 258, 263, 265, 268, 273
  printing revolution and, 94–95
  religious convictions and, 146–51,
    153–54, 181
  risks and difficulties in, 47–50
  shipwrecks and, 177
  of Spain, 248, 252, 265
  and taste of food in past, 82
  of Venice, vii, 29, 32–34, 37, 40,
    43–47, 50–52, 57, 59–60, 62–70,
    76, 82, 92, 94–95, 98, 102–5, 111,
    115–19, 121, 124, 133–37, 149,

About the Author

❦

MICHAEL KRONDL is a chef, food writer, and author of *Around the American Table: Treasured Recipes and Food Traditions from the American Cookery Collections of the New York Public Library* and *The Great Little Pumpkin Cookbook*. He has published articles in *Good Food, Family Circle, Pleasures of Cooking,* and *Chocolatier,* and has contributed entries to *The Oxford Encyclopedia of Food and Drink in America.* He lives in New York City.

About the Type

⚜

This book was set in Baskerville, a typeface which was designed by John Baskerville, an amateur printer and typefounder, and cut for him by John Handy in 1750. The type became popular again when The Lanston Monotype Corporation of London revived the classic Roman face in 1923. The Mergenthaler Linotype Company in England and the United States cut a version of Baskerville in 1931, making it one of the most widely used typefaces today.